breaking free

breaking free

Public School
Lessons
and the
Imperative of
School Choice

Sol Stern

ENCOUNTER BOOKS
SAN FRANCISCO

Published by Encounter Books, an activity of Encounter for Culture and Education, Inc., a nonprofit tax exempt corporation.

Encounter Books website address: www.encounterbooks.com

Manufactured in the United States and printed on acid-free paper.

The paper used in this publication meets the minimum requirements of ANSI/NISO Z39.48-1992 (R 1997)(Permanence of Paper).

FIRST EDITION

Library of Congress Cataloging-in-Publication Data

Stern, Sol, 1935–
    Breaking free : school choice and the new civil rights movement / Sol Stern.
    p. cm.
    Includes bibliographical references and index.
    ISBN 1-893554-07-4
1. School choice—United States. 2. Poor children—Education—United States. 3. Education, Urban—United States.

    LB1027.9.S84 2003
    379.1'11'0973—dc21
    2003040779

10 9 8 7 6 5 4 3 2 1

To Ruthie, Jonathan and Dani—
my eyes and ears in the public schools.

Contents

Introduction

I entered the New York City Public Schools three months before the Japanese attack on Pearl Harbor. On the appointed day in September my mother took my hand and walked with me the two blocks from our five-story walkup in the South Bronx to my designated elementary school. She turned me over to my first-grade teacher, Miss Banks, a tall, rail-thin Irish woman in her fifties. Certain that I was in good hands, my mother quickly left the building. She rarely stepped inside again during the eight years that I was a student there.

Miss Banks was a no-nonsense disciplinarian. She spent the first few days instructing us how to enter the room in neat lines and sit at our assigned desks with our hands folded. Not until this was accomplished did she get down to the business at hand: teaching us to read through drill and repetition of letter sounds— now known as the "phonics" method.

P.S. 6 was the number a city bureaucrat had assigned to my school earlier in the century; it had no other name. It was housed in a nondescript four-story brick building situated on a bluff overlooking the corner of Vyse and Tremont Avenues. With the entrance elevated above street level, the school had the appearance of a fortress guarding the crossroads of our white ethnic, working-class neighborhood. Our two most important cultural landmarks were the RKO Chester Movie Theater and the Paradise Ballroom, later immortalized in the 1950s film *Marty*, starring Ernest Borgnine.

About half of my classmates were Jewish, the rest Irish and Italian, along with a smattering of other European nationalities.

Virtually no black or Hispanic children attended the school. I was a brand-new immigrant, having arrived by boat from Israel (or Palestine, as it was then called) two years earlier, speaking only Hebrew. My classmates' parents were first- and second-generation Americans. Like the Italian family portrayed in *Marty,* many of the Catholics in the neighborhood sent their children to parochial schools. Almost every other child attended P.S. 6, having no choice in the matter.

For the Jewish children, the public schools were a haven. We regarded the Catholic schools as forebidding places. There were stories of the nuns meting out classroom discipline with rulers or other blunt objects, and some of us were convinced that among the lessons the Catholics taught in their separatist schools was that the Jews were "Christ-killers." That didn't seem to affect my friendship with the Catholic kids on my block, however; we played stickball together on the street and sometimes visited each other's homes. Still, I felt uneasy whenever I passed the local parish school with its huge crucifix hanging over the entrance.

Since no preschool or kindergarten programs were available, we all entered P.S. 6 in the first grade. Students were assigned to tracked classes based on the results of standardized intelligence tests. After completing eighth grade, most of my classmates went on to the zoned secondary school, Theodore Roosevelt High School in the Fordham Road section of the Bronx. Those children thought to be deficient in academic skills were directed to one of the city's many excellent vocational schools. A few (myself included) passed the entrance exam for the specialized science high schools, Bronx Science, Stuyvesant or Brooklyn Tech.

My parents didn't participate in the PTA (I'm not even sure there was one at P.S. 6) or other school activities. It wouldn't have occurred to them that they could have a voice in their child's school. It wasn't that they were uninterested in my education. Rather, they trusted the people in charge of the schools—the "experts," as they called them—to make the important decisions affecting my academic progress. Indeed, it was a fact of life to most parents in my neighborhood—like paying taxes—that their children would be assigned to a school by the city government and then sorted out by standardized aptitude tests. The "experts" would take care of the rest.

The agency that did the sorting and set the rules for everything else in the schools, right down to classroom instruction, was the New York City Board of Education, located at 110 Livingston Street in downtown Brooklyn. The board also controlled teaching licenses. Successful applicants were selected not merely on the basis of their academic credentials, but on demeanor and character as well. Teachers were expected to set a "proper example" for students. This meant mandatory jackets and ties for men and no facial hair. Female teachers who became pregnant were asked to leave the classroom immediately and take maternity leave. Each day, marching orders were sent out from the board's headquarters to the more than eight hundred schools spread out over the city's five boroughs. Lacking union representation, classroom teachers were under the near-dictatorial control of the system's principals, who in turn were relentlessly micromanaged by the bureaucrats at central headquarters.

Serving more than eight hundred thousand pupils, the system dwarfed the next-largest school district in the country by a factor of at least three to one. The nation's leading educators believed that a top-down command-and-control system was the most efficient way of providing education for the urban masses. They called it the "one best system." The guiding assumption was that the professionals at the top would insure that scientifically sound pedagogical methods were implemented in every one of the city's classrooms.

The schools were also charged with bringing together children of different social classes and religious and ethnic backgrounds and then initiating them into the common civic culture. At least that was the theory. In my recollection, the civics lessons taught by most of the teachers at P.S. 6 were actually quite parochial. We were required to stand next to our desks every single morning, face the flag and recite the Pledge of Allegiance, but the teachers rarely probed any deeper into the historical underpinnings of American patriotism. Nor were the schools sensitive to the diverse backgrounds of the students.

Several of my Irish teachers, themselves only one or two genera-
tions removed from being immigrants, were often dismissive of
the accents or dress of the newer European arrivals. Blacks in
particular could not have felt that they were participants in a
common civic culture, since our textbooks were full of crude
racial stereotypes, along with egregious misinformation about
the institution of slavery. And despite the ideal of commonality,
most black children in the city were relegated to segregated and
neglected schools.

Nevertheless, the mere existence of the public schools was
reason enough for my parents to have blessed the day they
arrived in this country. I never asked them, but I am sure they
believed that centralized, government-run schools similar to
those I attended in New York City had always been part of the
American political system.

They were wrong, of course.

As historian Diane Ravitch reports, the unification of all
New York City public schools under one administrative roof did
not occur until the beginning of the twentieth century. The "one
best system" was the brainchild of a group of Protestant reformers, led by Columbia University philosophy professor and later
president, Nicholas Murray Butler. Surveying the chaotic conditions of the public schools at the turn of the century, these
upper-class Republicans and self-styled progressives believed that
drastic measures were needed to cope with the hordes of poor,
unsocialized immigrant children flooding the city.

The reformers were able to convince the state legislature
that the existing neighborhood school councils were often under
the corrupt influence of Tammany Hall and not up to the job of
providing a proper civic education to the masses. Thus was created the largest school district in the country. The new
hierarchical system was based on modern ideas of managerial
efficiency. According to Professor Butler, the purpose was to
insure that the children of immigrants and the poor were
"brought under American influences and instruction."

★

By the time I entered P.S. 6 forty years later, Professor Butler's system was working like a well-oiled machine. It had weathered the demographic and social storms brought on by the last great wave of European immigration. One of the Depression's legacies was that a secure civil service job was considered a prized possession. Thus the public schools had a stable, highly qualified and contented teaching staff. Average class size in the 1940s was down to an all-time low of thirty-four students. Elite high schools such as Stuyvesant and Bronx Science were considered among the best in the nation. Not every child received an academic diploma (the dropout rate was even higher than it is today), but even those who didn't were likely to find opportunities in a manufacturing economy that provided jobs for workers lacking academic skills.

The 1940s and 1950s—including the twelve years that I attended P.S. 6 and Stuyvesant High School—are viewed by education historians as the golden era of the New York City public schools. I graduated from Stuyvesant High School in 1953 and went on to the City College of New York. "City" was known as the "Harvard of the poor." Located in the middle of Harlem, it boasted a world-class faculty and was filled with brilliant young people—all of them graduates of the public high schools. At City I met up again with some of my old P.S. 6 classmates who had gone on to Theodore Roosevelt High School. It was a testament to the public schools of the era that these graduates of the regular zoned high schools not only made it to top colleges but then went on to remarkably successful careers. I sometimes watched the Pershing Rifles, the elite ROTC drill team, performing their routines on the one piece of open space on the campus. One of the only African Americans among the Pershing Rifles was a graduate of Morris High School in the South Bronx named Colin Powell.

In the college's cafeteria many of us debated the hot political issues of the day—McCarthyism, Stalinism, the Cold War—and we divided ourselves up by political ideology and affiliation. At the time, we identified ourselves as communists, Norman Thomas socialists, unaffiliated radicals, liberals and libertarians. Each group even had its own table. Despite our differences we understood how much we owed to the New York

City public schools. We were part of the realization of Professor Butler's dream of educating and Americanizing millions of immigrant children.

The sixties were around the corner, however, and the consensus would soon be shattered.

★

After City College I moved on to graduate school, eventually ending up at the University of California at Berkeley. There I became one of the charter members of the New Left student movement. By the mid-1960s I was an editor and writer with the New Left's banner publication, *Ramparts* magazine, reporting about American and international politics, the Vietnam War and the national security state. In 1967 I published an article exposing the CIA's penetration of the National Student Association that caused major embarrassment to the U.S. government.

In a classic case of biting the hand that fed us, we sixties radicals extended our assault on all things American to the institution of public education. We embraced Paul Goodman's view in *Growing Up Absurd* that the schools and universities were stultifying to the young and that public education in America reflected the values of an acquisitive capitalist society. That was my ideological premise when I participated in and wrote about the Berkeley Free Speech Movement in 1964. I proclaimed that students at Berkeley were fed up with being "processed" for careers in the corporate world, and that we owed no loyalty or respect to the "multiversity" (Chancellor Clark Kerr's immortal term) because it functioned primarily as a service center for the corporations and the imperial U.S. government.

While on the staff of *Ramparts,* I read a book about the Boston Public Schools written by a young author named Jonathan Kozol. He was about my age and I detected a kindred spirit. Kozol's book, *Death at an Early Age: The Destruction of the Hearts and Minds of Negro Children in the Boston Public Schools,* described the six months the author spent as a substitute teacher in a predominantly black public school in Boston. With its graphic description of the white teachers' racism, this book seemed to reveal the grim truth about the damage being done to black children in every urban public school district in America.

It was exactly this assumption that black children were failing because of white racism that led New York's Mayor John Lindsay and McGeorge Bundy, then of the Ford Foundation, to try to dismantle the "one best system" in the late 1960s. The two patrician white liberals' answer to the alleged racism of white educators was to bypass the Board of Education and turn the public schools in black neighborhoods over to local leaders, who would then institute a curriculum better suited to black children's learning style and culture. Or so the theory went.

Mayor Lindsay began by setting up an experimental school district in the all-black Ocean Hill–Brownsville section of Brooklyn. The leaders of the community school board then fired a number of tenured white teachers—in violation of civil service rules and the teachers' union contract. The United Federation of Teachers, which had won the right to represent all teachers in a collective bargaining election in 1961, responded by calling out its entire membership in a citywide strike.

Amidst charges and countercharges of white racism and black anti-Semitism (most of the fired teachers were Jewish) along with sporadic violence in and outside the schools, Lindsay's experiment in decentralization exploded into one of the nastiest racial and political confrontations in the city's history. I wrote about the conflict for *Ramparts.* Because of my leftist political sympathies at the time, I sided with the black leaders and the young radical white teachers who defied the union and stayed on the job.

I later came to regret much of what I had written about the strike, particularly my willingness to explain away the anti-Semitism of black activists. Nevertheless, what I reported on in Ocean Hill–Brownsville reflected two dramatic developments that would soon radically change the face of urban public education. The first was the demographic transformation of the student population in the city. In the decade and a half since I had left the public schools, over a million whites had migrated out of the city to the suburbs. An even greater number of blacks and Hispanics moved into the city. A school system that had been majority white when I was a student became majority black and Hispanic. The bitter, racially inflamed struggle over control of the Ocean Hill–Brownsville schools only served to accelerate further the flight of whites out of the city schools. Within a few years the white student population would shrink to less than 20 percent of the total. From then on, the system that successfully assimilated the children of European immigrants would be judged by how well it educated the children of the city's new black and Hispanic poor.

The other change was the emergence of the teachers' union as a center of power within the school system. Led by its brilliant strategist, Albert Shanker, the United Federation of Teachers was strong enough by 1968 to face down City Hall and force it to end the Ocean Hill–Brownsville experiment. The union eventually agreed to a compromise decentralization plan, resulting in the creation of thirty-two elected community school boards with limited powers over the schools in their districts. Saddled with ineffective and sometimes corrupt school boards, the city schools remained stagnant in overall performance, and the biggest losers were poor minority children.

The big winner was the UFT. Within the following two decades, the 100,000-member union became the most powerful lobbying group in Albany and was able essentially to write entire sections of the state's education law. The union was also able to swing elections for mayor and other political offices. By the 1980s the UFT was powerful enough to veto the Board of Education's selection of schools chancellors. The union also used its political muscle to rearrange the balance of power within the schools. No longer could principals or other administrators tell teachers how to dress or even what to teach. The teachers now had an ironclad contract that made it virtually impossible to fire incompetents. The school system would never be the same again.

★

Another two decades passed before I once more found myself in a New York City public school. In September 1987, I took my five-year-old son Jonathan by the hand and walked with him the fifteen blocks from our home to his kindergarten class at P.S. 87 on the Upper West Side of Manhattan. P.S. 87 was then the "hot" elementary school in Community School District 3 (extending along the West Side of Manhattan from 65th Street all the way up to 125th Street in Harlem). There were at least five public schools closer to our home than P.S. 87 that my wife and I could have selected.

The policy of public school choice had first appeared in the predominantly poor and minority District 4 in East Harlem in the early 1980s. At the time Jonathan entered P.S. 87, it had become the de facto policy in several other white, middle-class enclaves of the city, including our own District 3. The opportunity to choose which school to send your child to (limited by availability) was one of the inducements offered by the system in order to prevent the flight of the dwindling number of white, middle-class families.

The "one best system" had undergone other profound changes since my student days. At schools like P.S. 87, parents involved themselves in the day-to-day activities of the school to a degree that the parents in my old neighborhood in the Bronx would have found unfathomable. After Jonathan was enrolled at P.S. 87 I discovered that parents could walk into the school at almost any time and easily obtain an appointment to speak with teachers or the principal. Some parents spent many hours in the classrooms as volunteers helping with reading groups or art instruction. Others devoted their time to outside fundraising for the school or putting out a parent newsletter. At least when it involved their own children, parents thought of themselves as knowledgeable education critics. Many lobbied with the principal to get their children into classes taught by the preferred teachers. They certainly did not believe that those my mother had called "the experts" always knew what was best for their own children.

Change was also evident when I stepped into P.S. 87's "child-centered" classrooms. My first shock was that there were no desks lined up in rows. From kindergarten through fifth grade, children sat in little clusters, either on the floor or at tables. The young teachers often dressed in jeans and T-shirts. They spent very little time in front of the room offering instruction; instead they wandered around the room observing the children working on their assignments in small groups. Reading was taught through the "whole language" or "holistic" method rather than the more traditional phonics approach of sounding out letters that Miss Banks had used at P.S. 6. On my first visit to P.S. 87, one teacher told me she was helping the children "construct" their own knowledge.

It wasn't only the public schools that had changed, I discovered as I became involved in my children's education. The Catholic schools of my childhood fears had also undergone a startling demographic transformation. The huge exodus of white Catholic families from the city had taken away much of the Catholic education system's traditional student base. But the parish schools did not close their doors and follow their students to the suburbs. Instead they beckoned to the new minority poor, including many who weren't even Catholic. By the 1990s, blacks and Hispanics accounted for almost 60 percent of the enrollment in Catholic schools in the city. In Manhattan and the Bronx it was close to 85 percent. Moreover, according to numerous studies published in the 1980s and 1990s, Catholic schools were doing a better job of educating poor minority children than were public schools in the same neighborhoods.

Some of the changes I saw at P.S. 87 reflected countercultural trends that had been transforming the country since the 1960s. From the military to the workplace to corporate boardrooms, American institutions were reinventing themselves, becoming more "client friendly," focusing on cooperation and teamwork rather than top-down management. Some school districts were trying public school choice and also creating experimental small schools, or "schools within a school." The changes also represented a desperate thrashing around by an institution that seemed to have lost its sense of mission. No one dared call it "the one best system" anymore. Everyone was looking for the magic bullet of reform that might make the system that had worked so well for my generation somehow work again for the children of the new poor.

There were some amazing successes. Inspired school principals—legendary leaders such as Deborah Meier, who started the Central Park East schools of District 4, or Lorraine Monroe, founder of Frederick Douglass Academy in Harlem—were able to create schools of extraordinarily high achievement in the most daunting of neighborhoods. But these remained isolated islands of excellence in a vast archipelago of failure and despair. The system either couldn't or wouldn't figure out how to use the lessons of the exceptional public schools or the Catholic schools and apply them to the vast majority of schools serving the city's black and Hispanic poor.

The dimensions of the failure were contained in the system's own published statistics. Fewer than half of the city's third graders could read at grade level—itself not a very high standard. Less than half of the high school students were able to graduate in four years and 30 percent dropped out altogether. And during the entire time my children were in the public schools—fifteen years—those grim statistics hardly changed. In the late 1990s, the Public Education Association, the city's oldest and most venerable education advocacy group, began using the phrase "education dead zones" to describe those expanding areas of the city where almost every school was failing.

Yet as bad as the situation was in New York, it was far worse in Los Angeles, Detroit, Newark and Washington, D.C. The economic and social consequences of public school failure and what to do about it became one of the dominant themes of the national political discourse of the late 1980s and 1990s.

Until my children entered school I paid little attention to those broader education debates. And for a time P.S. 87 seemed to be living up to its exalted reputation. Yet even though I was satisfied with my son's teachers, I had both a parent's and a journalist's curiosity about what looked like some very strange institutional arrangements at our school. One of the most annoying was the behavior of the school's custodial staff. To put it mildly, they didn't seem to be working very hard. I soon learned that the custodians' union had become a power unto itself within the school system.

There were other perplexing discoveries. I couldn't help noticing that Jonathan's school had three or four teachers who never had regular classroom assignments. Apparently these teachers were too dysfunctional to be trusted with the children and thus had to be given something to do, like babysitting a class when a regular teacher had a prep period or patrolling the cafeteria and the schoolyard. I also learned that because of the labor contract negotiated by the city with the teachers' union, it was virtually impossible for our school to get rid of these unproductive employees. In fact, several teachers had been forced on the school against the wishes of the principal. This was due to a provision in the contract giving teachers with seniority the right to transfer into other schools when a vacancy was posted. Since P.S. 87 was located in one of the most desirable neighborhoods in Manhattan (three blocks from Zabars) our school became a sought-after destination for transferring teachers.

Most parents at P.S. 87 were annoyed about the stranglehold that employee unions seemed to have clamped on our school. But as a political constituency, parents were disorganized and virtually powerless compared with the unions. I decided to register my protest and press for reform in the only way I knew how: by writing about it. I began by publishing an article about the teachers' contract in *City Journal*, a quarterly magazine published by the Manhattan Institute—the first of many essays on education I would publish as a contributing editor of the magazine. Drawing on what I observed at my son's school, I dissected the 250-page document, showing how it rewarded mediocrity and perpetrated a slacker culture in the schools. In writing about the contract, I had the advantage of entering a journalistic vacuum. Regular education beat reporters for the New York dailies rarely covered the realities of workplace practices in the schools.

Another subject hardly ever reported on by the press was the Catholic school sector. The success of Catholic schools in educating poor black and Hispanic children at less than half the cost of the public schools was a story waiting to be told. My article about the Catholic school phenomenon received a great deal of public attention; Mayor Giuliani mentioned it when he came out in support of a privately funded program that provided tuition vouchers for poor children stuck in failing public schools. I doubted that I deserved the honor of "most influential education critic in the city," as John Tierney of the *New York Times* called me, but I knew I was making headway when UFT president Randi Weingarten attacked me in the union newspaper.

★

Readers will notice that in this book I dwell at length on my own children's schools. In truth, I don't think I was any more obsessive about my kids' education than the other parents. The reason for my emphasis lies in a slogan we used in the sixties: "The personal is political." I came to believe this was true in education, and that what my children were enduring was a metaphor for problems with the entire American educational system. They were lucky to attend several of the city's best public schools, a far cry from the education dead zones; yet it was from their experiences that I learned about the lethal combination of a self-interested and powerful teachers' union, a dysfunctional bureaucracy and progressive education fads that was damaging all children. The message here is that public school lessons are best learned at the source.

If I started out—as I believe all responsible parents should—trying to understand why my children's schools and teachers were not all they should have been, I soon found myself on a personal and professional quest that eventually led me to report on the alternatives, especially the national school choice movement and the voucher schools in the minority neighborhoods of Milwaukee and Cleveland. In this journey I felt that I had rediscovered a new civil rights movement that was completing the unfinished business of the 1960s movement I had once been part of. I hope to convince readers, particularly other parents, that this new movement—and the moral imperative to liberate poor kids from dysfunctional schools—is our best hope of reviving the public school dream and creating the schools that our children need in the twenty-first century.

MY PUBLIC SCHOOL
LESSONS

1

P.S. 87: The Dream School
of the Upper West Side

When my firstborn son was accepted at P.S. 87, also known as the William Tecumseh Sherman School, my wife and I felt as if we had secured his educational future. After all, P.S. 87 had just been written up by *Parents* magazine as one of the country's ten best elementary schools, public or private. Two *New York Times* profiles puffed it as one of the rare public schools that white middle-class parents still clamored to get their children into. But it was actually the real estate section of the *Times* that offered the best testimonial to the school's allure. Ads for apartments for sale or rent on the Upper West Side often carried the line: "P.S. 87 catchment area."

P.S. 87 was considered the Holy Grail of urban public education because it was providing quality instruction to a racially and economically mixed student body. During the time my two children were in attendance, it maintained about a 40 percent minority enrollment. My sons had many black and Hispanic friends, some of whose parents had immigrated to this country from Ethiopia, Ghana, Colombia and the Dominican Republic. The parents of their classmates were, variously, high-powered lawyers, well-known writers and college professors, custodians, factory workers, even welfare mothers. The school's progressive "child-centered" philosophy was supposed to serve all students, not merely the elite.

Even if my wife and I had been able to afford private school tuition, we would probably not have considered that option for our sons. The public schools had worked well for both of us. More importantly, we believed in their historic role of forging a common democratic and civic culture out of the nation's diversity. P.S. 87 seemed the perfect vehicle for accomplishing that goal.

P.S. 87 had languished through the 1970s, when middle-class parents shunned the school. As in any other enterprise, new leadership is almost always needed to revive schools that have fallen on bad times. In the case of P.S. 87 the rescuer who appeared on the scene was a middle-aged woman given to wearing long, flowing black dresses. Her name was Naomi Hill, and she soon became one of the legends of the New York City school system. At the time Mrs. Hill was appointed principal, enrollment at P.S. 87 had dropped from a high of 850 to a skeletal 350. The school was in disarray; Hill's predecessor had pitted parents and teachers against each other, and the children were out of control, straggling into the building late and sometimes maliciously setting off fire alarms. Music and art instruction had virtually disappeared, as had after-school programs.

Hill insisted that she had no master plan when she took on what looked to be a daunting task. "I never studied this stuff," she once told me. "I just made it up as I went along." In fact, she could have written the book on turning around a failing city school. The key to reviving P.S. 87 was to lure back the middle-class parents. Recruiting at neighborhood fairs and nursery schools, Hill turned out to be a superb salesperson. She sometimes brought along a poster board that said: "Have you considered the public school alternative?" To skeptical parents she offered this challenge: Take a chance on my school, and you can be partners in rebuilding it.

Hill was also not above offering extra inducements. One mother recalled how Hill made her pitch to a group of parents at a nursery school located on the Columbia University campus: "It never would have occurred to me to send my child to a school thirty blocks downtown. But she provided us with a sense of discovery. She really seemed to know early childhood education and convinced us she had a plan to meet the needs of our children. She also promised that our children would get the school's best kindergarten teacher. Eventually eight of us decided to go as a group." Within a few years, P.S. 87's enrollment was back up to seven hundred students, about half of them white and middle-class. "We had to bring the parents back into the school actively and we had to make alliances with them," said Hill.

Since parents were welcome to visit classes, to volunteer, to drop in on the new principal anytime with problems or suggestions, they soon developed a feeling of "ownership." Even Mrs. Hill's office, furnished with comfortable couches and over-stuffed chairs she had inherited when her mother died, offered a warm and friendly embrace. "It gave me a place where I could meet with parents and teachers that felt human," Hill said.

In turn, the parents provided Mrs. Hill with a powerful instrument to help effect the school's resurgence. By the time my son Jonathan enrolled in 1987, the Parents Association was taking in over $100,000 per year through street fairs, raffles and auctions. The money was used to pay for a full-time music teacher and a part-time art teacher and librarian, plus many other needed items and services. New parents flocking to the school also brought important connections. Some were active in local Democratic politics or worked for powerful law firms or had jobs in the media.

Hill had an uncanny knack for discovering which of her parents could be useful to the school. Knowing that I worked for the New York City Council president's office, for example, she drafted me to get city parking privileges restored for her teachers. I spent several months trying to convince my boss, Andrew Stein, that this was a major issue. I even got him to appeal to the city's transportation commissioner to remedy this injustice to one of the city's best schools. In the end, alas, the commissioner didn't owe my boss a favor and wouldn't restore the parking permits.

Anton Klein, the West Side community school district superintendent during most of Hill's tenure at P.S. 87, recalls several occasions when she dispatched her most assertive parents to lobby him for something extra that the school needed and that required him to overlook the rules. "Three very imposing-looking women would march into my office," said Klein. "One was a lawyer for the ACLU, one was an opera singer and one was an influential political activist. They were persuasive in terms of what they wanted for their school, and they would often get it."

Among the rewards of being a P.S. 87 parent was becoming a member of an embracing community. Many parents were veterans of 1960s activism, and the school was a little like revisiting those heady days again. Not only was your child in a happy, nurturing place and receiving what looked like an excellent education, but the integrated school you were helping to build seemed to be accomplishing one of the key objectives of the 1960s civil rights movement.

At a time when the cause of school integration was in retreat almost everywhere in the country, P.S. 87 showed that public schools could still provide equal educational opportunity for children of all races and economic classes. "Being a P.S. 87 parent changed my life," recalled Barbara Horowitz, one of Hill's first Parents Association presidents. "It was an intense personal experience. We worked together to create a real democratic and community school." My wife, Ruthie, and I joined hundreds of other parents one memorable spring weekend to help build a playground for the school—a kind of urban community barn-raising for the benefit of our children. It felt like Berkeley in the sixties all over again, but without the violent histrionics and anti-Americanism.

Yet the school's communalism would have made no difference without our chief executive's gift for finding and inspiring talented young teachers. Hill made clear to prospective teachers that despite the teachers' union contract limitation of the school day to six hours and twenty minutes, in P.S. 87 many teachers showed up long before the students arrived and stayed long after they left. Bending the rules, she often hired bright young people with only a B.A. degree and a substitute teaching license, and then protected these gifted beginners until they had accumulated the necessary graduate credits to obtain their permanent licenses. And she had the gritty determination to confront mediocre and incompetent teachers. Though she couldn't fire them, she occasionally was able to embarrass some into transferring out of the school.

I first gained an appreciation for Hill's abilities during Jonathan's very first days in the school. Over the summer we had learned that his kindergarten teacher would be an African

American woman named Ursula Davis, reputed to have won a "teacher of the year" award. When I brought my son to his classroom on opening day, however, we were greeted by a very young, white woman named Lisa Golden. My heart sank as I realized that my son was not getting the "teacher of the year," who had moved on to a district staff development job over the summer, but a raw rookie.

Lisa Golden was all of twenty-three years old, didn't have a proper public school license and had never taught kindergarten before. Nevertheless, as is sometimes the case with so-called "uncertified" teachers, she turned out to be superb in the classroom. She was full of creative energy and figured out quickly how to manage a class of 25 five-year-olds. That first year, somewhat to my own surprise, I found myself telling friends that my son was receiving as good an education as he would have had in any $12,000-per-year private school.

Deborah Meier, one of the nation's leading progressive educators and the founder of several successful small schools in East Harlem, has written: "Every child is entitled to be in a school small enough that he or she can be known by name to every faculty member in the school and well known by at least a few." This seems quite sensible. Yet Naomi Hill concluded that in order to turn P.S. 87 around, she would have to enlarge the school back to what reformers like Meier have derided as "factory" size. "One of the advantages of recruiting more students," Hill told me, "was that I had more positions for teachers. That meant that I had more teachers whom I personally selected and more teachers who really wanted to be in the school and shared our philosophy."

Had she kept the school at 350 students, in other words, she would have been stuck with an unacceptably high percentage of incompetent, demoralized teachers protected by a state education law that guaranteed them a permanent job in the same building for life. But she could dilute their negative force by piling in students, opening new classrooms and hiring new teachers. Creating more staff positions also gave her a higher number of "cluster" positions for teachers who were supposed to cover classes when regular teachers were on their preparation periods. Thus she could shunt dysfunctional teachers out of the classroom into such less-than-demanding tasks as cafeteria or yard duty.

My optimism about Jonathan's education was tempered somewhat by the perception that burnt-out or incompetent teachers occupied a disproportionate amount of Hill's time. Each year, she and her parent "lobbyists" conspired over what to do about teachers who, under the union contract, were entitled to be assigned to the school as "seniority transfers." With the cooperation of a friendly district superintendent like Mr. Klein, the contract provisions could occasionally be ignored. One ruse was to hide any openings until shortly before the school year began, making it impossible for union transfers to file for the positions before they were already filled.

Still, for all of our principal's genius at skirting onerous union work rules, this remained a New York City public school. Always some unlucky children ended up in classes with teachers so bad that an entire year out of their educational life would be wasted. P.S. 87 never had enough cluster positions to hide all the incompetents. And despite our best efforts, some seniority transfers did succeed in getting jobs at the school without the principal's approval.

In the *New York Observer,* writer and new P.S. 87 parent James Lardner recounted his dismay at discovering that one of the school's nastiest "cafeteria operatives" was actually a veteran licensed teacher drawing top salary. Dubbing her "Mrs. Lungworthy," Lardner wrote that her "Marine Corps training camp methods" of dealing with small children made her seem an inappropriate choice for even the job of patrolling the school lunchroom. He expressed his outrage about the situation to a more experienced parent, who levelly replied, "Do you want her in the classroom teaching?"

Like Lardner, I quickly learned that the interests of employees often trumped the interests of children. One of the first things I noticed about the school was that the head custodian and his three helpers didn't always keep our building in tip-top repair. The janitors were allowed to run the school buildings as if they were their own property. Parent and community groups desiring to use the facility for after-school programs for kids were forced to pay exorbitant "opening fees" to the custodians. As a result, head custodians often made more money than the principals. Nepotism flourished among the custodial staff; many custodians hired their wives as secretaries. Principals who needed to get a light bulb or a window replaced and went to the custodian were told, "It's not in our contract." The principal would then have to wait—and wait—until the Board of Education's central maintenance department processed the work order.

If the board couldn't stand up to the thousand-member custodians' union, it was even less likely to take on the United Federation of Teachers, with its more than one hundred thousand dues-paying members. I was generally aware that in the years since I had last written about the teachers' union in *Ramparts* magazine in 1968 it had become the 800-pound gorilla of the school system, as well as a powerful force in city and state politics. P.S. 87 gave me my first up-close and personal look at how teachers' unions and their labor contracts impacted on the day-to-day operations of a school.

One morning early in my son Jonathan's fourth-grade year I noticed a bent, middle-aged man wandering around the school-yard as if in a stupor. He was carrying an old plastic shopping bag and his clothes were tattered and worn. My first thought was that a derelict had wandered onto the school grounds. Then, as the parents said goodbye to their children and started leaving the yard, I realized that he was actually a school employee on yard duty. I found out that this needy person, whom we all came to know by his first name (I will call him "Mr. B"), was actually a fully certified teacher who had recently transferred into the school under the seniority clause of the union contract. A gentle man, Mr. B was nevertheless deeply impaired and could not possibly have taken on a real teaching assignment. Other than yard duty, he was sometimes asked to cover a class while the regular teacher was on a prep period. He was so disheveled and smelled so bad that the children began to make up unkind songs about him. Nevertheless, he had been given a satisfactory rating by the principal at his former school in the Bronx, and thus was able to get his transfer to P.S. 87 without even being interviewed by our principal. If Mr. B had received an unsatisfactory rating, he would not have been allowed to transfer and the Bronx school would have been stuck with him. The name of the game, it seemed, was pass on the lemons.

Mr. B remained in our school for three years, his condition steadily deteriorating, while parent after parent expressed dismay. In order to try to get Mr. B dismissed, the principal would have had to assign him to a regular class and observe him for six months to document his teaching inadequacies. Meanwhile, the union would file an endless series of grievances contesting any negative entries in his teaching file. This process could drag on for years with no certain outcome. In the meantime, the unlucky students assigned to Mr. B's class would have been subjected to cruel and unusual punishment. Their parents would have either revolted or voted with their feet to leave the school. Finally, the quandary was resolved when Mr. B collapsed in the school in front of the children. He was then granted a medical sabbatical leave and never showed up again.

★

One of the early lessons I learned at P.S. 87 was that election-year debates about whether this or that candidate is "neglecting public education" are totally irrelevant to what happens each day in individual schools and classrooms. "Neglect" is defined almost exclusively as cutting education budgets. David Dinkins accused Ed Koch of such neglect, for instance; Rudy Giuliani did it to Dinkins; and mayoral candidate Ruth Messinger did it to Giuliani. In my recollection, no politician in New York City ever accused an opponent of neglecting education by supporting a system that protected incompetent teachers.

As Jonathan's experiences in P.S. 87 made clear to me, whether the city's education budget was up or down by a half-billion dollars had little impact on what happened in the classrooms. Such a cut—the equivalent of about $500 per pupil—paled in comparison with the scandalous waste and lack of productivity imposed on our school by the existing contractual arrangements. For example, just being able to fire the likes of "Mrs. Lungworthy" or Mr. B would have made up for all the cuts in our school's budget. And think of the productivity-crushing effect of the teachers' union contract requirement that virtually all staff development must take place during the prescribed six-hour-and-twenty-minute school day. Each year the children lost at least four full days of school because of that mandate.

It was also impossible to miss how little value the nonpedagogical staff—the custodians, cafeteria workers and security guards—brought to the school thanks to the contracts their unions were able to extract from the city. One small example: Our schoolyard was often unusable for days after a winter storm. This wasn't due to the ravages of nature. Rather, since the contract didn't specifically require it, our highly paid custodian and his helpers usually refused to clear the snow and ice.

If P.S. 87 had been operated as a rational enterprise dedicated to the interests of the children, we might have been able to relieve the overcrowding in the lunchroom—while enhancing the children's diet—by contracting with an outside vendor for food services. We could have saved money and made sure the yard was always usable by privatizing custodial services. We could have eliminated the security guard's job because we had no security problem in the school that the existing staff or parent volunteers couldn't handle. Despite their creativity in skirting some union contract rules, Hill and her successors had no authority to make crucial management decisions that would have dramatically improved P.S. 87's performance.

As a result, sooner or later many of the school's parents figured out how much our school was harmed by the system's special interests. The UFT had few friends among P.S. 87's parents. Even the most leftist of them put aside labor solidarity when the interests of their own children were involved. Yet many of those same parents had a harder time accepting that the school's underlying educational philosophy was harming their children and, even more damagingly, was crippling the minority students at the school. The mindset that found P.S. 87's communalism so congenial was also least likely to see through the egalitarian-sounding shibboleths of progressive education that permeated the school's entire program.

It took me a long time to recognize this. Like other P.S. 87

parents, I started out unfamiliar with pedagogical and curricular issues. At first it didn't seem to matter: Naomi Hill had a reputation as a "progressive" educator, as was *de rigueur* on the West Side. When my wife and I visited the school, the atmosphere in my son's "open" classrooms, where children worked together in constantly shifting groups of three or four sitting around a table, seemed both nurturing and productive. And though Jonathan was taught reading through the "whole language" approach rather than the more traditional phonics, my wife and I had no reason to complain. Partly because of some very good teachers in the early grades, he was reading ahead of schedule.

We first became uneasy when we learned that P.S. 87 was using a new method called "the writing process," based on the assumption that all children were "natural writers." The old-style concern about sentence drill, grammar and spelling squashed natural childhood talents, we were told, while the new method let children's creativity flow by dispensing with these stifling rules and letting kids write down in journals whatever came to their minds, including their own invented spelling. They would then revise these entries, with but a smidgen of guidance from the teacher.

P.S. 87 didn't seem to hold teachers accountable for making sure that students attained some objectively measured level of writing competence. Indeed, the parents of children who were less "natural" writers than others, who couldn't compose a correct sentence by third or fourth grade, were still hearing assurances that all children develop at their own pace and that there really is no "correct" way to write. In other words: don't worry, be happy.

The "writing process" was a product of Columbia University's Teachers College, which along with the nearby Bank Street College of Education trained many of P.S. 87's younger teachers. These citadels of progressive education taught them that teachers should "teach the child, not the text," that children, as "natural learners," can "construct their own knowledge." Thus teachers must not stuff children with "mere facts," but should help them "discover" useful knowledge on their own. The buzz words became congenial to teachers who didn't enjoy drilling grammar, spelling or penmanship anyway. But it was deadly for the children who ended up graduating without competency in these essential tools of language.

It was only after my older son's first three years at P.S. 87 that I began to suspect how readily the doctrine of "child-centered" education could lead to an abdication of pedagogical responsibility, especially in math. With its many hard-working teachers and bright students, P.S. 87 should have been thriving in this area, but math instruction at P.S. 87 was a wasteland.

Teachers automatically met parental anxiety with the bromide that the children were learning mathematical concepts by solving real-life problems and thus were also "learning how to learn." They assured us that the experts had proved natural, hands-on learning to be more effective than force-feeding children repetitive operational drills.

In the earliest grades, when children learned some of the rudimentary concepts of numeration by manipulating rods and blocks, this sounded reasonable. But by the time Jonathan reached the third grade, his school wasn't doing much to draw out his "natural" math abilities. In fact, he was hardly being challenged. His highly regarded teacher devoted months of class time to an across-the-curriculum project on Japan, which included— to the kids' delight—the building of a Japanese garden. Each day when my son came home, we asked him what he did in math, and every day he cheerfully answered, "We measured the garden." In answer to my wife's concern, the teacher assured us that constructing the garden required "real-life" math skills. Maybe, but my son's conscientious fourth-grade teacher later chafed over having to keep reviewing the multiplication tables that the children were supposed to have mastered the year before.

I soon complained to anyone in the school who would listen that although it was nice that our children were making Japanese gardens, while this was happening Japanese kids were leaving ours in the dust in actual math. Finally, my wife and I decided that we had to find a private solution for what we now realized was a serious institutional blind spot. Since we were frequent visitors to Israel, we used its excellent math workbooks to teach Jonathan ourselves. Needless to say, the very idea of a coherent, graded math workbook would have been anathema to most of the teachers at P.S. 87.

Just as we began our improvised version of partial home schooling, Naomi Hill threw the P.S. 87 community into turmoil: she announced that she was leaving to become principal of an elementary school in New Jersey. Such was the acclaim that P.S. 87 had achieved under Hill's tenure that her departure for the suburbs merited two articles in the *New York Times*.

The Parents Association lobbied hard to make sure that the district superintendent picked Hill's assistant principal, a younger administrator named Jane Hand, to replace her. Hand had been Hill's disciple for several years and thus would maintain the communal traditions and the child-centered pedagogy that had made the school so successful. Accordingly, Jane Hand was installed as the new principal in 1992. Three years later, she dropped another bombshell on the school when she announced that she was leaving to take a principal's position in Westchester. The various committees convened again and then elevated Hand's assistant principal, Steven Plaut—once again in the name of continuity.

For all the apparent seamlessness of these transitions, however, Hill's departure marked a significant turning point for P.S. 87. Veteran parents missed her charisma, her driving energy. Many grumbled that the school was losing its intimate, communitarian feeling. Hand provided a more bureaucratic, less personal style of leadership. With a uniformed security guard now at the front entrance (a new requirement imposed on the school by the central administration) it became more difficult for parents to gain access to the school. Hand was also less likely than Hill to confront an inadequate teacher, and more likely to get along with the teachers' union. Under Hand and then Plaut, teachers seemed to have almost unlimited autonomy in their classrooms. Some teachers gave tests, but most didn't; some assigned a lot of homework, and some assigned almost none.

Naomi Hill left the school at the end of Jonathan's third-grade year—the year of the Japanese garden. Up to that point, when West Side parents whose children were approaching school age asked me questions about the public school option, I would answer unequivocally that at P.S. 87 they could get the equivalent of a private school education for their children. After Hill's departure, I amended my answer: "P.S. 87 is fine for the first three grades, but after that you'd better be prepared to supplement it with some home schooling."

I had started out wanting to believe that innocuous-sounding catchphrases such as "learning to learn" and "child-centered" merely meant that high academic standards were compatible with nurturing, creative classrooms for young children. But I was beginning to understand what they really meant: teachers would never be held accountable for teaching any concrete body of knowledge. Without yet knowing it, I had become an education traditionalist.

★

As my older son began fifth grade (his senior year at our K–5 school) I joined a group of parents from other schools who wanted to start a new alternative junior high school for academically gifted students. We tried to convince the local school board that many brighter students were leaving for other districts because there weren't enough middle school choices. When Jane Hand learned that I was involved in this effort she was clearly annoyed. She said it was "elitist" and came close to accusing me of betraying P.S. 87's "progressive philosophy."

Hand insisted that all students could learn perfectly well in heterogeneous classes like those at P.S. 87. Indeed, in her articles in the school newsletter she often cited an academically respectable source in support of this idea, a University of Connecticut education professor named Joseph Renzuli. In defense of mixed classrooms, Professor Renzuli theorized that bright students could be pulled out of heterogeneous classes for some accelerated work in a kind of special education system for the gifted. But Hand (like many other defenders of the heterogeneous classroom) never implemented this part of the theory.

This omission was intentional. P.S. 87's principals wanted to redefine the very idea of giftedness, making it more democratic. Jane Hand wrote that P.S. 87 was "a school that believes that all children are gifted, talented, curious, capable and accomplished."

Fatuous as this sounded, parents were told it had the backing of yet another famous progressive educator, Harvard psychologist Howard Gardner, who had roiled the fields of education and cognitive psychology with his provocative theory of "multiple intelligences." His notion that every child is gifted in at least one of seven different "intelligences," including the nonacademic "bodily-kinesthetic" intelligence possessed by accomplished dancers and athletes, was a godsend for progressive educators. It meant that no matter how poorly some children might perform on objective tests, each had his own learning style and "giftedness" worthy of respect. Hand's successor, Steven Plaut, devoted several of his columns in the school newsletter to assuring parents that "Gardner would greatly approve of the way we group children for cooperative learning, treat each child as gifted and allow each child to develop his or her own particular talents."

But even Gardner cautioned about "some of the characteristic weaknesses of the progressive education movement," warning that "when [a] laissez-faire approach is carried too far, as it sometimes has been among progressive educators, one may be left with a large population at sea." Particularly after Naomi Hill's departure, P.S. 87 seemed increasingly adrift in this way, with no common curriculum or essential texts that each student was expected to master. After all, if every child was gifted in his or her own way, such uniformity made no sense. So while my older son's fourth-grade class studied the exploration of America by actually reading books and writing serious book reports, other fourth-grade classes (including my younger son's) meandered incoherently from one subject to another, without texts or book reports, but only hands-on projects. The notion that children should master a common body of core knowledge about our country or any of the major world civilizations or about the natural world was regarded as hopelessly outmoded. Under the doctrine of "learning to learn," it made no difference what subject matter was covered as long as all our "naturally gifted" children developed their "critical thinking" skills.

I was often struck by how little my children's very bright classmates knew about such foundational subjects of our civic culture as the American Revolution, the framing of the

Constitution, the Civil War. Sometimes as a prank I would ask my children's friends if they knew anything about William Tecumseh Sherman, for whom P.S. 87 was officially named. Of course, no one did, because they had learned virtually nothing about the Civil War. When I once told P.S. 87's principal, Steve Plaut, about my informal survey, he shrugged it off. "It's important to learn about the Civil War," he granted, predictably adding, "but it's more important to learn how to learn about the Civil War. The state of knowledge is constantly changing, so we have to give children the tools to be able to research things, to think critically, to use a library."

The idea that there are no facts about us as a people that our children must learn during their first five years of schooling had an important exception. As I was to discover, all children at P.S. 87 were expected to master those eternal verities sanctioned by the emerging doctrines of political correctness. Thus, while P.S. 87 children weren't expected to know anything about the dead white male their school was named after—the man who had helped turn the tide in a war that eliminated the institution of slavery in America—they were taught repeatedly about numerous African American heroes, about the suffering and extermination of the Native Americans and, increasingly, about women's rights and gay rights. To my knowledge, no progressive educator has ever suggested that children didn't need to know the "mere facts" about the contributions of African Americans to our society. If their school had been named after Harriet Tubman, you can bet that our children would have been able to identify her.

When a task force appointed by the New York State Board of Regents charged that the state's social studies curriculum was too Eurocentric and insensitive to the contributions of African Americans, I found myself remarking that anyone who believed that just didn't know what was actually being taught in the public schools. I cited my son, then a third grader, as an example, saying that he knew everything there was to know about Martin Luther King but probably didn't know much about George Washington. Then I decided to test my theory and asked Jonathan whether he had ever been taught anything about

George Washington. He looked at me in all innocence and asked, "You mean George Washington *Carver?*"

Despite the fact that P.S. 87 was already a living example of multiculturalism, that many of its children had developed cross-racial friendships, and that there were never any racial incidents in the school, many teachers nevertheless encouraged the children to think in racial categories and about latent racism. My younger son Dani's fourth-grade teacher directed her pupils to walk around the neighborhood for a week and to record in their notebooks any examples of prejudice that they witnessed. Dani came home grumpy with frustration: he was having a hard time finding prejudice on the streets of the Upper West Side. No P.S. 87 teacher ever told my children that the country they lived in was doing better than ever in the area of race relations, and far better than most other countries with a multiethnic population.

At the beginning of my younger son's last year I was astonished to learn that the third-grade teacher of Japanese garden fame would be leaving the classroom for a year to take over one of the cluster teacher positions. (The opening was created when one of the regular cluster teachers who could not be trusted in front of a normal classroom took a sabbatical leave.) I wondered why someone who was regarded as one of the school's more accomplished classroom teachers would be allowed to spend a year minding the yard and filling in for other teachers on their breaks.

It soon became clear that this was part of a larger plan: P.S. 87 was moving to create a formal school-based curriculum on the themes of political correctness. The third-grade teacher, a vocal gay rights activist, used his year as a cluster teacher to introduce a new schoolwide curriculum called "Peace Education and Global Studies." Its once-a-week sessions ensured that fourth and fifth graders had the right (or rather the left) perspective on issues such as racial prejudice, gay rights, world peace and environmentalism. Not content with mere academic instruction in these areas, the teacher also wrote a letter home to the parents promising to "infuse the idea of activism throughout this curriculum and explore ways for individuals to get involved and make a difference."

If there was one area in which most P.S. 87 parents definitely did want their school to make a difference, it was racial integration and equality. After all, ours was the school that prided itself on maintaining its racial balance and mixed classes. Its most deeply held credo was that all children, no matter what their family background, would receive the same quality education. Yet the saddest discovery I made at P.S. 87 was that its progressive pedagogy was undermining that objective. The biggest victims of the "don't worry about the facts; we are teaching your children how to learn" approach were poor minority children who desperately needed the basic skills and core knowledge that would allow them to compete in the real world.

Middle-class parents had choices, after all. When my children's teachers left them with intellectual gaps by wasting time trying to uproot nonexistent prejudice, my wife and I filled in with our informal version of home schooling, as did many other middle-class parents. And despite the school's progressive ideology, I noticed that many of the parents tried to get their children into the classes taught by teachers known to force the pace. Some P.S. 87 parents just gave up and, notwithstanding their support of public education in principle, moved their children to private schools. My friend Dan Polin, an Emmy Award–winning documentary filmmaker, was one of them. "Naomi [Hill] created a wonderful school for the first three grades," he said. "It wasn't that heavy on academics, but that wasn't so bad in the early grades, especially when you are a smart kid from an educated family background. Then by fourth and fifth grades you want your children to begin to be challenged academically. But there was little challenge there."

Years earlier my wife, Ruthie, had volunteered in Jonathan's third-grade classroom. She was assigned to work with the slowest reading group and was astonished to discover that all the children in the group were black and Hispanic. It made no sense to her that P.S. 87 should have a wide gap in achievement based on race. She became convinced that the single most important factor in those students' low performance was that they had never been taught—at school or at home—the basics of the English language. These kids were bright enough, but they had sadly impoverished language skills. They were missing what education writer E. D. Hirsch calls "cultural literacy."

In his book *The Schools We Need and Why We Don't Have Them*, Hirsch demonstrates that the most devastating consequence of progressive education doctrines is that they have widened, rather than reduced, the gap in intellectual capital between middle-class and disadvantaged children. "Learning builds cumulatively on learning," Hirsch writes.

> By encouraging an early education that is free of "unnatural" bookish knowledge and of "inappropriate" pressure to exert hard effort, [progressive education] virtually insures that children from well educated homes who happen to be primed with academically relevant background knowledge which they bring with them to school, will learn faster than disadvantaged children who do not bring such knowledge with them and do not receive it at school.

Hirsch also shows how the "thoughtworld" of progressive education guarantees that no educator ever has to face the music for this failure to raise the academic level of disadvantaged students. Education schools create an "impregnable fortress" of ideas and doctrines, which they, along with an "interlocking directorate that also encompasses the teacher-credentialing industry," transmit to prospective teachers. "Like any guild that determines who can and cannot enter a profession," Hirsch writes, "the citadel of education has developed powerful techniques for preventing outside interference, not least of which is mastery of slogan."

As I read these words I had the eerie feeling that without ever having stepped into our building, Hirsch was vividly describing P.S. 87's school culture. Our principals and many of our teachers kept invoking the same self-serving slogans so as to avoid any objective analysis of whether the school was really accomplishing its goals of helping all its students succeed. They constantly reassured parents that "all children are gifted." If some of these "gifted" children nevertheless did poorly on standardized tests, the explanation was that standardized tests didn't measure what was truly important—namely, "critical thinking" skills. And thus, few parents ever dared ask whether P.S. 87 was really successful in narrowing the academic achievement gap between poor and middle-class children.

During my last year as a P.S. 87 parent, some of us were disturbed when the state education department released results of the school's reading tests. A mere 53 percent of our third graders read at grade level, which was not a demanding standard. By now I was convinced that the children who performed poorly on the reading test were mostly minority, confirming what my wife had observed years earlier. Though the school could easily have broken down the children's test scores by race and family background to see if this was true—which might have occasioned some worthwhile self-scrutiny and reevaluation of teaching methods—it did no such thing. At a Parents Association meeting shortly after the test scores were released, our principal, Mr. Plaut, reassured us there was no cause for alarm; the test was only "a snapshot in time." What really mattered was whether the children went on to become "lifelong learners"—which he was confident they would do.

★

On a daily level, getting a child educated had now become low-intensity warfare. One day my son Dani brought home his fifth-grade homework packet for the rest of the week. I could see that this was going to be Christopher Columbus–bashing week. The social studies part of the assignment consisted of a few photocopied texts. One took the traditional view that Columbus was a great explorer who opened up the New World; all the others expressed the revisionist critique of Columbus as a mean-spirited treasure hunter who brought pestilence and genocide to the innocent native population. Without being given any historical background on the Renaissance age that produced Columbus and other New World explorers, the children were asked to compare the different texts—thus supposedly building up their skills in "critical thinking."

The math homework then took up the same theme in the grand P.S. 87 tradition that all learning should be cross-disciplinary and that the study of math should be relevant to real life—from Japanese gardens to Western imperialism. Titled "Math Challenge," the homework assignment for the entire week read as follows:

> Historians estimate that when Columbus landed on what is now the island of Hati [*sic*] there were 250,000 people living there. In two years this number had dropped to 125,000. What fraction of the people who had been living in Hati when Columbus arrived remained? Why do you think the Arawaks died?
>
> In 1515 there were only 50,000 Arawaks left alive. In 1550 there were 500. If the same number of people died each year, approximately how many people would have died each year? In 1550 what percentage of the original population was left alive? How do you feel about this?

We sent the teacher a note saying that our son would not be doing the "Math Challenge" that week. As politely as we could, we explained why we thought the assignment was foolish. Not surprisingly, we received no response.

Nor did it really matter anymore. Dani was about to graduate from P.S. 87, and we had long since dealt with the growing divide between us and the school by accelerating our home schooling efforts. During his fourth and fifth grades we kept him home between twenty and thirty school days a year, including all the half-days set aside for "staff development," when virtually nothing was accomplished in school anyway. Using our Israeli math workbooks and other study guides, we were able to create two-to-three-hour study sessions for him on those days. In math alone he was able to move further ahead during each of these brief home sessions than in weeks in his regular classroom.

Our modified home schooling project had made P.S. 87 work well enough for our children. Both of them scored very high on standardized tests and were accepted into selective junior high schools and then Stuyvesant High School. They benefited from P.S. 87's diversity, and both had several excellent teachers, guided more by common sense than by the catchphrases of progressivism. And P.S. 87 remained a decent, civil place, free from the violence and rancor that mars so many public schools.

Even so, my wife and I could no longer say, as we would have during those first euphoric years at P.S. 87, that we were unqualified supporters of the existing public school system. In our experience it had put the interests of its adult employees ahead of the needs of children. I could never again argue with a straight face that our public schools must be defended at all costs on the grounds that they were the only institutions capable of instilling a common civic and democratic culture in our children. After all, P.S. 87, the best of the best, rejected the very idea of teaching the foundational principles of the Republic.

In June 1997 my wife and I attended the second, and last, of our P.S. 87 graduations. We choked up with emotion as we spotted our youngest son, Dani, ten years old, in his first-ever white shirt and tie, marching into the auditorium with his beaming classmates of every color and hue. It was a moving ceremony, the children displaying the city's diversity at its most hopeful.

The valedictorian representing my son's homeroom class was a striking dark-skinned girl named Svati Lelyveld. After she read her charming speech (including a joke about her teacher's spelling lapses) we turned around to congratulate her doting parents, seated behind us. Svati's mother, Meena, was dressed in an elegant sari. An immigrant from India, she is a professor at Hunter College. Svati's father, David Lelyveld, is Jewish and a college professor. (More pertinent to West Siders, he is also the brother of the former *New York Times* executive editor.)

Addressing the graduates, our principal, Steven Plaut, said he was confident that all of them had "learned how to learn" and would continue to be "critical thinkers" for the rest of their lives. It was the same mantra I had heard over and over again for ten years. I found myself shaking my head sadly.

The idea that schools can starve children of factual knowledge and basic skills, yet somehow teach them to be "critical thinkers" defies common sense. As E. D. Hirsch has written, adults with high-order thinking skills are, "without exception, well informed people." So while it was true that many—perhaps most—of P.S. 87's graduates will be both successful and "lifelong learners," many other children in that auditorium without adequate family supports, who had to make do with what they received at school, will continue to lag behind. These were the children who were the neediest, yet they were getting the least. As social critic Shelby Steele has ruefully noted, "Every single progressive education fad of the past thirty years has hurt poor black children."

This was not the public school dream my children's generation was promised.

2

In the Middle

Parts of the previous chapter were published in *City Journal* and then reprinted in a two-part series in the *New York Post*. After the *Post* series appeared, I began to hear from P.S. 87 parents, past and present. The most surprising telephone call was from Jules Feiffer, the cartoonist and playwright. "I liked your article," he said. "You really captured some of those teachers." He then asked me for the name of my son's teacher who had assigned math homework on the number of Arawak Indians exterminated by Columbus. When I told him, he laughed and exclaimed, "I knew it!" Then he regaled me with stories from his daughter's year with the same teacher. (According to Feiffer, the teacher once gave the fifth graders a list of the most important feminist books of the twentieth century, but confused Betty Friedan with Gloria Steinem. When Feiffer's daughter called the error to the teacher's attention, she merely shrugged and said it didn't matter.) I asked Feiffer which school his daughter was now attending. He said that after their academic disappointments at P.S. 87, he and his wife decided to transfer her to one of the city's elite private schools for girls. For a moment I thought of asking Feiffer, a well-known liberal, what he thought about helping poor kids stuck in much worse schools than P.S. 87 escape to private or parochial schools; but I decided to leave well enough alone.

I received other calls that were similar in tone to Feiffer's, but many P.S. 87 parents thought my criticism of the school and its staff was too harsh. A few were simply upset that I had gone public with my complaints. Many of the parents who contacted me acknowledged that P.S. 87 was saddled with some incompetent teachers and agreed that something should be done about it. Yet they believed that their children were happy and were prospering academically. I recall one parent saying that, despite a few bad teachers, P.S. 87 was "about as good as it gets" in the current system.

Principal Steven Plaut played to that sentiment when he responded to my article in *Backpack News,* P.S. 87's biweekly newsletter. He began by acknowledging the merits of some of my complaints: "No sane and seeing person would argue that the New York City Board of Education is without failings," he wrote. "Unfortunately, all of us in this school are more than aware of them—the strangling bureaucracy, the ever shrinking budget, the layers of frustration and inconsistency." Plaut had once confided to me that the union contract was a major impediment to improving the school, but he didn't mention this in his column. Instead, he went on to insist that the school's "progressive" teaching methods and its "child-centered" philosophy were working. To prove the point—and take a shot at me—he reminded the parents that after graduating from P.S. 87, my sons had gone on to some of the most selective schools in the city, including the nationally famous Stuyvesant High School. "Not a bad record for former P.S. 87 boys," he exulted.

In this, at least, Principal Plaut was right. My wife and I were able to steer our children through the complicated selection process and into some of the system's limited number of desirable schools. Indeed, they were virtually guaranteed a seat at some of those schools merely by dint of the fact that they had graduated from P.S. 87, had scored high on standardized tests, and were white and middle-class.

The other P.S. 87 parents also had a range of choices for their children, and a surprising number, like Jules Feiffer, transferred their children into elite private schools. Still, these liberal parents continued to count themselves as fervent supporters of the public education system. In their view, public schools provided the only means of breaking down America's class barriers and ending racial segregation. They were also opposed to using tax money to provide private school vouchers to poor kids trapped in bad schools. After I had written an article in favor of vouchers, several parents told me that under any voucher program, private schools would unfairly "cream" the most motivated kids out of the poorest city schools, leaving the remaining children even further behind and more isolated. Yet besides having their own private school options, and sometimes using them, these parents were benefiting from an arrangement that—whatever its intent—resulted in "creaming" their own children into the city's best *public* schools. At the same time, hundreds of thousands of the city's poor children, with no decent choices at all, were being relegated to racially segregated and failing schools.

One of the only reasons that any choice at all was available was that the system was afraid of further middle-class defection. Interdistrict choice was pioneered in the 1980s by Anthony Alvarado, the whiz kid who, at the age of thirty-two, was appointed superintendent of the East Harlem School District. Alvarado's schools were allowed to recruit students not only from outside their traditional catchment areas within the district, but from anywhere in the city. He was given a free hand partly because the East Harlem district was performing so badly that nothing could make it worse. Alvarado also granted his principals a greater degree of freedom than any other superintendent in the city. Under the twin policies of choice and expanded school autonomy, and with Alvarado's knack for attracting and then empowering visionary school leaders, many dynamic new schools were created. Some even attracted a significant number of white middle-class students from other districts. Reading and math scores in the district zoomed upward from dead last among the city's thirty-two community school districts to the rank of fifteenth—a feat that led some education writers to call it the "Miracle in East Harlem."

The accolades that Alvarado received helped to elevate him to the position of schools chancellor in 1985. Unfortunately, he never had the chance to bring the changes he pioneered in District 4 to the system as a whole; he was forced to resign following the disclosure of personal financial improprieties. After a few years out of the system Alvarado made a comeback. He accepted the position of superintendent of District 2, an upscale area running all the way down Manhattan's luxurious East Side from 96th Street to 14th Street and then up the West Side to about 59th Street.

It was Alvarado himself who advised my wife and me about middle school options in his district. At a party at a mutual friend's home, he urged us to try to get our son Jonathan into a school his own daughter attended. It was located on West 17th Street, at least four miles from where we lived. The school had a very long official name reeking of progressive education jargon: "The New York City Laboratory School for Collaborative Education." Most people just called it the "Lab School" or "Lab."

Alvarado boasted that Lab was the best middle school in his district, and likely in the city. He was full of superlatives about one of the school's co-principals, Sheila Breslau, whom he had known for years. My wife and I took Alvarado's advice. After graduating from P.S. 87, Jonathan applied to the Lab School.

Lab operated in some respects like a private school. It was small enough (about 230 children in three grades) so that Ms. Breslau and most of the teachers knew almost every child in the school. And Alvarado had so much confidence in Ms. Breslau that he gave her as much freedom as possible to set her own rules. He then ran interference for her with the central bureaucracy.

Alvarado was an outspoken supporter of education equity and was on the left politically; so it was odd that he allowed Breslau a free hand in her admissions policies. This was public school choice with a twist: it was Breslau who actually made the choices. When my son Jonathan applied he was asked to provide his fourth-grade standardized test scores and a letter of recommendation from his fifth-grade teacher. He then had to sit for a special writing test and a math test administered by the school. The final step in the admissions process was a face-to-face interview with the principal. To my knowledge Ms. Breslau (or her co-director, Rob Mencken) personally interviewed every one of the more than 200 students who applied for the 35 seats that were then available in the sixth grade. This was the same gauntlet that children applying to elite private schools charging $20,000 per year had to run.

Of course we were elated when Jonathan was notified that he was one of the lucky few admitted to the Lab School's sixth grade. Still, we didn't have a clue as to why he was chosen while many other seemingly qualified students, including some P.S. 87 students with higher test scores, were not. It was only after Jonathan was at the Lab School for many months that we were able to see more clearly that Ms. Breslau, like any private school admissions director, had handpicked the students according to her personal criteria for what was best for the school. (The one clear difference from a private school was that no child was admitted to the Lab School because he had "legacy" or because his parents might make big financial donations.) Ms. Breslau seemed to be looking for children who were lively and verbal or who caught her eye with a certain spark.

The kids in Jonathan's class seemed not only bright but mature beyond their years. Lab's fame spread quickly as prospective parents who were considering having their children apply visited the school. After wandering around from classroom to classroom, these parents walked away in awe. No one could miss the academic seriousness in most of the classrooms, combined with an atmosphere of civility and trust between students and teachers.

In evaluating any school's effectiveness it is easy to fall into the trap of extrapolating from data about the performance of the students and using it to measure the school's success. When a particular school's admissions process is rigged so that it takes in students who score very high on standardized tests, for instance, the school can hide some of its problems and shortcomings behind the students' performance. To some degree that became the case in the other two schools that my children attended after graduating from P.S. 87—Robert Wagner Junior High School for Dani and Stuyvesant High School for them both. These schools had exalted reputations based on the achievement of the students they enrolled and, to an extent, both schools coasted on those reputations.

Lab was the one school that either of my children attended in which I was confident that most of the staff were working hard to bring some added value to their students' knowledge and skills. Of course, there was a malingerer or two. For example, Jonathan's sixth-grade math teacher finished the prescribed curriculum a few weeks early and then showed Fred Astaire movies in the classroom. But most of the school's teachers prodded the students to think much more deeply, to become better readers and writers.

One reason for this was the tone set by Lab's leader. Sheila Breslau had energy and vision in abundance. She was regularly in the school at six in the morning and rarely left before five or six in the evening. That example seemed to percolate down to the staff, most of whom also worked very long hours. Breslau modeled the serious, engaged classroom performance she expected from the other teachers in the school. My son was lucky enough to have her for sixth-grade English. She set high standards, asking her students to read serious literature and write papers, and she never fell into the usual clichés of progressive education.

Even with all the freedom granted her by the superintendent, Anthony Alvarado, Breslau had to cope with the suffocating work rules of the teachers' contract. But she was willing to go to the mat with the union over the incompetents on her staff. Eventually she pressured the sixth-grade math teacher who liked Fred Astaire into leaving. Perhaps the most egregious case involved an African American gym and health teacher who had come into the school under the "integration transfer" provision of the teachers' contract. This clause gives minority teachers the right to claim a job vacancy in a school when that school's teaching staff is deemed to be insufficiently "diverse." Because there are very few African Americans in the teaching force in New York City, the provision effectively forces any school to take in a black teacher who wants to claim rights to a posted vacancy, regardless of that particular teacher's qualifications for the job.

The teacher in question at Lab was verbally and physically abusive to students. In the required health class he regularly expounded his own crackpot ideas about subjects like nutrition and personal hygiene. One of his pet theories was that it was dangerous for the students to drink milk because it was likely to be contaminated. Another was that students should never touch the doorknobs on the doors to the school's lavatories, because there might be bacteria left by other students who might not have washed their hands. (He never explained how one could get in and out of the toilet without turning the doorknob.)

Ms. Breslau made a concerted effort to document this bizarre behavior and to initiate disciplinary proceedings against the gym teacher. She stuck to her guns even after he played the race card, charging her with trying to get rid of him because he was black. Breslau pursued the case for years, putting in dozens of hours in grievance proceedings to even get to the point where this teacher could be charged with incompetence. He was still there when Jonathan graduated, but a few years later I heard that Breslau's determined efforts had finally convinced him to leave the school for another position.

In another case the irrationality of the teachers' union contract actually worked in Lab's favor. The best math teacher in the school, indeed one of the best that either of my children have ever had, was a young Chinese American woman named Ms. Tam. She had begun her first year teaching at Robert Wagner, another middle school in the same District 2, but she was bumped out of her job at the end of the year by another teacher with more seniority. Ms. Breslau then hired her and figured out how to hide the teaching slot so it couldn't be claimed by another seniority transfer. Eventually Ms. Tam was able to accumulate enough years in the system to receive tenure protection.

When my son was at the Lab School, Jonathan Kozol's latest book, *Amazing Grace,* was making its way up the bestseller lists. Kozol is arguably America's most popular writer on education. In *Amazing Grace* he dramatized his point about the systemic underfunding of inner-city schools by focusing on "Mario," one of the book's most sympathetic characters. Mario is an angelic little boy from the Mott Haven section of the Bronx who is trapped in a failing, segregated public school.

Why is Mario's school so awful? According to Kozol, it's because the rich, white taxpayers of New York are unwilling to spend more than a paltry $6,000 on his education. "We say that in the eyes of God all children are of equal value," Kozol said in a speech, "and in the eyes of God I am sure they are. But in the eyes of America, little Mario has a price tag on him. He is a $6,000 baby. If you want to see a $16,000 baby, you have to go out to the suburbs."

I realized that my son was also one of those poor "$6,000 babies." Actually, during the three years that Jonathan was at Lab, the school was run on an average per-pupil expenditure that was even less than Mario's school in the Bronx. That's because Lab's student body was predominantly middle-class and didn't qualify for the additional federal funds available to Title I (high-poverty) schools like Mario's. Thus, the expenditure gap between my son's school and those suburban schools was actually wider than the one that so offended Kozol.

Nevertheless, the Lab School was more than holding its own. The college admission rates of Lab graduates, their SAT and New York State Regents Exam scores, and other performance indicators compared favorably with the very best suburban schools. And when I quizzed our friends who lived in the suburbs about their children's schools, it became clear to me that Lab's curriculum was as rich and its academic standards at least as high as theirs.

Of course I would have been happy if the Lab School had more money to spend. When I visited those suburban schools with their lush green lawns and acres of football and soccer fields, their swimming pools and modern science labs, I felt a twinge of jealousy. I certainly agreed with Kozol that my sons and their classmates and all the city kids deserved those amenities every bit as much as the children in the suburbs. But Kozol's money-is-everything theory cannot explain the success of the Lab School.

★

Nor could Kozol's theory explain the mediocrity of District 2's Robert Wagner Junior High School.

A year after Jonathan left the Lab School for Stuyvesant High School, our younger son, Dani, graduated from P.S. 87 and moved on to Wagner, located on Manhattan's gilded Upper East Side. Wagner was considered District 2's flagship middle school. It had a total enrollment of 1,300 students in three grades and attracted many of the neighborhood's white middle-class children, plus a large cadre of Asian students who traveled up from lower Manhattan.

Considering my rave review of the Lab School, the reader may wonder why my second child ended up somewhere else, specifically a big, traditional junior high school. The answer has to do with the vagaries of school choice in the real world of the New York City school system. In the four years since Jonathan had first applied to Lab, the school's popularity zoomed. Competition for the sixty seats for incoming students was now extremely intense. Since we knew that the Lab School gave no preference to siblings, we concluded that the odds were against Dani's being among the lucky few accepted. Moreover, we had to consider the complex rules governing the middle school selection process. If we designated Lab as our first choice in District 2 and Dani didn't get in, then all of the seats for out-of-district students at Wagner—a school with a good reputation—might be gone by the time the second round of the selection process started. Calculating that it was better to be safe than sorry, we designated Wagner as our first choice.

In our preliminary visits to Wagner we had seen a tantalizing hint of a time when educators were unashamed to be called "traditional" and believed that there actually exists a body of knowledge that they are duty-bound to introduce their students to. We were relieved because we thought this school stood firmly against the "progressive" teaching approaches that had horrified us at P.S. 87. We never again wanted to hear a school principal tell us that it was more important for children to "learn how to learn" than to accumulate "mere facts" (such as why the Civil War was fought).

Nothing seemed more old-fashioned and yet so reassuring as the presentation made to prospective parents by John Wettekind, Wagner's burly, white-haired principal. Wettekind was a former gym teacher who had worked his way up through thirty-five years in the system. Always neatly dressed in a tweed sports jacket, starched white shirt and tie, he seemed like a throwback to principals I remembered as a child in the public schools. Wettekind made you feel he was the unquestioned captain of a very tightly run ship, and he was blunt about what parents could expect. The children would be divided into tracked classes based on academic ability as measured by objective tests. They could move up to one of the higher-tracked SP (special progress) classes if they did well and could be dropped from those classes if they didn't keep up. Mr. Wettekind boasted that the tracked approach was working; he ticked off the latest impressive statistics on the number of Wagner students admitted into Stuyvesant and Bronx Science High Schools. Mr. Wettekind even announced proudly that the school had an honor roll with the names of the students who earned the highest grades on their report cards posted on the school's bulletin board. Hearing this, I thought I was being transported back to the 1950s.

Parents who were impressed by the buzzwords of progressive education were put off, of course. Surprisingly, however, many parents were eager to have their children at a school that stuck to the basics and rewarded high academic achievement.

The sense of being in a time warp was reinforced when I accompanied Dani to Wagner on his first day of school in September 1997. As we approached the building's main entrance on East 76th Street, we could see that a crowd of children and some parents were massed on the sidewalk waiting for the doors to open. I soon noticed, however, that there were no boys waiting, only girls. Somewhat puzzled, I asked one of the adults what was going on. I was told that under Wagner's rules, girls always entered through the main entrance, while the boys were required to come in through the schoolyard on 75th Street. I smiled at this archaism, but my son and I dutifully walked around two corners and a long city block to the schoolyard. Sure enough, all of Wagner's boys were there, some playing hoops on the outdoor courts, some smacking handballs against the side of the building.

After saying goodbye to my son, I walked back to the front entrance and found one of Wagner's assistant principals still guiding newly arriving girls into the building. I introduced myself as the parent of a new sixth grader and asked him about the gender-separate entrances. He explained that it was impossible to get all the children in through one entrance and Mr. Wettekind believed that both boys and girls would be better behaved if they were separated. He said that the policy had been in effect as long as he could remember. Jokingly, I asked him if the school had ever been sued by the American Civil Liberties Union or the National Organization for Women. He laughed and replied that they probably hadn't heard of the policy.

Alas, I quickly discovered that Mr. Wettekind's traditionalism did not extend to Wagner's classrooms or curriculum. In fact, our principal was hardly ever seen in the classrooms. The only time he seemed to venture out of his office was at the lunch hour or at the end of the school day, when he stationed himself outside the school to make sure that 1,300 students moved in and out of the building without causing any disruption. The principal I thought might have some steel in him as an educator had established what amounted to housekeeping rules, but then left day-to-day educational decisions and the supervision of teachers up to his three assistant principals. Each entering sixth-grade cohort was assigned one of those assistant principals. For continuity, that assistant principal stayed with the same group of students until they graduated from Wagner.

There really was no definable school culture at Wagner. Depending on the teacher, each class might be completely different in style and method from every other one. In fact, except for the academic tracking, plus trivial matters such as how the kids entered the school, Wagner was neither progressive nor traditional, That didn't mean there weren't some good moments at the school. Dani's classes were full of very bright kids, and he was blessed with a few excellent teachers. Nevertheless, everything important about his academic experience at Wagner depended on the luck of the draw. It was only by chance, for example, that the best of the three assistant principals, a smart, energetic young educator named Eric Byrne, was assigned to Dani's grade. Mr. Byrne was one of the few saving graces at Wagner, almost making up for the overall lack of educational leadership. He was always accessible to parents and took the time to monitor what was happening in the classrooms. However, not even he could do much when our luck ran out.

Dani's first year at Wagner gave only a hint of the disasters to come. Out of his five academic subjects, only his social studies teacher turned out to be inadequate. My wife and I decided that wasn't such a bad percentage. We wrote off the social studies class and gave our son some extra readings about the Greeks and Romans.

Two of Dani's other teachers in sixth grade were exceptional. The science teacher, Max Yerger, a middle-aged man with a southern drawl given to wearing cowboy hats, provided the sixth-grade students with a remarkably sophisticated introduction to physics and chemistry and engaged them with his enthusiasm about the subject. But the real unexpected bonus that first year was Dani's French teacher, Ms. Kaufman. *Voila!*— she actually taught the kids French. This was remarkable because the teaching of foreign languages had become a lost art in the New York City Public Schools. Most junior high schools and an increasing number of high schools in the city no longer even offered French (not to speak of German, Latin, Russian et cetera). Moreover, the school system's irrational regulations about certification made it almost impossible to do something about the acute teacher shortage in foreign languages. (More about this later.)

Starting in the second year, our lucky streak began to run out. The first bad omen was discovering that Ms. Kaufman would not be teaching Dani's seventh-grade French class. Instead, Dani was assigned to a veteran Wagner teacher named "Mr. S." After the first few weeks of the term, Dani began to tell us stories about Mr. S's bizarre classroom behavior. For starters, it appeared that the teacher couldn't stay awake. He would put an assignment on the board for the children to do in class and then, while they were working, he would put his head down on his desk and doze off. This was happening several times during each period. Indeed, the kids had turned this into a game. They would all keep absolutely quiet to see how long the naps would last. The record, we were told, was eight minutes.

I had heard enough to put in a call to Mr. Byrne, the assistant principal for the seventh grade. He took my call immediately and indicated that he was already aware of the situation. From his tone I gathered that this was not the first time a parent had complained about the French teacher. Byrne promised to monitor the situation and let me know if anything could be done.

A week went by and I was about to call Mr. Byrne again, when Dani reported that his narcoleptic French teacher had been absent for a few days. The class was told that he had been hospitalized. For the next few weeks, the French class had a succession of day-to-day substitutes, none of whom knew a word of French. So I called the assistant principal, although without much hope. As expected, Byrne said his hands were tied: as long as the French teacher was taking sick days and had not resigned or taken a leave of absence, he couldn't be replaced with a regular teacher.

After a few weeks, the French teacher showed up again. As my son reported, he dramatically announced to the class that someone wielding "a blunt metal object" had attacked him on the street, and he showed the students the long scar on his face as proof. For about the next week and a half, he showed up regularly. He also continued to doze off in class. And then he disappeared for a few days. This off-again, on-again pattern continued for weeks. Once again I called Mr. Byrne, who informed me that the teacher had now officially applied to the Board of Education for a medical sabbatical. Under confidentiality rules, Byrne couldn't tell me anything about the reason for the sabbatical, but I inferred that Mr. S must be suffering from some chronic impairment or substance abuse problem.

One day, about three months into the school year, my son announced that he had a new permanent French teacher. She was a recent immigrant from the Caribbean and her French was impeccable; but unfortunately, her command of the English language was not. To make matters worse, she didn't have a clue about managing a classroom. Confused and unsure of herself, she resorted to screaming at the kids. As she became more frustrated, the pitch of her voice climbed until she could be heard up and down the hallways. One day she gave the students a test that contained material they had never learned (partly because the class was always in chaos). When one of the students raised his hand and politely pointed this out, she tore up his test, told him he had a zero for a grade and ordered him out of the room.

Once again I placed a call to Mr. Byrne and repeated some of the anecdotes I heard from my son. Before I could finish, Byrne interrupted and, sighing, said he was aware that the new French teacher had "classroom management problems." This was such a transparent euphemism for the madness that had enveloped the French classroom that we both started laughing. Byrne said he was doing his best to rectify the situation, but we both knew how difficult it would be to find a French teacher with proper credentials in the middle of the year.

It occurred to me at the time that if our school had been dedicated solely to the good of its students and if it were run rationally, it would have been possible to solve the French problem. For example, the school might have hired someone from Berlitz on a contractual basis, or a teacher with private school experience could have been brought in. The children would at least have learned some French. But of course, this solution was ruled out in advance because it would have violated the sanctity of the teachers' contract and the system's arcane teacher certification rules. It was another instance of the interests of employees trumping the needs of the children.

Against all odds, however, Mr. Byrne did succeed in finding yet another French teacher with credentials. With about four months left in the school year, French teacher number three took over. She turned out to be the least damaging of the three permanent teachers and countless subs that Dani was subjected to that year. She had reasonable control of the classroom and was able to fill in some of the lacunae in the students' instruction. On the other hand, she had some very strange ideas of what was appropriate literary and cinematic fare for seventh graders. Before the spring break, she assigned a French language movie and its English language counterpart. Given the fact that the kids had had almost no instruction all year, the assignment itself was a big leap. Even more bizarre was the fact that one of the movies she recommended was the R-rated *La Cage aux folles*, far racier than its American version, *The Bird Cage*. If any of the eleven-year-olds had picked this movie, they wouldn't have understood one word of the dialogue but they would have witnessed a lot of suggestive scenes involving gay sex.

At the end of Dani's second year at Wagner, my wife and I did some damage assessment. We wrote off French as an almost total loss. Dani and the other children were basically no further along in understanding the language than they had been at the end of the sixth grade. We decided that Dani probably would have to start from scratch with another language in high school. Social studies was also a lost cause. The seventh-grade curriculum called for covering American history from the European explorers up to the Civil War. The teacher was actually quite intelligent and well informed about American history, but unfortunately he was trapped in the social studies department's penchant for projects and skits. He was particularly obsessed with the role of the spice trade in the early colonial period, so for weeks on end the class was dispatched to supermarkets to find spices and bring them in to class. The students then spent hours analyzing the properties of saffron, cloves and such. Another of his favorite projects was to have the children bring in examples of the essentials that the early settlers would likely have brought with them on the ocean voyage to the Americas. For several days the children came to school dragging valises full of old clothes, candles, pots and pans. So much time was spent trying to get the students to "feel" what it was like to be an early settler that they had few hours left to understand the American Revolution and the writing of the Constitution. The class never even got to the Civil War.

★

Coming back in September for Dani's last year at Wagner, I discovered that both Mr. Wettekind and Mr. Byrne were no longer in the school. Wettekind put in his retirement papers over the summer. Byrne had been promoted to a principal's job at another school in District 2. The new interim acting principal was Elizabeth McCullough, formerly the math department chair at Brooklyn Technical High School. Replacing Byrne as the assistant principal for the eighth grade was a former Spanish teacher whom I will call "Mr. C."

I was aware that the high turnover rate of principals was one of the school system's biggest problems. With over 1,100 schools in the system, administrators were constantly looking for openings to improve their personal or professional situation. Nothing in the principal's contracts or Board of Education rules required them to make any kind of commitment to the school. (One of the things that made the Lab School so exceptional was the long-term personal commitment of Lab's co-principals.) We had experienced the departure of principals before at P.S. 87, but at least parents there had the opportunity to have some input into the succession. In the case of Wagner, the two new administrators were picked at the last minute by the District 2 superintendent's office and then dropped on our school. Unfortunately, Tony Alvarado was no longer the superintendent, having left for a job in San Diego a year earlier. As it turned out, his knack for picking innovative principals was sorely missed.

My first taste of the respective administrative styles of Ms. McCullough and Mr. C came over what was now turning into the perennial issue of my son's French teacher. My hopes had risen during the first few days of the new school year when Dani reported that he had a new teacher, a tall African American man named Mr. Augustine, who actually seemed competent to teach the language. Alas, our elation didn't last very long. About a week into the semester, Dani announced that yet another French teacher had replaced Mr. Augustine. She was a woman who spoke both French and English with an almost undecipherable Chinese accent. Unable to control the class, she also resorted to screaming at the students as well as using other outdated methods of discipline. Among her first assignments was to ask the students to write the class rules ten times (in English, not French). One of my son's friends had a cast on his writing hand and couldn't grip a pen, but the teacher refused to accept this as an excuse.

After a few days of such depressing reports, I could see the direction in which we were heading again. I first made an effort to reach our new principal, Ms. McCullough, to let her know about the situation. She never answered my calls. Instead, I received a message from one of the school clerks directing me to take my problem to the eighth-grade assistant principal, Mr. C. I finally briefed him about the previous year's succession of French teachers. I told him that since Dani's class had received virtually no French instruction in over a year, the school had a moral obligation to make sure the class had first claim on any reasonably competent French teacher available to the school. But my plea fell on deaf ears. I asked Mr. C why Mr. Augustine had been pulled out of the class and replaced by someone with limited language proficiency. Mr. C said it was because of a scheduling problem. He rejected my request to assign Augustine to the class again, but said that as a former language teacher himself, he would personally help the French teacher with her "classroom management issues." He assured me that it would all work out for the best.

Of course, it didn't work out at all. The only time that Mr. C actually stuck his head inside Dani's classroom was when it had degenerated into total chaos and he had to come in to restore order. I'm not sure whether it was Mr. C or the new French teacher who finally realized that a divorce was in order. But at the end of the first marking period, all the parents received a terse letter from the principal announcing that the latest French teacher had left Wagner and the school was trying to find a replacement. There was no reference to the fact that this had happened five times in the past year and certainly no apology for ignoring the repeated warnings from parents.

Then, after several more weeks of day-to-day substitute teachers, a miracle occurred. A real French teacher with impeccable credentials named Ilana Laurence showed up at Wagner. She had a master's degree from the French Institute at NYU, had spent a year honing her skills in Paris and was taking the education credits necessary to qualify for a permanent teaching certificate. In the remaining months of the academic year, Ms. Laurence did a remarkable job of closing the gap. Many of the children caught up and passed an equivalency test for first-year high school French.

Rather than thank Laurence for the terrific work she had done and make an effort to retain her as a permanent French teacher, the Wagner administration apparently decided that no good deed should go unpunished. When I spoke to Laurence at the end of the year, she told me that she was reluctantly taking a job in a private school; she explained that although she had made it clear that she wanted to return to Wagner, she had received no encouragement from anyone at the school. Finally, a few weeks before the end of the year, she was informed that there was no job for her the following year because a veteran Wagner teacher was coming back from an extended sabbatical. And who was this teacher that the school was saving a position for? It was none other than the narcoleptic who had created the problem in the first place.

While the appearance of Ms. Laurence two months after the start of the school year saved the French class, three of my son's other academic classes—math, English and social studies— were now headed in the opposite direction, toward mediocrity and worse. What made this situation even more bizarre was that Dani's class—"801"—had been designated as the number-one- tracked academic class in the eighth grade. The reader might wonder why any rational educator would have gone to the trou- ble of herding the so-called smartest kids into the same class, only then to turn them over to some of the least effective teach- ers in the school. The answer is that no educator at Wagner actually made such a decision consciously. Since there was no controlling intelligence at Wagner, it was something that hap- pened by default. The school had an established (and arguably defensible) policy of tracking students by academic ability, but staffing decisions were made as if the tracking policy didn't exist. They were based on seniority provisions in the teacher contract, on bureaucratic convenience and on the teachers' own prefer- ences—with no thought given to students' needs. For Dani, the only honor about being placed in 801 turned out to be that he and his classmates lived through a year of trial by fire together.

Some of the disasters that occurred in the eighth grade could have been partially mitigated if one responsible and caring administrator like Eric Byrne had still been around. But Elizabeth McCullough ventured out of her office even less than Mr. Wettekind. She almost never took calls from parents, refer- ring most problems to the assistant principals. (I did get her to answer my calls later in the year, but only because she found out I was a journalist who wrote about schools, and because I had some access to officials in the District 2 superintendent's office.) Mr. C, in turn, seemed completely overmatched by his new job supervising four hundred students and about twenty teachers. He did put in many hours and he did take calls from parents, but he always appeared to be agitated and overwhelmed. Sometimes he would successfully take care of some bureaucratic detail concerning a child, but raising issues related to a teacher's classroom performance was about as useless as shouting at a brick wall. The last thing that Mr. C wanted to do was confront any of the school's teachers about what they were doing in the classroom.

The teacher assigned to Dani's high-school-level algebra class was probably the most inappropriate choice for instructing a group of highly motivated and advanced math students. He had been an accountant before turning to teaching and had a very weak academic background. It soon became clear that he was barely ahead of the kids in the algebra lessons. Moreover, he insisted that the students solve equations in only one way. These were some of the smartest kids in the school, yet he wouldn't allow them to use any creativity in coming up with a solution. Instead he drilled them relentlessly, step by step, in the basic problems that were most likely to show up on the statewide Regents Exam at the end of the year.

Micah Brashear was one of the most academically accomplished of Dani's classmates. In addition to having made Wagner's highest honor roll for two straight years, he attained the 80th-highest score in the city (out of 20,000 students taking the test) on the special science high school test. Here is how Micah's mother, herself a teacher, described the math teacher's classroom methods in a letter she sent to the district superintendent:

> Mr. J ascribes to a particularly rigid teaching style; it is basically his way or no way. There were instances in which Micah and/or his classmates would point out mistakes they felt Mr. J had made. Mr. J's response would be to argue with the students and ultimately call a halt to the discussion. There was an instance in which Micah was called to the board to solve a problem. In doing so, he redefined the variables (as x and $2x$, instead of $\frac{1}{2}x$ and x).

Mr. J criticized him saying that he knew his way worked all the time and could Micah say the same about his method. Micah responded that he was certain that his way would work. He was then thrown out of class for being disrespectful.

Notwithstanding their teacher's deficiencies, nearly all of the students in the math class scored very high on the Regents Exam, and naturally the teacher took credit for their scores. In reality, all of these talented kids were terribly shortchanged. Some of them, including my son, went into the next level of high school math at tough schools like Stuyvesant and found that a year of solving algebraic problems by rote had left them struggling at the next level.

But nothing at Wagner was as appalling as the social studies teacher the school so thoughtlessly assigned to class 801. She was young and immature and not very well educated, so she worked entirely from the canned lesson plans handed to her by the social studies department.

Under the state-mandated curriculum, the eighth-grade course was supposed to cover American history from the end of the Civil War to the present. The students were given a standard textbook on the period, but almost all of the class activities and homework assignments came from a foot-high stack of packets, titled "A Blast from the Past," that had been developed at Wagner with the assistance of a paid consultant. Each packet, about forty to fifty pages in length, covered a particular historical unit. In the "Industrial Revolution" packet, for instance, there were two pages with some sketchy information on historical figures such as Edison and Westinghouse. This was followed by a multitude of worksheets for the students to complete. The point of the exercises was to get the students to view the past through the prism of their own surroundings and interests. To understand the transition from the era of artisanship to the manufacturing age, for instance, the students were required to visit stores and draw up one list of items made by hand and another list of machine-made goods. To understand the concept of capitalism and economic competition, the students were asked to "make note where competition exists. Do you see one supermarket near another, one bank near another, one fast food store next to another? Describe what you notice."

Of course there were also lots of skits and classroom simulations. One day the students lined up the desks in a long row, each representing a station on a nineteenth-century assembly line. The student at the first desk traced a figure on a sheet of paper and then passed it on to the second station, where another student cut out the figure and gave it to the next student, who colored the figure, and so on. One of the students got to play the straw boss walking up and down the line to make sure everyone was working fast enough. Another lesson, on the infamous 1903 Triangle Shirtwaist Factory fire, was turned into a Ricky Lake TV show, featuring interviews with survivors of the fire.

Dani's social studies teacher favored the project method even more than the other Wagner teachers because she was incapable of imparting any actual history lessons to the students. Whenever there was any substantive discussion in the class, she was frequently contradicted by a student and had trouble holding her own. She constantly misspelled words on the blackboard and became annoyed when these errors were called to her attention. She once went on for nearly an hour about the "Albanian genocide" committed by the Turks and then denied she had said this after one of the children pointed out that it was the Armenian people who were slaughtered by the Turks.

The social studies teacher was also class 801's homeroom teacher, and it soon became obvious that she was working not a minute past the contractual six hours and twenty minutes a day. As my son and several of his classmates reported, she would arrive each morning just as the kids entered the building, and be out the door just after the bell rang to conclude the school day. If the kids moved too slowly she would nudge them along, saying that she had to close the door and leave. In the social studies classroom she almost never commented on the students' written work, and she often used students (usually Chinese girls) to grade her tests. I found this amusing because one of the social studies department's favored subjects in the "Blast from the Past" curriculum was the evils of child labor in Asia.

(Things could have been worse, however. One of the other

classes, taught by another Wagner teacher, was completely hijacked to test-run a child labor curriculum developed by the teachers' union. The kids spent the entire year writing and producing a play about child laborers in Thailand and Pakistan. The play was then performed at Wagner and other schools. A worthy cause, no doubt, but the kids learned nothing about American history. On the other hand, they and their teacher had their pictures taken and were celebrated in the American Federation of Teachers' national magazine. Shortly thereafter the teacher capitalized on her newly won fame and took a job at higher pay in the suburbs.)

I spoke to Dani's social studies teacher only once during the year. It was a desultory phone call in which I suggested that rather than perform skits, she might consider having the class read a book and write a research paper. She then explained to me why it was accepted practice in the social studies profession to have students "learn through doing." I was perfectly aware that her profession favored "doing" over more academically challenging pursuits. Indeed, of all the national professional teacher groups, none was more anti-intellectual, more committed to "constructivist" approaches to teaching than the National Council for the Social Studies.

There was no point in protesting, because no one in the school was supervising the teachers. By early May the social studies teacher had not even covered these essential components of the state-mandated curriculum: U.S. imperial expansion, World War I, the Roaring Twenties and isolationism, the Great Depression, the New Deal, the origins of World War II. With only six or seven weeks left in the year, however, she was determined to get to the Holocaust. Acting on advice given by the NCSS, she announced that in order to understand the Holocaust properly, the students must first be able to recognize "intolerance"—not the history of European anti-Semitism or Nazi racial doctrines, but ordinary, everyday prejudices that we are all guilty of. So she distributed a "Survey on Tolerance" that all the students were expected to fill out. A few sample questions:

- You walk into a crowded theater. Row seven in the mid-section has an available seat, next to a hunchback and a dwarf. Row twenty-four in the back aisle, in a corner has an available seat next to a young couple. Where do you sit?

- You walk into a restaurant where two tables are all that is available. Next to one available table, which is located by a good view sits a family whose one child has severe Downs syndrome. The other table is in the back by the bathrooms and kitchen, and there are two young couples to the left and right. Which table would you choose?

- You are the manager of a hotel that is completely booked for a busy weekend, with only one room available.... Two travelers approach the front desk requesting accommodations for the night.... The first woman to ask is very fat and weighs over 200 pounds, is untidy and frumpy, plainly dressed and is perspiring so heavily that blotches are discoloring the frock she's wearing under her armpits. The other woman is slim and graceful.... A scent of jasmine pleasantly teases your nose, as she stands close by. Whom would you choose?

With this foolishness in the background, the social studies teacher moved into the Holocaust unit. Naturally, the students weren't provided with any historical background on the rise of Nazism or twentieth-century totalitarianism generally, or insights into the history of European anti-Semitism or racialism. The teacher jumped right into the maelstrom and turned the class into a mini Holocaust museum. Each student plus a partner were assigned a main aspect of the Holocaust—some of the death camps, the Warsaw Ghetto, the Danish rescue of Jews, for instance—and asked to do a visual presentation, preferably a diorama. My son and his partner's assignment was Auschwitz and, yes, the teacher insisted that they do a diorama of the death camp.

After seeing the tolerance survey and hearing about the Holocaust assignment, I lost it. I had a discussion with Dani and we agreed that he would not do either of the assignments. Instead, he voluntarily did a research paper on the Holocaust. The teacher refused to consider the paper and gave him a failing grade for the Holocaust project. I then addressed a short letter to the teacher that was admittedly insulting: I said that the tolerance assignment was "one of the most moronic things I have seen in years of writing and commenting on education" and that it was "an insult to [the students'] intelligence." I also said that the idea of a diorama of Auschwitz was "offensive in the extreme." I added that my wife and I would be glad to meet with her if she wanted to discuss the matter.

Soon enough I received a call from the supervisor in charge of the social studies department. Ms. Ellis said she thought my letter was "a little strong" and "offensive" and requested that I come in to see her. I reiterated that it was her teacher's assignments that were "offensive," and I suggested that Ms. Ellis take a hard look at the social studies teacher's classroom. However, I added that my wife and I could come in any day after 3 P.M. to talk about the assignments with the social studies teacher and at least one Wagner administrator. I explained that my wife was also a teacher and needed time to get from her own school to Wagner. I never heard back from Ms. Ellis.

The meeting didn't transpire because the social studies teacher announced to both the assistant principal and the principal that she wasn't going to remain in the school for one minute past 3 P.M. When I asked Ms. McCullough (who was now taking my phone calls) if she supported such behavior on the part of one of her young teachers, she sighed and said, "There's nothing I can do. It's in the contract."

At that point I realized that Wagner, the flagship junior high school of the famous District 2, had turned into a loony bin. Our principal simply had washed her hands of any responsibility for what happened in the classrooms. The assistant principal was completely distracted and barely able to handle day-to-day bureaucratic details. Educational issues seemed to be completely over his head. Unless things completely blew up, as they did in the French teacher's classroom, the teachers could expect no scrutiny and no supervision.

Throughout that year, Wagner was a place without energy, without rationality or the human touch; it was an institution running on bureaucratic rules and the rhythms of the union contract. Like Dani's social studies teacher, many teachers were out the door with the students exactly at 3 P.M. Over twenty kids in 801 had passed the tests for the specialized science schools, but in most of their classes these kids were denied any opportunity to exercise their intellectual curiosity.

Dani and his friends were contemptuous of their teachers and angry at the administration. They frequently swapped stories about their most absurd experiences at Wagner, and at one point discussed boycotting the graduation. Finally they decided to attend, but a few of them declined to shake hands with some of the teachers when they were given their diplomas.

I watched the graduation rites from the balcony of the cavernous auditorium on the Hunter College campus. The dismal ceremony seemed to be emblematic of everything that the school had become. Ms. McCullough said about a half-dozen words and then retreated to her seat, turning over the microphone and the MC duties to Mr. C, who was dressed tastelessly in a garish white suit with wide lapels. Mr. C gave a semicoherent speech about what the kids could achieve with hard work and determination.

The guest speaker was a city councilman from Brooklyn named Herb Berman, who was preparing a race for city comptroller. Mr. C called him a "true leader" of education and cited almost every trivial piece of legislation he had authored. Berman let us know that this was the eighth graduation ceremony he had spoken at that week, but these were "the most awesome graduates, and the most awesome school, with the most awesome educational leaders, and the most awesome teachers." He went on in this vein for about five minutes, referring to our school all the while as the "Robert F. Kennedy Middle School" instead of "Robert Wagner."

Berman's self-serving and irrelevant speech was the perfect coda to a year that had been not awesome, but awful. He was a Democratic politician always supported by the UFT, and in return he never made an education proposal that discomfited the union. He positioned himself as "pro education" by calling for more money for schools and higher salaries for teachers, but never uttered a word about the strangulating work rules that allowed teachers like the narcoleptic French teacher and the social studies teacher to avoid any accountability for their classroom performance.

That summer after the graduation, I thought about the two

middle schools my sons had attended. How could the Lab School have soared academically while Wagner wallowed in mediocrity? Certainly the standard explanations of Democratic politicians like Berman and education writers like Jonathan Kozol—money and resources—made no sense. Both schools were in District 2, widely respected for its extensive staff development programs for teachers. Both schools had the same amount of money to spend per student. Both attracted lots of very bright students from middle-class families who scored high on standardized tests. Of the two, Wagner actually had much more extensive physical facilities and resources: better gyms and laboratories, a large, well-stocked library, an orchestra, more after-school programs and teams.

The answer was unavoidable: it was the leadership, stupid, not money. And freedom. With inspired, hands-on, dawn-to-dusk leadership, the Lab School was able, in some measure, to break the shackles of bureaucracy and union work rules and create a culture of high expectations for teachers and students. Lacking that dedicated leadership, Wagner degenerated into just one more school in the slacker culture of the union contract.

3

Stuyvesant High School's Dirty Little Secret

O n a bitterly cold Saturday morning in December 1995, I wished my son Jonathan good luck and then watched him squeeze behind the police barriers outside the entrance to Stuyvesant High School in lower Manhattan. He joined a long line of students already waiting to take the admissions test for New York's three specialized science and math high schools. Even after their children were safely inside the building, hundreds of parents continued to mill around nervously on the street next to the school.

The admissions process for the three schools is one of the last bastions of pure meritocracy in American education. Each year about 20,000 out of a total of over 90,000 New York eighth graders report for the three-hour math and verbal aptitude exam at testing sites around the city. The grand prize, a seat at Stuyvesant, is offered to those with the top 800 scores. The next 600 are admitted to the Bronx High School of Science. Another 1,000 students get into Brooklyn Technical High School. There are no "legacy" or affirmative action admissions. Political connections can't get your child in. Special consideration is given only to a small group of students who qualify as "economically disadvantaged" and come within a few points of the cutoff score. These students are given a summer course and allowed to take the test a second time. If they achieve the required score, they are admitted.

The high school options in the city are so limited that thousands of middle-class and working-class parents find themselves left out in the cold when their children fail to make the cutoff for the test schools. Some will then move to the suburbs, while others endure heavy financial sacrifices to send their children to private or parochial schools. Attending a regular zoned public high school is usually the option of last resort.

Of course, the situation could always be worse; and it would have been much worse if New York's iconic liberal mayor, John Lindsay, had gotten his way in the 1970s. As if anticipating the current controversy over the use of SAT scores for college admissions, Lindsay complained that the entrance exam for the three specialized high schools was "culturally biased" against black and Hispanic children. Therefore he wanted Stuyvesant and the other special test schools eliminated. Lindsay's own children attended exclusive private schools where money, connections and "culture" played a major role in the admissions process. Nevertheless, our patrician mayor believed that it was a serious civil rights violation for the city's elite public schools to use what in fact were race-blind admissions standards.

To Lindsay, the crusade against the elite high schools was a matter of ideology and politics. What was at stake for parents at the three schools was a lifeline for their children. Making an end run around the city's education establishment, the parents were able to convince two obscure state legislators from the Bronx, Burton Hecht and John Calandria, to intervene to preserve the special character of the test schools. The result was the Hecht-Calandria Bill, now Article 12 of the New York State Education Law. It reads in part: "Admissions to the Bronx High School of Science, Stuyvesant High School and Brooklyn Technical High School shall be solely and exclusively by taking a competitive, objective and scholastic achievement examination, which shall be open to each and every child in the city of New York."

Two decades later, Stuyvesant High School received another unexpected gift: a brand-new building. Even when I attended Stuyvesant back in the 1950s our turn-of-the-century building on East 15th Street was so overcrowded that we went to school in shifts. By the 1980s the building was falling apart. A committee of Stuyvesant parents and alumni then lobbied state and city officials for a new home. Remarkably, the city agreed to spend $150 million for an ultramodern building on a sliver of land next to the Hudson River in lower Manhattan.

The new Stuyvesant was designed by one of New York's leading architectural firms. When my wife and I first toured the building, we couldn't believe that we were in a city high school. Walking into the tan-colored brick structure, the visitor first sees a pair of marble staircases sweeping up to the second floor and two classic black columns extending up the entire height of the building. Escalators and elevators whisk the students up through the ten floors, each with wide corridors and spacious classrooms. The building contains a competition swimming pool, three gymnasiums, a modern high-tech theatre and ten fully equipped science laboratories. Some classrooms boast views of the Hudson River and the New Jersey shoreline. The fifth-floor cafeteria has a balcony with a vista of New York harbor and the Statue of Liberty. Finally, this property comes with central air conditioning.

The Parents Association raises more than $300,000 each year to help pay for a smorgasbord of extracurricular activities, including one hundred clubs and publications. The school offers a hundred-piece symphony orchestra, a symphonic band, a Renaissance choir and a number of chamber ensembles. The debate and math teams regularly score at or near the top in national and regional competitions. Despite its reputation as a refuge for "nerds," Stuyvesant also fields more athletic teams (girls and boys) than any other school in the city, including a highly successful football program that has been a school tradition for more than eighty years.

When my wife and I learned that Jonathan had been admitted to Stuyvesant we felt as if we had won the state lottery jackpot. At the time, I was writing magazine and newspaper articles criticizing the public education system, focusing particularly on the damage inflicted on schools by the teachers' union contract. Yet as new Stuyvesant parents we believed that the quality of the students, plus the beautiful building and the bounty of extracurricular opportunities, would make Stuyvesant one of the few points of light in an otherwise dreary education system.

Walking into this palace-on-the-Hudson every morning, our sons (our second child, Dani, entered Stuyvesant four years after his brother) were surrounded by three thousand of the city's best and brightest students, representing more than fifty different nationalities and ethnic groups. The students seemed to exemplify the spirit of an achievement-driven city with its succeeding waves of striving immigrants. Though many students did not count English as their first language, the graduating seniors regularly attained average combined verbal and math SAT scores of around 1,400—topping every other school in the country, public or private. Stuyvesant also usually ranks number one in the New York State Regents exams for all academic subjects and frequently leads the nation in National Merit Scholarships and in semifinalists for the prestigious Intel science awards.

But while the Hecht-Calandria legislation of 1970 preserved Stuyvesant as a meritocracy for students, it offered no relief from the bureaucratic regulations and corrosive work rules that plague every public school in the city. From the perspective of the Board of Education, Stuyvesant was just another cog in a rules-driven system. For example, the single most important decision affecting the quality of education offered by Stuyvesant is the selection of a principal, yet there never has been a truly open national search to find an educator with the vision to lead this nationally famous school. Instead, the process is stacked in favor of time-servers from within the system.

The standards of excellence that Stuyvesant's students are expected to meet are undermined by the seniority provisions of the teachers' contract. As many as half of Stuyvesant's teaching vacancies each year may be set aside for teachers seeking transfers from other city schools, and these vacancies are supposed to be filled solely on the basis of seniority. The fact that many of those selected lack the academic qualifications to teach to the level of Stuyvesant's students is irrelevant to the union and the system. The underlying premise of the contract is that any teacher with a state license is fit to teach at Stuyvesant.

Most parents, basking in Stuyvesant's aura, find it hard to acknowledge the school's dirty little secret. I was so grateful that my son was at this beautiful, safe and challenging school that for some time I too was in denial about the corrupting effect of the work rules. Jonathan was very happy with his classes. He joined the school's excellent debate team and quickly made friends with a group of wonderful kids, including first- or second-generation immigrants from Russia, China, India and Korea. Each had an amazing life story about family perseverance and hard work.

Jonathan also had an improbable streak of good luck with his freshman year teachers. The most memorable of them was Iftimie Simion, a refugee from Romania who was also in his first year at the school. Not only was he a brilliant mathematician, but he had a magnetic effect on the students. After complaining for the first few weeks that he was having trouble understanding his math teacher's accent, Jonathan eventually came home praising Mr. Simion's ability to unravel the mysteries of quadratic equations, logic tables and the like.

Simion had taught at the university level in Romania for thirteen years, was one of the coaches of the Romanian national math team and published papers in professional journals. As a recent immigrant, however, he hadn't yet accumulated enough education credits to qualify for a state teaching license. An education system that truly cared about the welfare of kids would have immediately recognized Mr. Simion as a unique asset for a place like Stuyvesant. But in the Alice-in-Wonderland world of the New York City Board of Education and the teachers' union contract, he was just another file number without the proper credentials. For two years in a row Simion came perilously close to being pushed out of Stuyvesant by an incompetent math teacher whose only claim was that he had toiled in the system for nearly forty years.

The union contract eventually became one of the flashpoints in a bitter struggle splitting the Stuyvesant faculty down the middle. The first shots in this educational civil war were fired after Abraham Baumel, Stuyvesant's revered principal of thirteen years, announced his retirement in 1994. The opportunity to take the helm at a brand-new hi-tech facility with the highest-performing students in the country would surely have attracted qualified applicants from all over America had there been a wide-open search. Instead, the choice was effectively restricted to two favored insiders. Murray Kahn, Baumel's second-in-command and a longtime physics teacher at Stuyvesant, had the support of the veteran teachers and many parents. J. (Jinx) Cozzi

Perullo was the other "inside" candidate. She had never taught at Stuyvesant, but had been an administrator in the system, including seven years as deputy to the superintendent of Manhattan High Schools.

Perullo's connections in the superintendent's office probably helped push her over the top. She was the first woman ever to serve as principal at one of the three specialized math and science schools, and the first principal in anyone's memory who was not a science or math teacher. She had a master's degree in Romance languages from Middlebury College and had started out teaching Italian, French and Latin in the system. Some of Stuyvesant's veteran teachers worried that this newcomer might neglect the school's elite science and math programs in favor of the humanities.

In fact, Perullo actually tried to upgrade the teaching of science and math at Stuyvesant. For example, by bending the rules she was able to save a job at the school for Iftimie Simion. Later she did some more creative interpretation of rules to get the best possible person appointed as head of the math department. She also worked to extend the time that students spent in some science classes from 5 to 7.5 periods per week.

What really bothered many Stuyvesant teachers, however, was that Perullo attempted to undermine the culture of the union contract. She didn't like the seniority system and the contractual work rules, believing they subverted academic excellence, and she said so in public. For this she made enemies.

Perullo once described to me a conversation she had with the outgoing principal, Abraham Baumel, as she was preparing to take over the school. Baumel told her that she now had the best principal's job in the city. At first Perullo was flattered; Baumel seemed to be suggesting that working at Stuyvesant was an exciting challenge, demanding vision and leadership. She soon realized that he meant something else altogether: that Stuyvesant was a great place to be a principal because there was virtually no way to fail. The quality of the students who passed the admissions test guaranteed the school's academic success. No matter what the principal of Stuyvesant did or didn't do, the graduating seniors would still achieve average SAT scores of

1,400 points; 99.5 percent of the graduates would go to college; and hundreds would be accepted to Ivy League schools or the equivalent.

Baumel's message to the new principal seemed clear: If the machine isn't broken, don't try to fix it. This school runs itself.

Perullo conceded that Baumel had a point. "There's never been a discipline issue here," she told me. "The kids always do their homework. In some ways Stuyvesant isn't a 'real' school. A teacher could fake it here for thirty-five years, because even when the teaching is inadequate the kids will find a way to do well on their tests."

I'm still not sure what made Perullo ignore the advice of Stuyvesant's elders. She was in her mid-fifties when she took what would likely be her last job in the system. No one expected this soft-spoken and dignified woman to rock the boat by taking on the school's union leadership.

One of Perullo's first targets for reform was the process for selecting applicants for "compensatory time" positions in the school. These jobs, including crucial positions in the guidance and college offices, were traditionally reserved for veteran teachers anxious to get out of the classroom. Everyone at Stuyvesant knew that the most suitable teachers for these assignments were never selected. For example, there were persistent complaints by students and parents about the cavalier treatment they received from the longtime head of the college office. "My frustration was that the philosophy of those who managed the college office in terms of dealing with kids was diametrically opposed to mine," Perullo recalled. "Kids would cry and parents were outraged. No matter how I tried, I felt helpless."

Perullo had the notion that as principal she should have some say in filling an in-school assignment that affected the well-being of the students. That would be nothing more than commonsense management in any other enterprise, but in the public schools it was a radical, even dangerous idea.

Anyone familiar with successful private high schools recognizes that the position of college advisor is critical. Elite schools market themselves partly on the effectiveness of their college offices. It would never occur to such competitive schools to encumber themselves by limiting eligibility for the position to senior teachers looking to escape the classroom. That a school like Stuyvesant was forced to do so was another indication that the public school system's rules and regulations were intended to benefit the employees rather than the students.

Adding insult to injury, Stuyvesant's UFT chapter had inserted yet another wrinkle into the already restrictive rules. To qualify for the compensatory time positions, an applicant had to meet a "residency" requirement: a minimum of ten years teaching in Stuyvesant. In other words, these key jobs were reserved exclusively for Stuyvesant's old-guard teachers. By excluding such qualities as individual merit, productivity and ability to communicate with students and parents, the process led inevitably to the arrogance and insensitivity that parents and students were complaining about.

Perullo failed in her efforts to revamp the college office. However, merely by challenging the union's prerogatives she incurred the wrath of the UFT chapter leader, a veteran biology teacher named Dorothy Suecoff. As the enforcer of the union contract, Suecoff stood guard at the ramparts to make sure that seniority—and its twin, mediocrity—always received their due at Stuyvesant. In some respects, especially in her ability to block reform, she was as powerful as Stuyvesant's principal. "Her role in the school is to defend the indefensible," said one of Stuyvesant's assistant principals.

The biggest weapon in Suecoff's armory was the elaborate grievance machinery available to the union if—god forbid—a principal should disregard any of the contractual work rules. In the schools that I was familiar with up to then, the chapter leader tended to file grievances against the principal only over issues dearest to the union's heart—for example, if a principal gave unsatisfactory ratings to an incompetent teacher. But once Perullo made clear her intention to try to change some of Stuyvesant's old ways, Suecoff became a ferocious grievance monger. She objected to almost every directive coming out of the principal's office. If Perullo proposed experimenting with block scheduling (i.e. double periods for some classes), Suecoff countered with a grievance. If the student newspaper ran an article critical of the union or a particular teacher, a grievance was filed against Perullo on the ground that the principal was supposed to protect teachers from students' criticism. Responding to the official grievances was time-consuming and distracting from the responsibilities of running a school of three thousand students. For Suecoff, who was relieved of some teaching duties to do her union work, filing grievances was the name of the game.

At the same time, Jinx Perullo was immensely popular with the students. She stood at the entrance to the building almost every morning, personally greeting students, many of them by name. We never discussed politics, but there was definitely a touch of the 1960s idea of "participatory democracy" about her. She even voiced some reservations about Stuyvesant's elitism. Yet she also believed that Stuyvesant students could be entrusted with many more responsibilities, including a voice at the school's planning council. Perullo even proposed having the students rate teachers in an anonymous survey—a widespread practice in colleges—as a means of providing useful feedback on classroom methods. She tried to convince the teachers that this was an idea that would become irresistible and that teachers would be better off embracing it than fighting it. But the union wouldn't hear this.

Representing the school's old guard, Suecoff regarded any privilege or concession given to students as a loss for teachers. It was all a zero-sum game. According to Perullo, some students once offered her a large campaign-style button saying "Kids First," which they had created for an upcoming school celebration. Perullo not only accepted the button, she wore it prominently for several days. When Suecoff spotted the button, she asked Perullo, in all seriousness, "What about the teachers?"

At the heart of this increasingly bitter confrontation was Perullo's refusal to drop the issue of the seniority clause. The *New York Times* quoted her as complaining that she had no say in filling as many as half of the teacher vacancies at Stuyvesant. Without the power to hire and fire teachers, she insisted, principals couldn't really do their job.

Another part of the contract that troubled Perullo was the "Transfers to Further Integration." This granted transfer rights for "minority" teachers—i.e. blacks and Hispanics—into any school that was deemed not to have a fully integrated teaching staff. It was affirmative action plus. Because there was a dearth of blacks and Hispanics in the profession, this meant that a school like Stuyvesant was forced to set aside its openings for any licensed black or Hispanic teacher who put in for the job. Perullo supported the goal of bringing in more minority teachers, but she bridled at the fact that the process was corrupted by the seniority rule. Integration transfers frequently displaced younger, dedicated minority teachers at Stuyvesant who had been groomed by the principal, but had no seniority rights.

UFT leaders usually argue that the seniority clause is insignificant because only about 300 to 400 teachers actually transfer from one New York City school to another by virtue of the contract each year. Against a total teaching force of 80,000 that's obviously not a great number. The problem is that the transfers are concentrated in a relatively small number of the system's most desirable schools. For those schools the impact can be great. After moving into its new building, Stuyvesant was particularly inviting for transfers. Which veteran teacher wouldn't want to end his or her career among students who virtually taught themselves, in a luxury building located in one of the city's most interesting and accessible neighborhoods?

Perullo kept a running tally of how many transfers were able to get into Stuyvesant and offered the numbers to various interested parties. According to her count, between 1995 and 2000 Stuyvesant took a total of twenty-four UFT transfers, amounting to 16 percent of the school's total teaching force. If that rate were to remain constant for another five years, it would mean that over a decade as many as one-third of Stuyvesant's teachers would have received their jobs because of seniority (or race and ethnicity) rather than professional accomplishments or proven ability to teach. At Stuyvesant, at least, the transfers were far from a negligible problem.

Even more compelling than the raw statistics was a story Perullo often told that dramatized the sheer stupidity of the system's personnel policies. One of its two main characters was the brilliant Mr. Simion, my son Jonathan's first-year math teacher.

By the end of Simion's first year of teaching, Perullo and the chairman of the math department knew they had a rare gem, someone who significantly upgraded the level of math instruction offered at the school. Simion was soon teaching college-level courses such as multivariate calculus and differential equations to the most advanced math students. He also coached the math team and supervised the math research program at Stuyvesant. Math department chairman Danny Jaye, a big baseball fan, referred to him as "my MVP" or "my indispensable franchise player."

In the public school league, however, talent doesn't count for much. Stuyvesant's MVP was vulnerable to being dropped from the staff because he had neither seniority nor a permanent teaching license. One applicant for a transfer who came close to bumping Simion was a seventy-one-year-old math teacher from Seward Park High School. Though he had thirty-five years in the system, this teacher had apparently never taught at a level higher than first-year Regents math—which 90 percent of Stuyvesant's entering freshmen have already taken in junior high school. Perullo and the math department were successful in convincing him that he was not up to the task of teaching the accelerated Stuyvesant curriculum, which far exceeded the state requirements. At the last minute, the elderly man declined the transfer that would have been his by right and returned to Seward Park.

Unfortunately, that wasn't the end of the story. A year later he again was approved for a transfer to Stuyvesant. Apparently, his union colleagues at Seward Park told him not to let the administrators at Stuyvesant intimidate him. After all, didn't the union contract stipulate that he had an absolute entitlement to transfer to any school he preferred? Now seventy-two and apparently beyond embarrassment, he joined the Stuyvesant math faculty. Fortunately, Mr. Simion had received his license so his job was safe. Not safe academically were the students (eventually including my younger son, Dani) who were assigned by the program office computer to the new arrival's classes.

Not all of Stuyvesant's teachers were happy with the union's definition of their rights and responsibilities. A physics teacher named Van Caplan was so embarrassed by Suecoff's confrontational tactics and personal attacks on the principal that he decided to run against her for the position of chapter leader. Caplan had taught physics at West Point for twenty years before taking a job at Stuyvesant, where he quickly developed a reputation as a superb teacher.

Contested elections for the chapter leader position are extremely rare in New York City schools, mainly because most teachers don't really want to be bothered. In this case Suecoff's policies became the issue. The election was essentially a referendum on two competing visions for the faculty: allowing the principal to make reasonable changes in staff assignments to benefit the students versus maintaining the status quo for the benefit of the veteran teachers. The status quo won by a vote of 72 to 63.

Although the final count was surprisingly close, the election sent Perullo a message: Suecoff had enough support from the staff to continue erecting roadblocks to her plans for reform. The endless grievances and the hostility they engendered were also wearing the principal down. "On a personal level, I had never experienced anything like this in twenty-eight years as a teacher and administrator before I arrived at Stuyvesant," she told me. "I was not accustomed to my person coming under attack because of my position as principal." A year after the union election, Perullo called a staff meeting and announced her retirement after five years at Stuyvesant. She minced no words in explaining that obstructionism from the union chapter made it impossible for her to fulfill her goals for the school.

Perullo's resignation received a surprising amount of coverage in the press. In interviews she continued to press her contention that principals needed the power to hire and fire teachers to accomplish their mission. This was so abhorrent to Suecoff that she was still waging war against Perullo a year after the resignation. At a union executive committee meeting, Suecoff introduced a resolution that Perullo (who still showed up at Stuyvesant from time to time because she was assisting her successor and had other unfinished business) should be physically barred from the building.

The reaction to Perullo's resignation was split. Members

of the hard-core faculty group that supported Suecoff could hardly contain their glee. On the other hand, many teachers and most parents were devastated. Among the many calls Perullo received from Stuyvesant parents asking her to reconsider was one from New York's senior U.S. senator, Charles Schumer. In a follow-up letter to Senator Schumer, Perullo explained that "the System's inability to allow instructional leaders to be just that without strangling them, put me over the edge after 32 years." Perullo attached a copy of her study showing the impact of the transfer policy on Stuyvesant's teaching staff and expressed hope that Schumer would look into the issue. "How can a principal be accountable when he or she cannot choose staff?" Perullo asked at the end of the letter. As far as I know, Senator Schumer, who has had the rock-solid support of the UFT in all his election contests, never said a word in public about the fact that his daughter's school was forced to accept unqualified teachers.

A year after Perullo's resignation, my wife and I attended Jonathan's graduation at Avery Fisher Hall in Lincoln Center. Just before the ceremony was due to begin, there was a noticeable buzz through the audience when Ms. Perullo walked onto the stage and took a seat with the honored guests and dignitaries. When she was introduced by the new principal, the entire class of the year 2000, all 750 boys and girls, rose as one and gave her a standing ovation.

It seemed to me that these smart young people were expressing not merely their appreciation for someone who really liked them (though liking kids is an underappreciated asset for teachers and principals) but for someone who had always leveled with them. In my view, Perullo's legacy is that she never tried to make believe that all was well at Stuyvesant because the trains ran on time. She wasn't satisfied that Stuyvesant kids had super-high SAT scores and that many were admitted to Harvard, Yale and Princeton. She knew that was the kids' achievement, not the school's. She always made it clear that she knew there were teachers at Stuyvesant who didn't belong there in the first place and others who weren't carrying their weight. She never threw up her hands to say (as so many principals throughout the system do): "That's the way it is. It's in the contract and there's nothing I can do about it." From the time she occupied the principal's office until she left, she tried to do something about it.

★

Jinx Perullo's successor, Stanley Teitel, represented a return to normalcy of sorts. He was the ultimate insider with all the proper credentials. Selected for the top job after serving as assistant principal and chairman of the department of physics and chemistry, he had taught both subjects at Stuyvesant for eighteen years. By reputation he was a demanding but fair teacher and a strong department chair. Rail thin, with a trimmed black beard and a deep gravelly voice, Teitel projected an image of youthful energy despite his nearly thirty years in the system. In contrast to Perullo's soft, almost motherly countenance, he was all hard edges.

My first reaction to Teitel's appointment was guarded. Certainly, I thought, it could have been worse. Jonathan never had Teitel as a teacher, but I had two encounters with him during his time as department chair that led me to believe he did care about the welfare of students. The first time I called Teitel was to inform him that Jonathan had an opportunity to attend a debate institute at the University of Kentucky but the scheduling of the state Regents chemistry test that year created a conflict. I asked when the test was being offered again. It was Teitel who then volunteered a much more convenient but unconventional solution: if we could arrange for a responsible person to proctor the test, he would fax it to the university, Jonathan could take the test and the proctor would then fax back the answer sheet for Teitel to grade. That is exactly what happened and my son was very grateful for this intervention.

On another occasion Jonathan received his schedule on the first day of classes and discovered that his physics instructor would be someone known as the most inept teacher in the department. I called Mr. Teitel to see if there was any chance to switch Jonathan to another class. I thought it revealing that Teitel didn't even ask why I wanted the transfer, nor did he come to his teacher's defense. Instead, he went directly to the point, as if it were common knowledge that one of his teachers should not be at Stuyvesant. He said that Jonathan would get the transfer, but only if there was space in one of the other physics classes. Fair enough, I thought. The next day, Jonathan was transferred to another physics class.

Teitel made it clear that he would be a "science and math first" principal. He announced that if the budget allowed, he would add more science electives rather than another course in English or the social sciences. To the veteran teachers and union activists who thought that Perullo, among all her other sins, had undermined Stuyvesant's elite science traditions, this had the sound of a restoration. To me the arguments about just how much the sciences should dominate at Stuyvesant always seemed silly. I was less interested in how many science electives were offered than in what our new principal was going to do about unqualified teachers in either the sciences *or* the humanities.

In the spring of 2000, my younger son Dani and I attended the half-day orientation held each year at Stuyvesant for the eight hundred eighth-grade students who passed the test but had not yet officially accepted the offer of admission. At one of the sessions Mr.Teitel addressed several hundred students and their parents. Playing the elitism card to the hilt, and in his deepest gravel voice, he promised the kids four years of blood, sweat and tears at the premiere math and science school in the country. He warned them to think seriously about whether they were ready for such a big commitment. Having scared the kids half to death, Teitel then pronounced, "Why wouldn't you come here? It's a no-brainer. You're the eight hundred top students in the city."

Teitel and an assistant principal, Eugene Blaufarb, then took questions on index cards from parents and students. After four or five predictable queries about courses, homework and the like, Mr. Blaufarb read out a question that almost propelled me out of my seat: "How do you hire and fire teachers here at Stuyvesant?" For a moment Blaufarb looked at Teitel. But the new principal wasn't eager to handle this hot potato. Blaufarb then said, "Well, we have the union contract, just like any school.... " I held my breath. Was Blaufarb about to own up to

Stuyvesant's dirty little secret? After a short pause he added, "But we're sure that teachers don't come to Stuyvesant unless they really want to be here."

I was amused by Mr. Blaufarb's assurance that the seniority transfers "really want to be here." Of course they do. Why *wouldn't* they want to be at Stuyvesant? As Jinx Perullo observed, teachers can fake it at Stuyvesant for years because their students bail them out with their high test scores.

Of course, not every seniority or "integration" transfer was a bad teacher. Jonathan continued to be very lucky in this regard. He had an African American English teacher who came into the school as a transfer but turned out to be a highly effective and caring classroom teacher. Jonathan's excellent Advanced Placement physics teacher was also a seniority transfer. The point about these two teachers, however, is that they would probably have been appointed on their merits, with or without seniority.

Not so with the five transfer teachers that Dani was stuck with in his freshman year—especially the seventy-four-year-old math teacher who had transferred from Seward Park High School. He was in his third year at Stuyvesant when Dani had him for the Sequential 2 Mathematics course.

Dani described him as a decent, gentlemanly old man who struggled to get things done in each forty-three-minute period. Whatever he did came straight from the textbook, but he avoided the more complicated problems and proofs. The scuttlebutt in the school was that there was an unspoken tradeoff for those students who found themselves stuck in his class: they would end up with a gap in their math education, but were guaranteed a high grade. The teacher seemed to hint at this by telling the students not to worry about their test grades, because he was more concerned about their "integrity."

I took advantage of open school week to observe the math teacher myself. It was obvious to me that he was completely out of his league. He worked at a snail's pace with kids who were ready to sprint. In the class I observed, he put quadratic equations on the board and then assigned some students to do the problems. The teacher used a crib sheet to steer himself methodically through the steps of the solutions. Throughout the exercise

I saw kids in the class rolling their eyes as if to say, "Let's move on already."

With this math teacher the seniority transfer issue at Stuyvesant reached a level of comic absurdity. His lack of mastery of the curriculum he was being paid to teach was so glaring that he had to sit in on two lower-level math courses at the school. For an entire semester he went to classes with the students (mostly sophomores and juniors), took the tests and was graded just like anyone else.

Nevertheless, it was impossible for an administrator to document that he was unprepared to teach at Stuyvesant. The only proof of his qualifications required by the system was the state license he had obtained over thirty years ago. Stuyvesant's administrators were prohibited from asking for a college transcript to see what level of math proficiency he had actually attained at the time the license was granted. Nor did the teacher have to demonstrate that he had kept up with his subject after all those years. As far as the system was concerned, he had a license from the state to teach high school math—the same license that Mr. Simion had.

There were many others at Stuyvesant like the elderly math teacher and the inadequate physics teacher, who made a mockery of Teitel's insistence on waving the flag of math and science elitism. On the other hand, incompetence was randomly distributed at the school. A case in point was the music teacher my son was assigned in his freshman year. She was an elderly woman with almost thirty years in the system when she was deposited at Stuyvesant for the duration of the fall 2000 term.

I use the word "deposited" advisedly. The music teacher was technically not a seniority transfer because she never actually applied for an opening at Stuyvesant. Instead, when she was let go from her previous school because of a cutback in music positions, she was then entitled to use her seniority rights to displace any other music teacher who was lower in the pecking order. She had done this many times in the past, moving around from one school to the other like a wandering minstrel. At the beginning of the semester, and with virtually no advance notice, the central board sent her to Stuyvesant, where she bumped a young, exceptionally talented and beloved voice teacher.

Unlike Dani's math teacher, his music teacher did know something about the subject she was paid to teach—the history of Western music. She was a well-meaning, decent lady anyone would love to have as next-door neighbor. Unfortunately, she was hapless in the classroom. Distracted and disorganized, she could hardly communicate with her students. Her speech was so muted that kids in the back rows had difficulty understanding her. She regularly lost students' papers and tests. She told Dani that one of his tests was missing but she remembered grading it and giving him a 76. When I saw her at the parent-teacher conference I asked how she could be sure that his grade was 76 and not 86 or 96. "Oh don't worry," she said in a kindly voice. "He's a nice boy and he's not going to have his average lowered because of music." (Music was counted as a full course unit for purposes of computing students' grade point averages.)

At the end of the semester, the music teacher was supposed to review the material to prepare the students for a comprehensive two-day departmental final. The problem was that she suddenly stopped coming to school. Dani reported that a substitute who knew nothing about music was the designated babysitter for the last few classes. Nor was the music teacher there on either day of the final exam. When Bernard Lieberman, the chairman of the art and music department, showed up to proctor the exam, the kids asked him what happened to their teacher. He shrugged his shoulders and said, "I don't know." Dani also told me that he was sure he bombed the test and so did almost all the kids in the class.

I didn't know whether to laugh or cry. I decided to call up Mr. Lieberman, a nice man who runs a pretty decent department. Following are excerpts from our surreal conversation:

Me: "What happened to the music teacher?"

Lieberman: "I don't know."

Me: "What do you mean, you don't know? You're the chairman of the department. She's your teacher."

Lieberman: "She just stopped showing up at school. She hasn't even picked up her check. We keep calling her home, but there's no answer."

Me: "So what are you going to do about the grades?"

Lieberman: "I don't know. I've never had a situation like this. Do you have any ideas?"

Me: (laughing) "You're asking me?"

Lieberman: "Yes."

Me: "You could give pass/fail."

Lieberman: "That's a possibility."

Mr. Lieberman then tried to explain the seniority system to me. I told him that I had written articles about the union contract and was well aware of how it worked. But he kept talking: "Then you know I have no control of something like this. I have no say about teachers like her coming to the school. She pushed out a wonderful young voice teacher. The UFT believes that teachers are like interchangeable parts—you put one in, you take one out. It's a disgraceful situation."

A few days later, Lieberman told me that the music teacher finally showed up at school. The following week I saw Dani's report card: He had a final grade of 90 for music. The space where his score on the final exam was supposed to be posted was blank.

I didn't ask and didn't tell.

★

As the reader will have long since realized, I was deeply (some of my kids' school administrators would say pathologically) involved in my children's schooling. Yet I sometimes regret that I wasn't more involved organizationally during the years at Stuyvesant. The truth is that I never viewed parent associations as effective instruments for bringing about school change. I thought that I could have a greater impact by using material from my kids' schools to direct fire at the dysfunctional public school system as a journalist. And in fact, my articles in *City Journal* about the destructive impact of the teachers' contract seemed to be attracting attention. Many were reprinted in the *New York Post*, the *Daily News* and, occasionally, the *New York Times*. They were often referred to and quoted by other reporters. John Tierney of the *Times* devoted an entire column to my views on the monopolistic public school system and why it needed to be shaken up through outside competition. I also appeared on TV talk shows to debate teachers' union leaders or Board of Education officials about the work rules. I knew that my critique of the system was resonating each time union head Randi Weingarten attacked me in her column in the union newspaper.

During the spring semester of Jonathan's last year at Stuyvesant I was invited to participate in a panel discussion on the public schools sponsored by the New York City Council. One of the other participants was Harold Levy, the corporate lawyer who was recently appointed schools chancellor. I had met Levy several times and was still hopeful that he might become a powerful champion of reform. But on this night at the council we argued about what the system needed most, money or teacher accountability. Levy suddenly sounded less like a school reformer than a traditional liberal Democrat (which he was) taking care of his core constituency by arguing for more money to pay all union teachers higher across-the-board salaries.

According to Levy, the reason the city had a much higher proportion of uncertified teachers than any other school district in the state was that teacher salaries were lower than in the suburbs. In his view, the uncertified teachers partly accounted for the low performance of city schools and students. Thus, he reasoned, the first step toward school improvement was bringing the salaries of city teachers up to the levels paid in the affluent suburbs.

I disputed Levy's theory, which also happened to be the theory of the UFT. As my main exhibit to prove that "uncertified" doesn't necessarily mean "unqualified," I cited the case of Iftimie Simion, Stuyvesant's "MVP" math teacher who was not certified during his first years of teaching at the school. I said that Simion certainly deserved a lot more money because of his talent and accomplishments, but why should he be forced to take a lot of useless education credits that wasted money and resources that might be used elsewhere in the system? Levy countered that it was preposterous to suggest that teachers as a group didn't need pedagogical training in an academic setting. He asked if I would be satisfied being defended by a lawyer who had no law school training.

I pointed out that Mr. Levy's own choices as a parent

refuted his theory. Levy sent his children to the Dalton School, where—like every other elite private school in the city—virtually none of the teachers were certified or had degrees in education. Most never even took a single course in pedagogy. Yet neither Levy nor the other sophisticated education consumers who sent their children to these $20,000-per-year schools worried about the quality of the teaching.

My participation in the forum had the serendipitous result of reuniting me with the amazing Mr. Simion. (The last time I had seen him was at parent-teacher conferences when Jonathan had him for freshman math.) Eventually it led to my being able to do something to raise the quality of teaching at Stuyvesant.

The city council education forum was videotaped and shown on New York 1, the local cable news station owned by Time Warner. Mr. Simion had watched the show (probably the only person I know who did) and was "pleasantly shocked," as he put it, that his situation at Stuyvesant was being discussed on TV. He wrote me a touching letter thanking me for bringing up his case. "It is comforting to know that people in the highest offices are aware of my plight," he wrote, elevating my station in life somewhat. He asked if I could give him "some sound advice."

Although I was not the high official that Simion initially thought I was, I did meet with him and the chairman of the math department, Danny Jaye. What I heard was yet another lesson in the sheer stupidity of the system that Chancellor Levy had been defending at the forum.

Simion was now in his fourth year at Stuyvesant. At considerable cost and time he had completed all the ridiculous education courses the system required him to take, including credits in special education and "human relations." In return the State of New York had finally handed him a piece of paper that said he was qualified to teach high school math—as he had already been doing brilliantly. Still, the Board of Education would not acknowledge his unique talents and academic accomplishments. To the contrary, a bureaucrat somewhere deep in the bowels of 110 Livingston Street had decided that it was too complicated to evaluate his Ph.D.-level training in Romania (partly because some documents had been lost in his flight from his homeland). Mr. Simion thus was denied the salary increment given to teachers who have attained a master's degree plus thirty credits.

He was also penalized by one of the most senseless clauses in the teachers' contract. It stipulated that a teacher coming into the system from any other school district (either public or private) could not be given salary credit for more than five years of prior teaching experience. The cap on experience credit had been put into the contract at a time when there was a surplus of teachers rather than a shortage. Even the UFT was now against the clause and proposed eliminating it. With Chancellor Levy bemoaning an acute teacher shortage, the clause was an albatross preventing the city from recruiting more teachers. In fact, New York City was the only school district in the state that imposed this recruiting restriction on itself. It was yet another case of the Board of Education shooting itself in the foot.

Between not being credited for his prior years of teaching outside the country and the school board's unwillingness to recognize his foreign math education, Mr. Simion was earning about $20,000 less than he otherwise would have been entitled to. His salary was also $35,000 less than Stuyvesant's seventy-four-year-old teacher who couldn't hold his own in a freshman math class. In the meantime, two nearby suburban districts not only were offering Simion a generally higher salary scale, but also said they would recognize his prior years of experience in Romania. (Stuyvesant physics teacher Van Caplan had left for the suburbs a year earlier partly because the city wouldn't acknowledge his twenty years of teaching at West Point.) It was almost the end of the school year when I went to see Mr. Simion at Stuyvesant, and he already had one foot out the door. Although he loved teaching at Stuyvesant, he also had a family to support, including a son about to enter college.

It occurred to me that if reason and common sense didn't work at the Board of Education, plain embarrassment might. I put in a call to David Klassfeld, Chancellor Levy's top deputy and, coincidentally, a Stuyvesant parent. I knew that not only was Klassfeld aware of Simion's reputation in the school, but his daughter had experienced the trauma of having the unqualified math teacher who had transferred into Stuyvesant. Klassfeld knew what it would say about the school board if Simion left the Stuyvesant math department while the unqualified teacher stayed, all because of the idiotic rules enforced by our self-styled "reform" chancellor. Klassfeld also knew that I would reveal it in whatever media outlet would offer me the space.

Within ten days Klassfeld called back to tell me that a partial solution had been found for Mr. Simion. A permanent advisory committee of outside experts had been convened at the board to evaluate the course work of teachers who had attended foreign universities. In fact, the committee had already looked into Simion's case and ruled that he was entitled to the salary increment for education. He would even be paid the increase retroactively, dating back to his first year of teaching at Stuyvesant. The back payment of about $16,000, plus the extra $4,000 added to his base salary, convinced him to stay on at Stuyvesant for at least one more year.

It was amazing to see how quickly the rules can change when there is the will to change them. I felt that I had made a small contribution to Stuyvesant's legacy of math and science excellence, and I decided that I should do even more to undermine the oppressive rule of seniority and mediocrity at the school.

I first had to get a feel for the new political landscape at Stuyvesant. Mr. Teitel was now beginning his second year as principal. Unfortunately he was not demonstrating a great deal of vision or courage. He was already telling people that he was going to spend another four or five years on the job and then take his retirement. My sense was that he would try to make his tenure as risk-free as possible. Certainly he wouldn't take any reform initiatives unless he was pushed by the parents.

Stuyvesant had just put into place its School Leadership Team (SLT), as recently mandated by state education law. This was supposedly a vehicle for parents, teachers and students to collaborate in coming up with proposals for school improvement. It was intended to be something like a board of directors representing the collective will of the school's different constituencies, but with proportionately greater weight given to the parents, who were to have the same number of seats as teachers and administrators combined. Students were also to serve on the high school SLTs, but there was some disagreement as to whether the regulations intended that they be given a vote. In theory, if the SLT reached a consensus it could make major decisions about school practices that the principal (as the school's CEO) was then required to carry out.

Despite the promise of parent empowerment I had few illusions that the SLT would lead a breakthrough for reform at Stuyvesant. There was a big Catch 22 in the enabling legislation: a school SLT could not adopt any policy that conflicted with the union contract. This was like saying that the delegates to the Continental Congress were free to adopt their own laws provided they didn't conflict with the decrees of the King's Privy Council. Thus I wasn't surprised when I heard that the SLT had accomplished nothing in its first year of operation. I was told by some of the parents that the main reason for the stalemate was that the UFT chapter chair, Dorothy Suecoff, effectively blocked every proposal for change by filing a grievance or threatening to file one.

My expectations were low, but I decided it would be useful to attend as many SLT meetings as possible during the 2000–2001 school year. At these open sessions all of the school constituencies—parents, students, teachers and administrators— were supposed to set aside their parochial concerns and do what was best for Stuyvesant as an education community. I hoped that I might be able to lobby some of the parent delegates to be a little bolder and focus on the issues of teacher performance and accountability. The meetings would also provide an opportunity to see Suecoff in action. (She had declined my requests to interview her.) The chair of the UFT chapter had a permanent seat at the SLT, and by all accounts she was not shy about saying what was on her mind.

The first SLT meeting I attended was held in the school cafeteria. It had the look of a United Nations Security Council meeting, except that the twenty-five delegates sat at tables arranged as a square instead of a circle. The meeting opened with many delegates expressing frustration that almost nothing had been accomplished in their one-year-plus of existence. Much like the UN, this was attributed to excessive procedural wrangling or the power of one permanent member. Suecoff had apparently played the role of Vyshinsky, the Soviet Union's infamous UN ambassador during the Cold War who kept saying *nyet* and vetoed just about every resolution passed by the Security Council majority.

"This is a cumbersome legislature without the ability to make decisions," complained parent delegate John Wagner at the meeting. A teacher named Mr. Levin agreed, saying, "It's our third meeting this year and nothing has been accomplished." Math department chair Danny Jaye then chimed in with an even more succinct comment about the SLT's seeming paralysis: "This is making me crazy."

The parent delegates felt that the actions taken by the UFT chapter leader were largely responsible for the previous year's gridlock. The SLT would work on an issue through several meetings and arrive at an agreement about what should be done, only to be told by Suecoff that the proposed change violated the teachers' union contract.

In one such instance the SLT had adopted a resolution calling for the principal to start an experiment with block scheduling. The idea was to have some teachers voluntarily teach some classes for two periods in a row, that is, for an hour and a half, instead of one forty-three-minute period every day. (This was essentially the same proposal made by Jinx Perullo three years earlier.) A tremendous amount of time and effort went into drawing up the plan, including a visit by some delegates to Thomas Jefferson High School in Virginia, which uses block scheduling. But the proposal was killed at the end of this elaborate process when Suecoff filed a grievance with the superintendent of Manhattan High Schools. She claimed that the block scheduling would have meant that some teachers exceeded the contractual limit of teaching five periods in one day—even though this would be balanced by teaching fewer than five periods on other days. The grievance was upheld—even though the teachers in question would have *volunteered* to teach the block schedule.

Trying to head off a similar fiasco in the future, one of the SLT subcommittees proposed a resolution requesting delegates to inform the SLT very early on in the process if they believed that a proposed initiative would "contravene a union contract or state education law." The resolution was clearly aimed at the UFT chapter chair, the only person who was invoking the union contract to kill proposals. Suecoff was actually on the subcommittee that proposed the resolution and everyone believed she had agreed to it.

But Suecoff sat expressionless as the resolution was read, and then made the following announcement: "I can't be bound by this resolution. I represent the staff. I have the right to file a grievance against this committee." Many of the delegates were shocked by this response. As one parent delegate pointed out, no one disputed the right of the UFT chair to file grievances. All that was asked of Suecoff—as a courtesy and as a means of making the SLT operate more efficiently—was to let the delegates know when she thought they were headed into territory covered by the union contract. Suecoff wouldn't even offer her fellow delegates that crumb. She insisted that she wasn't going to provide the SLT with the benefit of her interpretation of the contract. "A grievance is a private matter," she added with emphasis.

I sat through four SLT meetings during the 2000–2001 school year. I never heard Suecoff say anything about education at Stuyvesant. She did, however, reveal some of her pet peeves about the school. At one meeting she took advantage of a very indulgent student who was chairing the meeting (the chair rotated between the different constituencies) and began venting about the condition of the Stuyvesant bathrooms. This had nothing to do with the agenda item on the table, but Suecoff insisted on telling a story about how one of her female students came out of the girls' bathroom gagging and complaining about the stench. Suecoff said she went into the bathroom with one of her petrie dishes and took a sample of the "fetid fluid" she saw gathering on the floor. Producing the petrie dish out of her purse, she announced that she had cultured some lethal-sounding bacteria. She then turned to Principal Teitel and pushed the petrie dish across the table toward him. "Do something about it," she said imperiously. Teitel sat there in stunned silence.

At the same meeting Suecoff interrupted a discussion about Stuyvesant's budget to send another shot across the principal's bow. She told Teitel that he could save money and bother by leaving the biology department alone and not starting a search for a new departmental chairman. (The department had been operating with a rotating coordinator for two years after its previous chairman, Richard Plass, was taken out of the building in handcuffs and charged with sexually molesting a female student. As part of a plea bargain, Plass pleaded no contest to the charges, served no jail time and was allowed to retire from the system.) "We're doing fine," Suecoff insisted. "We don't need anyone to supervise us."

No doubt she was reflecting the views of the veteran biology teachers who preferred not to have anyone looking over their shoulders. However, her claim that the department was "doing fine" was risible. The reality was that biology was the most disorganized of the math/science departments at Stuyvesant. It was the only department that hadn't managed to create its own website where students could obtain study materials and other important information.

My son Dani and hundreds of other freshmen found out just how "fine" the biology department was doing when they took the department's final exam a few days later. The multiple-choice questions were full of errors and typos. There was no correct answer for several questions. There were two different questions listed for the same number on the answer sheet. During the test, the proctors in the classrooms (who were not biology teachers) were besieged with requests for clarification and were constantly running out to the hallways to speak to the biology teachers. This created constant disruptions and affected the students' ability to concentrate on the exam.

I complained in writing to Principal Teitel about the biology test and about how this fiasco made it clear that the department needed a permanent chairperson. Teitel responded within a day, saying that I was right in my description of the test and that he had already begun the process of recruiting for a permanent assistant principal/biology department chair. "I believe this is the first step to rectify the situation," he wrote. True to his word, Teitel soon announced the formation of a C-30 committee, which constituted the first-level screening of candidates for a new biology chairperson. I served as one of the ten parent members on the C-30 committee. Although the proceedings were confidential, I can say that our committee did not support the candidacy of the Stuyvesant biology department coordinator who had been responsible for the disastrous final exam but was still favored by some of the old-guard teachers. The person eventually chosen came from outside Stuyvesant and at least gave some promise of bringing much-needed leadership to the department.

The episode showed that our principal would respond to pressure from parents. If Suecoff was going to lean on Mr. Teitel to preserve the status quo and protect teachers from any outside scrutiny, it was essential that parents push back to get the principal to do what was right. That's why I was appalled that the parent delegates had allowed the UFT chapter chair to set the parameters of permissible debate. At an informal meeting with some of the parents, I said that I didn't understand why they needed Suecoff to interpret the contract to them. I pointed out that she wasn't exactly a disinterested party. "The contract is written in plain English," I said. "Why don't you read it and decide for yourself whether something you want to get done for the school violates the contract or not?" I urged the parents to push ahead with proposals for reform even if Suecoff filed a grievance and advised them to face the fact that the contract itself was the issue. I proposed that they go outside the SLT and fight in the public arena against the restrictions that the union contract was imposing on our school.

Most of the parents were not prepared for anything like that. They almost all agreed that the contract created some of the school's most acute problems, but they couldn't imagine getting into a nasty fight with the union. Most felt that the more prudent course would be to continue to press for whatever modest improvements they could get out of the SLT structure.

The five student representatives on the SLT had a more

realistic view of the politics of school reform. In the first place, they provided a constant flow of personal testimony about the problem of poor teaching at Stuyvesant and the lack of accountability for the staff. The leader of the student delegation was Matt Kelley, a tall, handsome senior with blond hair falling below his shoulders who sometimes showed up at meetings looking disheveled. Kelley mocked Teitel's pretensions about Stuyvesant being a great science and math school. "A lot of us came to Stuyvesant because of the math and science," Kelley once pronounced, "but then we discovered that the worst teaching was in those subjects."

Kelley, with classic adolescent contrariety, often needlessly antagonized teachers and administrators. Nevertheless, I credit him with going directly to the heart of the matter on the subject of the union contract. At one meeting the student delegates pushed for teachers to set aside time during the day to meet with students who needed academic help or just wanted more personal contact with their instructors, in the same way that college professors are required to have office hours. This was an eminently reasonable request, since Stuyvesant teachers were notorious for leaving the building as soon as their last teaching period was over. Many even arranged their schedules so that they worked a five-hour day or less.

Suecoff's response to the students' proposal was that it was a nonstarter because all the hours of the school day permitted by the contract were already accounted for. A visibly frustrated Kelley then blurted out: "Every time the students try to bring up a program to improve education we are told it violates the teachers' contract. It seems like education improvement is itself a violation of the contract."

I thought these were the truest words spoken at the SLT all year and that they should have been hung on a plaque at the entrance to the school.

What I saw at the SLT confirmed that Stuyvesant teachers were fearful of being judged and found wanting. The union contract was like an amulet protecting them from outside scrutiny. That is why there was near-hysteria over any suggestion that Stuyvesant students be able to rate their teachers. The union chapter rejected the idea out of hand when Jinx Perullo first proposed it in 1997, and it was deflected again when it came up at the SLT.

Near the end of the 2000–2001 school year the ratings issue resurfaced from an unexpected source. A junior student named Gary He created his own website for Stuyvesant students, and among the services he offered were ratings of Stuyvesant teachers by students. There was nothing comprehensive about Gary's survey. He also made the mistake of allowing off-color remarks about some teachers to be posted, something he later said he regretted. Still, most people who saw the short-lived ratings thought they were pretty accurate. For example, Mr Simion received the highest number of rave reviews, while the math teacher who transferred from Seward Park High School drew overwhelmingly negative comments.

But it was neither the accuracy nor the fairness of Gary's rating system that unsettled Stuyvesant's faculty. It was rather the fear of being judged—period. At a staff meeting with the principal, several teachers demanded that something drastic be done. One teacher proposed that if Gary didn't shut down the website immediately, the faculty should refuse to write college recommendations for the entire junior class. Another teacher threatened to sue Gary for libel. After being called into the principal's office with his mother, Gary stopped posting the ratings.

The genie was out of the bottle in any case. First the student newspaper carried an account of the faculty's reaction, and then the story made it to the *New York Times* and most of the local TV news programs. Gary He's Chinese immigrant mother was quoted about Stuyvesant's muzzling of her son: "If there were no freedom of expression in this country, we wouldn't have come here in the first place." Lots of people now knew that teachers at the premiere math and science school in the country were so afraid of criticism that they were willing to muzzle free speech. Jinx Perullo's warning to the teachers that they would be better served by embracing a fair rating system than waiting for it to happen to them turned out to have been prophetic.

There was a deep sense of dismay over the incident among a few parents. "This is just disgraceful," said Marilena

Christodoulou, the president of the Parents Association, whose son, Peter, is a good friend of Gary He's. "Gary's a terrific, hard-working kid and he didn't do anything that justified the threats against him and the other students. What are the teachers so afraid of?"

Christodoulou and her husband, Ari, are Greek immigrants who climbed the ladder of success in this country, high enough to be able to send Peter to an exclusive East Side private school through eighth grade. When he passed the admission test, they helped convince him that attending Stuyvesant would be a double bonus: he would get the diversity of the public schools and the excellence in math and science. (This was an interesting reversal of the pattern I had seen at P.S. 87 and elsewhere—liberal parents switching their children from public to private schools.) Then Peter was assigned to the seventy-two-year-old transfer teacher for freshman math. "That's what got me active in the Parents Association," Marilena said. "I needed to find out how something like that could happen at a school like Stuyvesant and whether there was anything we could do about it."

Marilena's popularity among the parents was such that she was elected to the PA presidency for two straight years. After a frustrating first year attending meetings of the SLT, she was ready for something more useful and radical. She initiated meetings with the PA presidents of the other test schools with a view to pressuring the Board of Education to grant their schools relief from the stifling bureaucratic regulations and the union contract's seniority clauses. She had encouraged me to protest the biology department's ineptitude and then put me on the committee to recommend a new biology chairperson. During the summer of 2001 Marilena and I were meeting informally with other parents to think of ways to pressure Mr. Teitel to stand up to those in the school who were fanatically opposed to change. I joked with her about our little conspiracy to start a revolution at Stuyvesant.

We had agreed to meet again during the second week after the opening of school in September, but the meeting never happened. On the morning of September 11 both of our sons were in their classrooms and witnessed the second hijacked plane crash into the World Trade Center three blocks south of Stuyvesant. They were dismissed onto the street just before the second tower came down and then had to run for their lives. There is a video clip that was shown over and over again on TV news broadcasts showing hundreds of Stuyvesant kids running north up West Street just ahead of the huge dust cloud created by the tower's collapse.

After 9/11 our plans for trying to shake up the status quo were necessarily put on hold. Marilena and other PA activists were completely preoccupied in dealing with the consequences of the attack for the children's health and safety. After meeting in the Brooklyn Tech building for about three weeks, the students and teachers returned to Stuyvesant on October 9. To Mayor Giuliani and other political leaders, Stuyvesant was the most famous of the ground zero schools and it became a symbol of the city's recovery. But the political pressure to return the students quickly and the inept handling of the building's cleanup forced Marilena and other PA leaders into a series of nasty confrontations with the Board of Education and the school administration. It took the entire year and the threat of a lawsuit against the board to have the school finally cleaned of all the dangerous contamination from 9/11.

Stuyvesant was a bittersweet experience for the Christodoulous. "Peter eventually had a number of outstanding teachers, including Mr. Simion," Marilena recalled. "But my first disappointment was that the quality of the teaching was not up to the reputation of the school. Then in the year after 9/11 I was shocked at the bureaucratic ineptitude, starting with the school administration and all the way to the chancellor's office. I realized that dramatic change can come only through pressure from the outside, certainly not from within the system."

By the end of the year, Marilena's son had graduated and we had a newly elected PA leadership, far more passive and willing to accommodate the school administration. I went back to what I felt I did best—writing articles about the need for radical school reform and sometimes using Stuyvesant as an example of what was wrong with the system. Many people still couldn't understand how I could be critical of a school like Stuyvesant.

"Your child is in the best school in the city," they would say to me. I would try to explain by quoting Jinx Perullo about the kids making the school and how easy it was for teachers to coast.

My older son graduated with the first Stuyvesant class of the new millennium. My younger son is due to graduate at the same time that Stuyvesant is celebrating its one-hundredth birthday. Although I started out joking about it, I am convinced that Stuyvesant does need a revolution if it is to justify its exalted reputation into the twenty-first century. It needs to break free from the shackles of a union contract that was written for the industrial workplace of the 1950s and that undermines the ideal of academic excellence the school was founded on. It must then be guided by the fundamental principle that the interests of its students come ahead of staff claims to lifetime job security and the perks of seniority. This would mean, for example, that Stuyvesant's principal would be allowed to hire a teacher like Mr. Simion based on his academic attainment and his proven ability to perform in the classroom, regardless of whether he had a state license. It would also mean that Stuyvesant's principal would be hired after a national search that included candidates from private and parochial schools.

There is one final lesson that Stuyvesant teaches: If what I have described can happen inside the "best school" in the system, think of what the lack of accountability and the rule of mediocrity do to schools already under stress. My sons and Marilena's son will eventually forget the incompetents and remember Stuyvesant fondly for brilliant, caring teachers like Iftimie Simion and for their extraordinary fellow students. But for the children in the city's vast archipelago of failing schools, the effect of teachers who don't teach and school leaders who don't lead is devastating.

UNION DUES

4

Our Teachers and Their Union

What made the New York City school system that my sons attended so different from the system that educated me was, above all, the labor contract between the Board of Education and the United Federation of Teachers. The first teacher contract was signed on October 18, 1962, after a short strike by thousands of city teachers, a historic event for the nation's as well as the city's schools. It was the first time that a union representing teachers had achieved collective bargaining rights in one school district. Most of the thirty-eight-page contract dealt with the traditional wage and benefits issues, but the parties also agreed on some new "work rules" demanded by the union. At the time, these seemed like reasonable adjustments in areas such as school scheduling and teacher assignment. In fact, it was a foot in the door that led to fundamental changes in the governance of most public school systems. The emergence of teachers' unions marked the beginning of the third distinct era in the history of American public education.

Open markets and choice characterized American education from before the Revolution almost until the middle of the nineteenth century. While there were publicly funded schools during this period (particularly in New England and Pennsylvania), these were far from the norm. Private individuals or religious institutions operated most schools. In New York City, many schools were run by a single private charitable organization called the Free School Society. As Alexis de Tocqueville and other visitors to America observed, this loose system served Americans well, producing an extraordinarily high literacy rate.

The propriety of tax funds going to religious schools—as happened in many communities—was never a public issue at this time, nor did any lawyer yet dream of making the claim that it violated the U.S. Constitution.

The winds of change started blowing in the 1830s and 1840s. The nation's elites came to a consensus that the existing arrangements for educating the young were too haphazard for a growing country with a steady influx of new immigrants. The "common school" movement was spurred partly by the noble impulse to assimilate all children into a unifying civic and democratic culture. But as most education historians now acknowledge, it was also driven by less generous sentiments. The dominant Protestant majority feared the social consequences of hordes of unwashed Irish and Italian Catholics entering the country. It wasn't merely that mainstream Protestant groups wanted Catholic children to be Americanized; they also expected that the public schools would wean the young away from the despised Catholic rituals and the "foreign influence" of the papacy.

By the beginning of the twentieth century, virtually every big city in America had a hierarchical, centralized public school system run by civil servants claiming expert knowledge of the "best education practices." Government officials decided what was to be taught in every school in a given locality and who was qualified to teach in those schools. The system was undeniably successful in delivering a decent education to millions of new immigrants and thus helped them assimilate into the mainstream. The overt anti-Catholicism of the public schools of half a century earlier was gone and there was a genuine effort to teach the common civic culture to all children.

Until the 1960s most public school teachers belonged to a staid professional organization called the National Education Association, to which the words "unionism" and "strike" were anathema. This was true despite the fact that teachers were treated as interchangeable parts in a one-size-fits-all system, with no right to challenge arbitrary decisions by administrators. In New York City, prospective teachers were blackballed for exhibiting traces of a foreign accent or for looking slightly unkempt.

It was only a matter of time before teachers working in a factory-style system figured out they might as well organize themselves into factory-style unions. It is hard to imagine America passing through the 1960s without its public school teachers demanding more control over "the decisions that affected their lives"—as the countercultural student movement of those years put it. Nor is it surprising that the big break-through for teacher unionism came in New York City. After all, the Big Apple was a union town *par excellence.* City officials, from Mayor Robert Wagner on down, were proudly pro-labor and conceded in principle that public school teachers had a right to be represented by a union.

★

Small teacher unions, but without collective bargaining rights, had existed in the city since the early part of the century. (The philosopher John Dewey was a charter member of the United Federation of Teachers.) By 1960 several fledgling unions, including the UFT, were vying for the support of the city's forty-five thousand teachers. On the UFT's left was the Communist-led New York Teachers' Union. On the right, hell-bent on stopping the UFT and its "radical agenda," was the National Education Association. The leaflets it distributed to teachers warned against the evils of "Hoffa and Bossism." If the UFT won the upcoming collective bargaining election, according to one NEA tract, New York's teachers would be under the thumb of "corrupt and auto-cratic union bosses."

The UFT won the election by a wide margin, but not because of "labor bosses" twisting teachers' arms. The UFT's very smart rank-and-file leaders worked long hours for almost no pay and were willing to go to jail for their cause if necessary. (The law forbade strikes by teachers.) Many UFT officials were still class-room teachers. They understood how difficult it was to try to do good work in a bureaucratic system run from the top down. They were able to convince their fellow teachers that this was a battle for dignity and professionalism as much as for more money. The teacher ranks at the time were filled with highly educated people, including many women who had been effectively barred from other professions. The women in particular chafed under a system with illogical and demeaning rules, including the one that required female teachers to leave the classroom as soon as they became pregnant.

The most gifted of the UFT leaders was a young high school math teacher named Albert Shanker. The son of Yiddish-speaking immigrants, Shanker attended Stuyvesant High School and Columbia University and then received an advanced degree in philosophy. Unable to find an academic position, he took a job in the public schools and was swept up in union work. Many of the UFT's early leaders were socialists or radicals of one stripe or another. Shanker had learned his anticommunist social-democratic politics in one of New York's most esoteric left-wing sects, the "Schachtmanites" (after their leader Max Schachtman, a former protégé of Leon Trotsky).

Shanker was elected president of the UFT shortly after the first contract was signed and then quickly built it into the most powerful union local in the country. He envisioned the union as a positive force for improving the quality of public education and strengthening democracy. He was also confident that he knew more about what works in the classroom than the system's bureaucrats and administrators, and he was probably right about that.

Under Shanker the UFT played a heroic role in the civil rights movement. Many New York City teachers volunteered to go south for the Freedom Rides in the summer of 1964. Some were beaten by white mobs. Yet in 1968, Shanker found himself accused of racism because he led his teachers into a bitter strike over the arbitrary dismissal of Jewish teachers by black militants running Brooklyn's Ocean Hill–Brownsville community school board. The "limousine liberals" of the time were convinced that uncaring white teachers were responsible for the low academic performance of minority students. They assumed that learning could be improved by empowering the black community to make its own decisions on curriculum and who should teach in the schools. It was a misguided assumption. The short-lived experiment in "community control" left the city more racially polarized and the schools in worse shape than ever.

The UFT emerged from the strike more powerful, yet even more suspicious of education experiments that gave too much authority and discretion to principals and local communities. One of the lessons the union learned from the 1968 conflict is that it had to flex its muscles in the political arena to protect its members' job security. The UFT accepted a weakened and decentralized system for K–8 schools (high schools remained under the control of central administration) governed by thirty-two separate community school boards. In return, the union got changes in state education law that made it almost impossible to fire a tenured teacher on grounds of incompetence.

Shanker moved to Washington in the 1980s to take over the UFT's parent union, the American Federation of Teachers. Until his untimely death in 1997, he courageously promoted worthy proposals for education improvement. In contrast to his opposite numbers in the NEA, which had transformed itself over the years from a white-collar professional organization into a politically correct cog in the Democratic Party machine, Shanker frequently acknowledged that public education was a mess and needed reforming. On one occasion he even said the unsayable: that it was worth considering the efficacy of providing vouchers for poor children who were performing badly in the public school system. He was an early proponent of charter schools and supported a national curriculum, high academic standards and testing—even though this sometimes put him in the company of conservatives and at odds with some of his own membership.

Shanker used the union's treasury to publish his iconoclastic ideas in a monthly paid advertisement on the editorial page of the *New York Times*. One of his last columns was devoted to E. D. Hirsch Jr.'s new book, *The Schools We Need and Why We Don't Have Them*. Shanker endorsed—without reservation—Hirsch's attack on the progressive education idea that teachers should not be imparting factual knowledge ("mere facts") to children but instead should be encouraging them to learn "how to think." Mincing no words, Shanker declared that this abdication of responsibility was one of the main reasons for the high rate of academic failure in America's public schools. After I read that column, it occurred to me that if Shanker had been able to convince his members of this, the schools would be less likely to need radical education reforms such as vouchers and charters.

Unfortunately, Shanker's ideas about the crisis in American education were not the main legacy he left to his successors. Rather it was his organizing genius and understanding of political power. The UFT is now the largest and most powerful teachers' union local in the country, a political colossus that has forced itself on the city's schools as a full partner in their governance. The union represents over one hundred thousand school employees and takes in about $70 million annually from membership dues and other income. The dues the union charges every teacher through an automatic payroll deduction probably constitute the most regressive tax in the world; all teachers pay over $800 per year (after taxes) whether their salary is the minimum of $39,000 or the maximum $81,000. (The irony is that this fee is imposed by the same union that insists that federal and state income taxes have to become even more progressive in order to support a vast expansion of the welfare state.)

The UFT has used its leverage at the bargaining table to expand the number of teachers employed by the system from 45,000 in 1962 to 80,000 in 2002. This phenomenal growth in teacher ranks (and thus in the union's membership) occurred while the number of students in the system remained fairly constant. The union is now another gilded education bureaucracy. It owns two buildings on New York's lower Park Avenue and has a staff of over four hundred, with dozens earning more than $100,000 per year.

The union spends millions of dollars each year on media, lobbying and political contributions. New York City school chancellors come and go (their average tenure is about two years) but the UFT is forever. After the 1968 decentralization plan, the UFT moved into the local school board elections, running its own candidates and often dominating because of the low turnout (sometimes as little as 4 percent of eligible voters showed up). According to Norman Scott, a veteran UFT activist and publisher of the independent union newsletter, *Ed Notes:*

> The UFT in many districts threw itself into these local politics with a vengeance and also played a role in "making" supervisors. Some [UFT] District Reps became crucial point people. In some cases the district union set up machines of their own and had enormous influence. This process culminated with one District Rep actually becoming superintendent, completing a merger of the union and administration. Almost every [school] Chapter Leader that was part of that machine became a supervisor.

Harry Spence, who came from Boston to serve as first deputy schools chancellor under Chancellor Rudy Crew from 1996 to 1999, told me that his biggest surprise was how intimately involved the UFT was in the day-to-day operations of the central school administration. "The UFT is everywhere and they know everything," Spence said. "Their people sit in on planning meetings in several departments." Spence mentioned one vice president of the union, David Sherman, who was stationed at the board almost full-time and had the run of almost every important office in the building. Other former Board of Education officials told me that the chancellors they worked for would never make an important management appointment over the objection of the UFT. Schools chancellors accommodated the union for two very important reasons: First, they knew that the UFT could have vetoed their own selection for the chancellor's position if it had chosen to. Second, they realized they were going to need the union's lobbying power to help get additional resources for the system from the state legislature and the city council.

The UFT, together with New York State United Teachers, the state AFT affiliate, has the deepest pockets of any special interest lobby in Albany. In a typical election cycle, the teachers' union PAC reports over $1million in lobbying expenses and political contributions to legislators. That's three times as much as the next-highest group, the state's medical societies. The union makes contributions to those legislators—the majority Democrats in the state assembly and the majority Republicans in the senate—who are most likely to be in a position to help its legislative agenda.

In return, the union gets to set the limits of permissible

debate in education policy in the legislature. Vouchers, privatization and merit pay are forbidden subjects; and there are others. Debra Mazzarelli, the mother of two public school children and a parent activist, learned that lesson several years ago after she was elected to the state assembly from Patchogue, Long Island, on a platform calling for ending automatic tenure protection for public school teachers. "I was just fed up that we were paying teachers $80,000 a year but couldn't hold them accountable and certainly couldn't fire them if they were incompetent," she said. Her reasonable bill to modify teacher tenure won support from the New York State School Boards Association, which held hearings on the proposed legislation around the state. But in typical Albany fashion, the assembly education committee, led by Democrat Steven Sanders, a leading recipient of union PAC money, never scheduled a discussion on the bill. It eventually died in committee, taking its place in a graveyard littered with countless other worthwhile initiatives that might have improved the public schools.

The UFT newspaper once excerpted without comment an article from *Crain's New York Business* describing UFT president Sandra Feldman as someone who "wields more control over the education of New York City children than any mayor." Feldman's successor, Randi Weingarten, is widely acknowledged in political circles to have single-handedly blocked legislative proposals by Mayor Giuliani to abolish the Board of Education and make the mayor responsible for the education system.

Over the past four decades the union has played a pivotal role in electing (and sometimes defeating) mayors, governors and state and national legislators. In 1993 the UFT punished Mayor David Dinkins for not giving in to its contract demands by running a $1 million ad campaign against him at the beginning of his mayoral campaign. In addition, the union withheld the volunteer phone banks that had been an essential part of Dinkins' first winning campaign against Rudolph Giuliani in 1989. The UFT's withdrawal of support may have made the difference in Giuliani's very small margin of victory over Dinkins the second time around. In another sign of the union's clout, UFT president Randi Weingarten was probably more responsible than any other New Yorker for convincing Hillary Clinton that she could win a U.S. Senate seat in 2000. Clinton announced her candidacy at UFT headquarters with Weingarten at her side. The union then took the lead in mobilizing organized labor for a huge get-out-the-vote effort for Clinton's campaign. With the union's support, Mrs. Clinton was able to project herself as the "education candidate." Even the supposedly neutral schools chancellor, Harold Levy, accommodated Clinton by arranging frequent photo ops for her in city schools.

The most convincing testimonial to the UFT's political power in New York comes from one of the most astute politicians of our time, Mario Cuomo. In his published diaries about his 1982 campaign for governor, Cuomo penned this entry:

> Teachers are perhaps the most effective of all the state's unions. If they go all out it will mean telephones and vigorous statewide support. It will also mean some money. I would have had them in 1977 [in Cuomo's losing race for mayor of New York City] if it had not been for a clumsy meeting I had with Shanker. I must see that I don't make that same mistake again.

He didn't. Cuomo appeared at the union convention and appealed for its support with a rousing speech trumpeting the primacy of public education and the rights of teachers. He won the teachers' endorsement (and their phone banks) and went on to defeat Ed Koch in the Democratic primary and then the Republican candidate in the general election. But Cuomo has never acknowledged just how much trimming he had to do in order to win the union's support and keep it.

It isn't generally known that as a young lawyer starting out in politics in the early 1970s, Cuomo presented himself as a passionate supporter of government aid for Catholic schools. (It was a position that many urban Catholic politicians supported in the 1950s and 1960s.) On August 28, 1974, Cuomo sent a letter to his supporters that is worth quoting at length:

> I decided to run for public office because after nearly twenty years of trying from the outside, I feel now that it's necessary to do more to change the unfortunate directions our governmental policies have taken in some areas.

Specifically, consider the parochial schools and Yeshivas. As a father of five children, I feel deeply the need for a healthy religious pluralism in this nation. The private school system has been a vital instrument in keeping this pluralism alive. For that reason I've spent more than fifteen years as an attorney and professor of law, arguing for aid to private schools. Unfortunately, although there are millions of people in this nation who agree with this position, they've been outmuscled politically to the point where the Supreme Court of the United States was persuaded in a series of cases to take hard positions against various forms of aid. This is regrettable but it's no reason for surrender. The Supreme Court may change its mind—it has in the past. Moreover, there are still various forms of aid that have been declared constitutionally valid and that could be of some help. For myself, I'll continue to make the argument on behalf of aid and I'd call upon all of you similarly disposed not to weaken in your own resolve.

Edmund Burke said a long time ago that the best way to assure that evil will conquer is by enough good people to do nothing. If you believe [parochial school] aid is a good thing, then you are the good people. If you believe it, then it's your moral obligation as it is my own, to do something about it. And there are things that can be done. Let's try tax credit plans and anything else that offers any help. Of course the law being what it is, it's difficult to presume such plans to be constitutional. On the other hand, it's impossible to say with absolute assurance that they are unconstitutional and the law will not be changed unless the court is presented with opportunities to reconsider. At the same time, let's push for every available constitutional assistance: lunch programs, bus money, and all the rest.

Religious pluralism is too valuable to be frittered away by indifference: Let's not let it happen. Register. Listen. Learn. Argue. Vote.

When he was actually in office between 1982 and 1994, Governor Cuomo had many opportunities to "do something about it," as he put it in his letter. In private meetings with Catholic leaders the governor repeatedly said that he still supported tax credits for parochial school parents. But he always took a completely different position in public. In 1984 he acknowledged that giving tax credits for parochial school tuition was "clearly constitutional" under a recent Supreme Court decision, yet he refused to support such a plan. Cuomo was vigilant about cutting off unfettered debate in state forums about vouchers and tax credits—the education reforms most feared by the teachers' union.

Surprisingly, the voucher idea surfaced in 1989 in a preliminary draft of the "New Compact for Learning," a document of proposed reforms prepared for the New York State Board of Regents by the education commissioner, Thomas Sobol. This was a shock to the union because Sobol was assumed to be loyal to the Democratic Party establishment (including Governor Cuomo) that had boosted him for the commissioner position. A few years later Sobol told me that he included a modest voucher proposal because when the state had tried everything to improve its nonperforming schools and the children were still not learning, "Why not at that point step outside the traditional public school system and try the private schools? Under New York's Constitution, the state has a duty to educate the children. It is not a constitutional duty to protect the system."

Sobol quickly learned that the education establishment and Governor Cuomo did not agree with his reading of the state constitution. "The teachers' unions and the school board associations and the PTAs were up in arms," Sobol recalled. "They basically told us they were out to kill everything if we persisted with the voucher proposal. The message was, 'If you do this, nothing else will be done, and your agency will go nowhere.' I pulled the private school proposal off the board. It was a political decision. I said to the Regents, in effect, 'Ladies and gentlemen, this reform agenda will not go anywhere as long as vouchers are on the table. The opposition is just too strong' "

In the summer of 1991, alarm bells went off again at teachers' union headquarters and at the governor's office in Albany. This time the Board of Regents was about to consider a proposal from one of its members to liberate five thousand poor and minority students trapped in the state's worst public schools. Under the proposed pilot program, the children would have received tuition vouchers worth $2,500, usable at any private or parochial school. This could not pass, Cuomo determined—not after all the teachers' union had done for his political career. He used his considerable oratorical skills to try to convince the members that the proposal shouldn't even be on the Regents' agenda, that it was a "dagger aimed at the heart of public education." In public he called the limited voucher plan a form of "malign neglect."

Despite the governor's pleading, the Board of Regents went ahead and debated the experimental voucher proposal at its scheduled public meeting. After a spirited discussion in front of an overflow audience, the program was voted down by 8 to 6.

I was once in Governor Cuomo's office at the World Trade Center in New York City. The most striking of the paintings hanging on the wall was a large portrait of Cuomo's favorite Catholic saint, Sir Thomas More. Unlike his hero, Cuomo wasn't called upon to test his faith against an all-powerful head of state. He *was* the head of state, yet he declined to stand up to a union of government employees.

★

The UFT's growing political clout led to a shift in the balance of power at the bargaining table with the Board of Education. The union didn't always get what it wanted from the city in direct financial benefits; wages for city teachers remained lower than in the wealthy suburbs. But the union compensated by getting teachers relieved from more and more duties in day-to-day school operations. The first few labor contracts eliminated some onerous and clearly needless requirements, for example being forced to punch a time clock upon arriving and leaving the school each day. In the mid-1960s the union was able to gain a guaranteed number of preparation periods for teachers during the school day. Each successive contract, however, limited the principal's authority to make education decisions for the school, and this process fundamentally changed the institutional culture of the schools.

The UFT contract now runs to over two hundred small-print pages. The time clock and other relics of the factory system are gone, but so too is the idea that teachers work for the children. I call it the "we-don't-do-windows" contract because of the long list of things that school principals may no longer ask teachers to do. Teachers are not required to attend more than one staff meeting per month after school hours, to walk the children to a school bus, to patrol the hallways or the lunchroom or the schoolyard, to cover an extra class in an emergency, to attend a lunchtime staff meeting. Principals can't ask the staff to come in more than one day prior to the beginning of classes each September. As a result, the staff can't adequately plan for the new school year and rookie teachers are often thrown into the trenches with absolutely no help or preparation.

Teachers are the soul of the educational enterprise, but the labor contract undermines teacher professionalism, excellence and hard work. It assumes there's insufficient human intelligence and trust within each of the city's more than one thousand schools to order productive working relationships among teachers, administrators and parents. Thus every last detail of the school day must be regulated.

The contract's most damaging provisions are the seniority clauses, including the transfer plan. This requires principals to post half of their job openings and fill them with any applicant from another school who possesses the most seniority. As illustrated by the cases I cited in discussing my children's schools, the receiving school's principal often doesn't even have the right to interview the incoming teacher or get the teacher's personnel file. The process resembles a longshoremen's hiring hall of the 1950s, with the worker who has the most years of seniority getting the plum job.

Such rules can frustrate the best reform efforts by undermining the leadership that is crucial to creating a good school. I spoke with a principal who was trying to turn around a small alternative school in Manhattan and develop a challenging curriculum for its almost entirely minority student population. Although it had only twelve teachers, the school was sent five UFT transfers in six years.

"You have no say when the UFT transfers come in, and then they are here for life," the principal said. "You are stuck with them until they decide to leave or retire. So you try to take action against the incompetent ones or those who do no work. You spend six months going to their classrooms and writing them up and then going to grievances with the UFT district representative. And then nothing happens anyway—so what's the point? You just give up."

What's more, the transfer process creates perverse incentives for principals to turn teacher evaluations into a farce. Teachers are allowed to transfer out of schools only if they have not had an unsatisfactory rating from the principal. Thus, principals who want to encourage nonperforming teachers to get out will give them satisfactory evaluations. The principals call this exercise in cynicism "passing on the lemons."

Jorge Izquierdo, now a district superintendent in Manhattan, was one of the few principals who fought the system and tried to purge incompetent teachers. Even more rare, he was willing to risk the ire of the UFT by speaking out. He told me that in the case of one totally dysfunctional teacher, he spent close to one hundred hours over two years out of the building, in grievance sessions at the district office, at the Board of Education, and at arbitration sessions. At that point he was still at least two years away from having an arbitration board decide on terminating the teacher. For attempting to follow the rules and rid his school of incapable teachers, Izquierdo was attacked in the UFT newspaper as a principal who "harasses" his staff. Such tactics intimidate most principals, so they give up and accept it as a fact of life that they will have to carry their quota of incompetent teachers.

"I am like the CEO of a little corporation," Izquierdo said. "I am judged by whether or not I achieve the equivalent of a profit—how much the children gain in learning. But unlike any other CEO, I can't hire the people who work here or fire them when they're incompetent."

In the contract's sections on in-school assignments, the language becomes truly baroque. Consider the way in which Article 7C2e restricts the principal's prerogatives for assigning teachers:

> In order to make certain that teachers are not frozen into positions which are relatively easy or difficult, the following procedures should be adopted in making class assignments...on a particular grade level:
>
> (1) On each grade level, classes should be divided into two

categories, difficult and less difficult, in terms of reading achievement. In general, a teacher who has been assigned to a class in one category for a period of one year should be assigned to the other category for the next year.

Suppose the principal, the parents and a majority of the teachers at a particular school want to experiment with a longer school day. No way, says the contract. What if the principal suggests to the teachers that it would be helpful for the staff to get together once a week during a lunch period, send out for sandwiches and discuss school issues? The contract stipulates: "Every elementary school teacher is to have a duty-free lunch period of 50 minutes." The contract also micromanages such things as the number of lunchroom assignments that teachers can be given and how many periods per week they teach (twenty-five).

But what is most revealing about the UFT contract is what it does not say. Its two hundred pages of text breathe not a word about how many hours teachers must work. Article 6 stipulates only that the school day "shall be 6 hours and 40 minutes" and that the school year lasts from the Tuesday after Labor Day until the middle of the last week in June. (In the most recent contract, the length of the school day was increased by twenty minutes in return for a huge across-the-board salary increase for teachers.) School principals may not require teachers to be in the building one day before that Tuesday in September, one minute before the students arrive each day, or one minute after they leave.

The number of hours teachers work is not a trivial issue. Teaching is a labor-intensive occupation. Particularly at the elementary school level, teachers get results not because they are brilliant or have attended elite education schools, but rather because of the hours they spend with students in and after school, the hours they devote to reading students' work, and the hours they spend talking to parents.

So how many hours do union teachers really work? According to a survey by the U.S. Department of Education, public school teachers put in an average of forty-five hours per week, including time in the classroom, work with students outside the classroom, preparation time in the school building, and work done at home. But since the survey was based wholly on teacher self-reporting, any bias is likely to overstate the number of hours worked.

Doubtless, many public school teachers in New York do work long hours—at least during the thirty-six weeks that school is in session. One of the dirty little secrets of the system, however, is that there are many others who work close to, or exactly at, the contractual minimum. In and out of the school building at about the same time as the children, they rarely take work home, grading at school whatever homework they sporadically assign. Even assuming the teachers worked during all ten of the preparation periods provided for in the contract, if we deduct their 50-minute "duty-free" lunch periods, I estimate that these by-the-rules teachers work a maximum of 30 hours per week, or about 1,100 hours per year.

Many of these teachers have enough seniority and graduate-school credits to put them at $81,000, the top of the salary scale. Thus they are earning a wage, not including benefits, of more than $70 per hour, much higher than the rate earned by employees with the city's top civil service titles, or even commissioners of city agencies.

I don't know if 15 percent or 50 percent of the city's teachers work to the contractual minimum. And—scandalously—the Board of Education and City Hall are also in the dark about their productivity. In the past, the board's labor negotiators tried to raise the issue of monitoring the number of hours teachers work. "The union never wanted to discuss it," one former board official recalls. "They said that teachers were professionals and it would be an insult." The city's elected comptroller is legally empowered to conduct an audit to get at this vital piece of information. Unfortunately, every recent holder of the office was elected with the help of the UFT, and therefore such a survey was never conducted.

Could the managers of the city's police, fire, sanitation or transportation agencies (not to speak of private sector firms) improve their delivery of services without collecting data on worker productivity? The answer is clear, but in public education, the city has agreed to ignore such basic management information. Worse, it doesn't matter, since all teachers receive the same base salary, no matter how many hours they work or how effective they are in the classroom. Teachers get raises merely for showing up for another school year or for accumulating more education course credits, not for working hard and doing well.

The UFT often complains that teachers are paid less than other professionals such as lawyers, accountants and engineers, and that this reflects society's lack of commitment to public education. Usually left out of the discussion are two essential facts: First, teachers work far fewer hours than these other professionals. Second, lawyers, accountants and engineers work in a competitive employment market where their performance is constantly measured. They can be fired or denied higher pay when they don't produce. They are also laid off when the firms they are working for flounder. Teachers, on the other hand, are insured against such risks through their contract and state education law. The UFT and other unions have been loath to consider proposals that would offer teachers more competitive, merit-based salaries in exchange for measured gains in productivity and performance.

★

There is no greater testament to the success of Al Shanker and the early UFT leadership than the fact that their bitter rivals at the National Education Association soon decided that militant trade unionism was the way to go. It was a classic case of flattery by imitation. By the mid-seventies the NEA had dropped its white-shoe pretensions. It had a majority of the nation's teachers covered by collective bargaining agreements and became even more willing than the AFT to send its members out on strike. Today the NEA and the AFT represent more than three million school employees, including 80 percent of the nation's three million public school teachers. Teacher unions now dominate the American trade union movement, accounting for almost 50 percent of all unionized government employees and more than 20 percent of all union members.

The AFT and the NEA have been discussing a possible merger for the past decade. Even without formally creating one new organization, however, the two national unions continue to cast a giant shadow over American politics. They and their state and local affiliates take in $2 billion each year from dues and employ more than six thousand full-time staff members. In the 2000 election cycle, the teachers' unions contributed more than $20 million directly to Democratic Party candidates through their political action committees. But the PACs are just the visible tip of a vast iceberg of soft money, independent media buys, thousands of full-time campaign workers paid with union dues, and in-kind services such as phone banks and direct mail advertising. At the last Democratic convention, the teachers' union caucus constituted 11 percent of all delegates—a bigger share than the delegates from California.

The creation of the federal Department of Education was largely a payoff for the NEA's all-out support of Jimmy Carter in 1976 (the first time the NEA endorsed a presidential candidate). In the Clinton Department of Education, former NEA issues director Sharon Robinson was assistant secretary for research and educational improvement, shaping the national education debate with her office's research reports and assessments of student performance. In 1996, when the U.S. Congress was on the verge of passing legislation to offer private school scholarships to a few thousand poor students from Washington D.C.'s hopelessly broken public schools, the NEA, fearful that a voucher program in the capital city might encourage similar legislation in the states, furiously lobbied the White House. President Clinton had first indicated that he would sign the bill. Bowing to pressure from the union, he backtracked and said he would veto it, essentially killing the legislation.

I once spent a few days at an NEA national convention speaking with delegates from places like Cedar Rapids, Iowa; Birmingham, Alabama; Billings, Montana; Honolulu; Denver; and Storrs, Connecticut—all of them active classroom teachers. All believed with an almost religious passion that public education was under siege by the political right and profit-hungry corporations. One morning over coffee, the delegate from Connecticut told me that his school board was considering contracting with a private vendor to provide food services for the district's schools. His NEA local was mobilizing to fight this proposal because, according to him, it was "a step on the road toward privatizing" all the school district's education services.

The NEA wants public education preserved as a nonenterprise zone, even when public money is not involved. Former Jersey City mayor Brett Schundler came up with a plan in 1996 to give tax-funded scholarships to some poor students trapped in dysfunctional public schools. When the state blocked Schundler's initiative, a local Pepsico distributor offered to pay for some of the scholarships. The New Jersey NEA affiliate immediately organized a boycott of Pepsi products, and the company quickly backed down. The NEA affiliate in Florida was outraged when it heard that the local electric company was contributing money to a private foundation that was offering poor public school kids scholarships to attend private schools. In retaliation the union called for the school district to shut off the power to all schools for one day in order to punish the electric company. Speakers at NEA conventions frequently threaten similar boycotts of any company that dares to help kids who have no real alternative to abysmal public schools.

Moreover, the once-conservative NEA now favors a political and cultural agenda far to the left of the Democratic Party. It is as if the veterans of the Berkeley Free Speech Movement and other sixties causes had taken off their tie-dyed T-shirts, cut their hair, put on thirty pounds and taken over the Rotary Club. Each year, convention delegates spend their days passing resolutions on almost every issue under the sun—from federal housing and immigration policy, to nuclear testing and the World Court, to support for the special rights of every aggrieved racial, ethnic, gender, sexual-preference and "otherwise-abled" group, subgroup and tribe in America. In the midst of a Social Security crisis, the NEA wants to lower the retirement age and repeal all taxes on Social Security payments. It favors a national single-payer health plan supported entirely by tax revenues, full funding for Head Start programs, and a huge increase in federal spending on education—especially for "disadvantaged students," immigrant and American Indian students, and students with disabilities.

It would be an understatement to say that the NEA favors an expansion of the welfare state. Its economic program closely resembles those of the most radical European socialist parties. John Berthoud, a senior fellow of the Alexis de Tocqueville Institution, has calculated that if Congress passed all the NEA's legislative proposals, the annual additional charge to the federal treasury would be $800 billion, requiring an average tax increase of $10,000 for a family of four.

In the nation's school choice debates, the charge is often made by the teachers' unions that vouchers and other forms of subsidies for private schools would undermine public education and have a fragmenting effect on our common civic culture. All sorts of imaginary horrors are conjured up by the unions, including the specter of families using vouchers to enroll their children in "David Duke schools," black nationalist schools, even "witchcraft" schools. Sandra Feldman, Al Shanker's successor as president of the American Federation of Teachers, has said that if vouchers become public policy, "our rich diversity [will] become a source of balkanization and division, because common public schooling will no longer be the way into the American mainstream and will no longer hold our society together."

At least Feldman is evoking the original vision of the "common school," and the idea that public money is shared money and thus must be used for the furtherance of shared values in the interests of *e pluribus unum.* Today's NEA would allow no charter schools or vouchers; but in addition to denigrating the *pluribus,* the organization isn't much interested in *unum* either. NEA conventions typically celebrate not our common heritage but rather the disuniting of America. A standing NEA resolution requires a set-aside of 20 percent of the convention seats for certain designated minorities. The NEA also officially recognizes numerous caucuses of the fragmented and oppressed and encourages delegates to join one or another, from the African American caucus, Hispanic caucus, American Indian and Alaska Native caucus, or Asian and Pacific Islander caucus, to the women's caucus or the gay and lesbian caucus. Each of these identity groups proposes resolutions (almost never opposed) demanding special consideration for its particular ethnicity, race or gender. The resolutions add up to a massive assault on precisely those common ideals that were the historical justification for the creation of a public school system in the first place.

For example, the NEA supports the "movement toward self-determination by American Indians/Alaska Natives" and believes these designated victim groups should control their own education. It supports "the infusion of Black studies and/or Afrocentric curricula into the curriculum." Against the grain of the latest research and the popular will expressed in California and other states, the NEA strongly supports bilingual education for Hispanic students and opposes efforts to legislate English as the nation's official language. It believes that all schools should designate separate months to celebrate Black History, Hispanic Heritage, Native American Indian/Alaska Native Heritage, Asian/Pacific Heritage, Women's History, Lesbian and Gay History—which nearly takes up the entire school calendar, leaving scant time for plain old American history.

Some of the NEA's affiliate teacher organizations, such as the National Council for the Social Studies and the National Council of Teachers of English, carry on the struggle by training teachers to focus inordinate attention in the classroom on issues of "diversity" and "difference." Both organizations propose reconstructing schooling to reflect a race- and gender-centered philosophy of pedagogy and child development. The NCTE, in its conferences and publications, is obsessed with multiculturalism and "the Other." The socal studies organization's official policy paper, "Curriculum Guidelines for Multicultural Education," is one of the scariest documents in American education. In the tone of a commissar's lecture at a political reeducation camp, the NCSS exhorts teachers to think and act multiculturally during every moment of the school day, lest they become accomplices of America's lurking racism. School personnel should scrutinize every aspect of the school environment—from classroom teaching styles and the pictures on the walls, to the foods served in the lunchroom and the songs sung in the school assemblies—to be sure they reflect something called "multicultural literacy."

"The instructional strategies and learning styles most often favored in the nation's schools," the guidelines declare, "are inconsistent with the cognitive styles, cultural orientations, and cultural characteristics of some groups of students of color." These students flourish under "cooperative teaching techniques" rather than the "competitive learning activities" that work for white kids. At its heart this is a fundamentally racist assumption. It is dangerously close to City College professor Leonard Jeffries' rants about black "sun children" and white "ice children." For the NCSS, the ideal of a race-neutral classroom is a mirage; teachers who strive toward a single standard of excellence, who presume to treat all students equally, are doing something harmful, not admirable. The NCSS offers teachers this final Orwellian conclusion: "Schools should recognize that they cannot treat all students alike or they run the risk of denying equal educational opportunity to all persons."

The NEA's permanent bureaucracy takes the convention resolutions very seriously. Through its 1,300 field representatives assigned to state and local affiliates and through its permanent Capitol Hill lobbying staff, it works hard to get this agenda implemented by Congress and state legislatures and infused into the culture of the schools.

Most parents are completely unaware that the union representing the teachers in their children's schools has a far-left political agenda. But in the fall of 2001 the NEA made the mistake of posting guidelines for classroom teachers to discuss the anniversary of 9/11. It would probably be going too far to say that this document was out-and-out anti-American, but it certainly qualified as anti-anti-Islamic-terrorism. It was filled with multicultural psychobabble and stressed the need for children to respect and be tolerant of all cultures—to the extent of completely ignoring the fact that our country was engaged in a just war with a vicious enemy determined to destroy *our* tolerant and democratic civilization. This time the NEA had gone too far. The predictable public outcry forced an embarrassed organization to remove the guidelines from its website.

No matter that the voters don't support the NEA's left-wing political agenda. This is America, where anyone with a little money can go straight to the courts. The NEA budgets as much as

$20 million a year for its legal arm, headed by a brilliant Washington lawyer named Robert Chanin, who travels the land to intervene in major court battles involving the pet issues of the NEA's leftist majority. At the NEA convention Chanin received loud ovations from the delegates when he described the *amicus* briefs he had filed on behalf of gay rights in Colorado, sexual integration of the all-male Citadel in South Carolina, and racial preferences in admissions to the University of Texas School of Law.

But these efforts are just frosting on the cake. Chanin's primary mission is to throw up legal challenges to every piece of legislation passed by democratically elected bodies anywhere in the United States that might free some children from the monopolistic public education system. At a 2001 conference on vouchers sponsored by New York City mayor Rudy Giuliani, Chanin amazed the audience with his disarmingly honest recitation of the NEA's intentions. He stated that his client's first line of defense was to try to kill all voucher experiments (such as those in Milwaukee, Cleveland and Florida) on the basis of past Supreme Court interpretations of the First Amendment's "establishment of religion" clause. But Chanin said that even if the Court reversed or modified its position (which it did a year later) his mission would not change. No matter how much public support might develop for voucher experiments, the union was primed to fight forever to maintain the wall of separation between the public and private education systems. Chanin vowed to continue using every legal loophole to block implementation of any legislation that gave taxpayer funds to children from bad public schools so they could switch to a successful private school.

★

It has now been forty years since Al Shanker led his fellow New York City teachers out of the old factory system of schools. A new generation is in charge of the unions. But have we reached the Promised Land of better schools and greater dignity for the teachers?

The teachers' unions spend millions each year on advertising to convince the American people that we're almost there, that it's just a question of more political will and of course more money. "Let's roll up our sleeves…and work together to give our children the schools they deserve," reads a typical full-page *New York Times* ad taken out by the UFT. "We've tried everything else; now let's try what works," was the message of a second UFT ad a few days later.

But have they really tried everything?

In 1995 I interviewed Sandra Feldman, president of the United Federation of Teachers at the time, for an article I was writing on the New York City teachers' contract. Feldman already knew that I was very critical of the union contract because we had previously discussed the problem of incompetent teachers and of seniority transfers. I had even complained to her directly about the "derelict" teacher who had been forced on P.S. 87, my sons' elementary school.

Thus I was pleasantly surprised when Feldman agreed to talk to me on the record, and even more surprised by what she had to say about the system. When I proposed to her that the contract's rules resembled a longshoremen's hiring hall from the 1950s, with the union member who had the most seniority getting the plum job, she didn't try to defend the practice. "We do have a contract that was written out of a blue-collar ethos," she explained. She also said that "in principle" she would consider eliminating all seniority preferences and changing the hiring system into a free labor market for all teachers. She conceded that there was "a great deal of dissatisfaction with public schools and a lot of it is justifiable. Therefore you have to make the public schools better." She paused for a few moments and then offered the following thought: "If we don't improve the schools, we are going to get vouchers."

I was speechless. Feldman didn't say it exactly, but the logical implication was that if we don't improve the public schools, we *deserve* vouchers.

I was so taken with Feldman's candor about the problems of the schools and her seeming openness to change that when my piece appeared in *City Journal* it had a hopeful tone, also reflected in the title: "Let's Seize This Chance for Reform." I proposed that

Feldman and Mayor Giuliani use their upcoming negotiations to rewrite the contract completely and turn it into a guideline for promoting excellence and productivity in the schools. After the article came out and before the contract negotiations began, I even fantasized that before my two sons left the system (they were then in the third and seventh grades) they might be relieved of the burden of seniority transfers in their schools. That didn't happen, of course. As the previous chapter has shown, seniority continued to trump merit even in elite schools like Stuyvesant High School.

A couple of years after the article appeared, Feldman moved on to Washington as Al Shanker's successor. As president of the American Federation of Teachers she is now one of the most powerful voices in American education. But she never again made a link between the system's inability to improve schools and the possible remedy of vouchers. Instead, under her leadership the national union maintains a steady drumbeat of denunciation and invective against any reform proposal— whether it be vouchers, tuition tax credits, privatization of schools or services—that challenges the existing public education monopoly.

"We know how to fix the schools," Feldman now says repeatedly in her speeches and articles. Not surprisingly, the fixes that she and the union have in mind require lots of money and lots of new dues-paying union teachers. More money is needed for reducing class size (which of course means hiring more teachers), for higher teacher salaries and for staff development (which also requires hiring more teachers). Many of these measures were actually undertaken by school districts across the country in recent years. Since my interview with Feldman, the size of the teaching force in New York City has grown from 60,000 to 80,000 (while the pupil population has remained constant) and the overall education budget shot up from $8 billion to $12 billion. Yet there has been no improvement in the schools.

In California, a $1-billion-per-year statewide initiative in 1996 to reduce class size not only led to no improvement, but widened the performance gap between wealthier and poorer schools. The reason should have been obvious from the beginning: the mandate to reduce class size in every school in the state created a need for many more teachers. With more teacher jobs available in the richer districts, many good teachers from the poorer districts were able to take jobs in the higher-performing districts that could also pay them more. Thus, in teaching talent the rich got richer and the poor got poorer (while the teachers' union gained more members).

Yet none of this has stopped the union and its political allies from insisting that even more money must now be spent for what they claim are "tested and proven" reforms. The union's self-justification goes something like this: Driving up wages has made the teaching profession far more attractive to qualified young people. There's nothing wrong with the union's PAC activities and political lobbying because they help pressure elected officials to finance education adequately, so that school boards can pay teachers the salaries they deserve, hire more qualified teachers, reduce class size, provide staff development and purchase books. Result: better schools and improved student performance.

And true, the evolution of teachers' unions into political powerhouses did lead to huge increases in the resources devoted to public schooling. Between 1965 and 1990, average per-pupil spending in the United States increased from $2,402 to $5,582 in inflation-adjusted dollars. The average pupil/teacher ratio dropped from 24.1 /1 to 17.3 /1. The percentage of teachers with master's degrees increased from 23.2 percent to 52.6 percent. The median years of experience for teachers went from 8 to 15.

Unfortunately all that extra money didn't improve student performance. During the same period, average SAT scores for public school students declined by 10 percent. Dropout rates in urban school systems increased and American students scored at or near the bottom in comparisons with the other industrialized nations. After years of examining the data, one of the nation's leading education economists, Eric Hanushek of the University of Rochester and the Hoover Institute, concluded: "There appears to be no strong or systematic relationship between school expenditures and student performance."

Why did American public education go into the tank just as

all that extra money was pouring in? To put it simply: Adding powerful unions with exclusive collective bargaining rights to the existing monopolistic education system has been a lethal mix. In the private sector, unions know that if they insist on protecting incompetent workers and cling to outdated work rules, the company they are bargaining with is likely to end up losing market share. Union members will then lose jobs, especially in the global economy of the twenty-first century. In public education, however, collective bargaining takes place without the constraining discipline of the market. Even if the negotiated labor contract allows some teachers to be paid for hardly working at all and others to perform incompetently without penalty, there are no real economic sanctions on employers or employees. After all, the unions' political allies have made sure that most of the public school system's customers, the schoolchildren, have nowhere else to go. And taxpayer funds will continue flowing into the schools no matter how they perform. The worse that schools become, the more money they seem to receive; and the worse that teachers perform, the more they claim that more money is the cure.

It is worth recalling that teacher unionism was never supposed to be exclusively about economics. To Al Shanker and his New York City comrades, liberating teachers from the pettifogging rules of a bureaucratized central administration and restoring their professional pride would infuse a new element of caring and intelligence into the classroom.

In *Education through Partnership,* education scholar David S. Seeley offers this summary of what actually did happen in the schools after the emergence of teacher unions:

> Teacher unionism was a response to bureaucracy, not the cause of it. Nevertheless, instead of helping to cure or correct the ills of the present structure, it has increased many of its anti-educational aspects. The power won by the teachers has increased centralized power. As a stepchild of bureaucracy, teacher unionism has now become one of its strongest supports, since collective teacher power can most easily be exercised through centralized decision making.

I like Seeley's description because it captures the double bind of union work rules and bureaucratic regulations that dragged down almost every one of my children's schools like a negative force field. It's one of the main reasons that these schools accomplished less academically than they otherwise might have. It's also why the best of our teachers seem as troubled as the nonunionized teachers of forty years ago by the daily indignities they have to endure.

One of my sources on this has been my wife, Ruthie, a ten-year veteran teacher in a Manhattan middle school. For years she has been telling me horror stories about the thoughtless actions of higher-level administrators or bureaucrats. We could never decide which was more destructive to her school, the union work rules or the bureaucracy. In any event, the combination was crippling. Speaking for many thousands of his fellow UFT teachers, *Ed Notes* editor Norman Scott says, "We believe our union leaders have become defenders of a rotten system."

5

Public Education's Twilight Zone

"**Y**ou don't know whether to laugh or cry," proclaimed the headline of an April 19, 2000, newspaper column about New York City's public education system. The column began by recalling *The Twilight Zone*, a 1950s television drama "where weird, inexplicable things happened, things that made sense only in a world where nothing makes sense." The columnist continued:

> Such a world is our school system's byzantine bureaucracy, a world so out of kilter that we start to accept as normal the most outrageous happenings. This is a world where new computers are obsolete before they can be plugged in (because it takes so long to install adequate wiring); where elaborate, expensive science labs—or art rooms, or libraries, for that matter—are dismantled as soon as they are installed (because the room is needed for a class); where a contractor builds an Olympic-sized high school swimming pool only three feet deep. Perhaps the would-be swimmers should have tried the basement at IS 8 in Queens. At one point the water there was so deep, the custodian stocked it with fish.
>
> And of course, we all have our funny (sad?) stories about eccentric (certifiable?) administrators, who complain over the PA about too many classroom interruptions; who never used to read teachers' submitted lesson plans, but now lament their inability to collect them routinely; whose idea of leadership is daily memos that fill your file drawer, their blank sides often serving as students' first-draft paper when supplies are low.

New Yorkers have come to expect columns savaging the public

school system in the city's conservative tabloid, the *New York Post.* I've written a few of those myself. But this one appeared in *New York Teacher,* the United Federation of Teachers' biweekly newspaper. The writer was none other than union president Randi Weingarten. It is one of many educational ironies that the UFT newspaper is one of the best sources for damaging stories about the system's dysfunctional bureaucracy.

The union takes a certain risk in this. If too many people begin to suspect that the public schools' managerial system really is something out of the Twilight Zone, they might conclude there's not much point in throwing more and more money at the problem. The public might even begin pressing for radical reforms such as vouchers and competition.

So far the UFT seems to be comfortable living with the contradiction. In its multimillion-dollar media campaigns it tries to sell the idea that there is nothing fundamentally wrong with public education, except that more money is needed for smaller classes and higher pay for teachers. On the other hand, the message it conveys to its own members is that without the union's help, classroom teachers would be trapped in the educational Twilight Zone.

After my wife, Ruthie, began teaching, she received a large, expensively printed, multicolored poster from the UFT. It was a replica of a subway map, except that each of the more than fifty stations along the three imaginary subway lines described one of the cumbersome bureaucratic tasks that teachers in the public schools have to complete in order to achieve state certification. The title line at the top of the poster said: "The United Federation of Teachers Guide to…Riding the NYC Licensing Subway."

I thought the poster was brilliant. It captured the madness of state and city teacher licensing requirements that resulted in thousands of talented people deciding that teaching in the public schools wasn't worth the bother. Yet it was also great PR for the union. At the first station along the subway line there was an illustration of a young man dressed in his college graduation cap and gown and clutching a diploma. At the last stop, the "permanent license and tenure station," the same young man appeared again, now casually dressed like a teacher and with the UFT logo on his jacket. The message conveyed to new teachers was clear: Stick to the union and we will get you through this hellish process.

The joke of it all is that the UFT refuses to use its political power to streamline teacher licensing or to make it more rationally related to the personal skills and academic accomplishments needed to excel in the classroom. The union would never come to the aid of a brilliant but unlicensed teacher like Iftimie Simion. In fact, the UFT and other teacher unions are among the most strident opponents of alternative teacher licensing programs that permit liberal arts college graduates to bypass the traditional education school requirements and get into the classroom quickly. The unions actually prefer the long-drawn-out certification process in order to regulate and control access to the teaching profession.

Still, the problem that Randi Weingarten pointed to in her column is undeniable. The dysfunctional education bureaucracy undermines classroom teachers and thus harms learning. Whenever I wrote about the outsized political power of the UFT and the damage done by the teachers' contract, I heard from rank-and-file classroom teachers—not necessarily UFT boosters—who said the union was not the only villain. They complained about how badly they were treated by the system and how demoralizing this could be. They would recite horror stories about incompetent administrators or the bureaucratic follies at 110 Livingston Street. I didn't argue the point. In fact, I had a few horror stories of my own to tell.

I had spent some hours at Board of Education headquarters in Brooklyn completing the reams of paperwork my wife was required to submit as a new teacher. Not only did the clerks at the board not object to teachers sending surrogates to navigate this process, they encouraged the practice. It seemed to be understood that having someone share the burden would lower the new teacher's level of frustration.

On one occasion I sat through a mandatory two-hour orientation and paperwork session for newly appointed teachers (or their surrogates) jointly conducted by a UFT representative and a Board of Education employee. In the presence of the board official, the union rep warned the new teachers never to send any completed forms to the board by mail. Instead, she advised the teachers to deliver every important piece of paper by hand directly to the appropriate office at the board. "And don't forget to ask for a receipt," she added.

There was a stunned silence in the room. Some teachers had just been assigned to schools in areas of the city that were more than a one-hour subway ride from the Board of Education headquarters in Brooklyn. I heard someone say, "Are you kidding?" With the board official nodding, the union rep then repeated her warning: "I'm telling you, don't take a chance. Things have a way of getting lost around here." At that point I couldn't contain myself. "How does the IRS do it?" I blurted out. This elicited giggling by some teachers and a shrug of the shoulders by the UFT representative.

And so I made several more trips to Brooklyn to present my wife's papers to the board's Office of Personnel and Recruitment. It was a dreary place full of sullen clerks and felt like an Eastern European dead-letter office as portrayed by Kafka. Each time I traveled to the board it occurred to me that if the city's goal was to entice qualified teachers to work in the public schools, a good start would be to begin treating them like human beings.

My experiences with the Board of Education convinced me that the UFT had developed a symbiotic relationship with the very system it sometimes railed against. The inept bureaucrats were indispensable enemies for the union. After all, the endless and bothersome licensing requirements, the irrational regulations, the incompetent and sometimes crazy school administrators allowed the union to sell itself as defender of teachers' rights and dignity. This made it possible to keep raising union dues, expand the union staff and enlarge union political power.

There seemed to be no way out of the conundrum. School choice and vouchers would help by forcing the system to compete with the nonbureaucratized private and parochial schools. But the union was so powerful in New York that this would likely be the last state in America to adopt any radical school reform plan. Thus six different schools chancellors went through the revolving doors at 110 Livingston Street during the first twelve years that my children were in the school system, and each seemed to accept the dysfunction all around them as the way things are in public education. I had pretty much given up all hope that a reform-minded chancellor would emerge out of the Twilight Zone in Brooklyn.

Then in January 2000 the Board of Education did something that would have been unthinkable during the heyday of the "one best system." By a 4-3 vote it hired a corporate lawyer named Harold O. Levy as schools chancellor. Levy was not a professional educator—not even close. In fact, his selection was a violation of everything that Nicholas Murray Butler, the creator of the "one best system," believed in. One of Professor Butler's legacies is that the minimum requirements for obtaining a superintendent's license are very stringent; they include three years of teaching or administrative experience in the schools, sixty graduate credits in education courses approved by the education commissioner, plus an administrative/supervisory internship. Nevertheless, state education commissioner Richard Mills—a hawk about enforcing the maze of licensing requirements for every last teacher in the system—quickly granted Levy a waiver. If there had been a shred of confidence left in the existing system, Levy would never have been chosen as chancellor, much less received a waiver. It was as if everyone now agreed that the "one best system" had turned so bad that the old rules requiring a "professional educator" no longer applied. The question was: could an outsider make things any better?

After Levy was appointed, I participated in a panel discussion on NY1, the local cable TV news station. Asked to comment on the board's choice for chancellor, I shrugged and said that Mr. Levy was the seventh person to occupy the office since my children began attending public schools. Each of these men, including the recently departed Rudy Crew, was overwhelmed trying to manage a hopelessly dysfunctional system. I recalled that Ramon Cortines, the chancellor who preceded Crew, still hadn't figured out how many people worked at 110 Livingston Street after a year on the job. I had seen so many chancellors come and go that it was hard for me to believe any one person could make a difference.

Then, on reconsideration I decided that there really might

be something hopeful about this appointment. I had met Levy
once, when he was chairing a state commission studying the city
school system's construction needs. We had argued briefly about
whether lack of money was at the root of the system's problems.
(He said it was. I said it wasn't.) But most of what I knew about
the new chancellor came from the media. He was a first-genera-
tion immigrant from Germany (his parents were Holocaust
survivors) who attended the public schools and graduated from
the Bronx Science High School. After law school, Levy moved up
the corporate ladder, eventually becoming a top executive with
Citibank. He was also reported to have political connections to
the liberal wing of the Democratic Party.

Still, I hoped that coming from a highly competitive business environment, Levy might at least be shocked by the school
system's slacker culture, its stifling bureaucracy, the destructive
union work rules, the hostility to new ideas. Maybe as the first
chancellor of the twenty-first century Levy would understand
that it was time to dismantle the top-down factory model of
urban education created at the end of the nineteenth century.
Perhaps he would even insist that the board's employees learn
how to process mail without losing it.

Another part of Levy's biography I found intriguing was
that his own children were not enrolled in public schools, but at
Dalton, one of the city's elite private schools. Unlike some public
education activists, I didn't regard this as a case of hypocrisy on
Levy's part. To the contrary, I believed that in shopping around
for the best possible school for his children, he might have
learned something that could help the cause of reform for my
own children's public schools. I couldn't imagine Levy not noticing the freedom and autonomy that his children's principals
enjoyed compared with the straitjacket of bureaucratic regulations that public school leaders had to work under. And since
virtually none of Dalton's excellent teachers had state licenses
or had graduated from ed schools, it occurred to me that this
might lead Levy to question the state's inflexible certification
rules for public school teachers.

Just as I was thinking about all this, Levy began sending out
signals that he was indeed shocked by the dead weight he saw

around him. One story leaked to the media was that Levy discovered that the restroom on the executive floor at 110 Livingston Street was chronically filthy. He then asked one of the old civil service hands how this could happen right next to the chancellor's office. The answer was that the building's head custodian had many years of seniority and couldn't be transferred. Each of Levy's predecessors had taken this in stride, knowing that's the way things are in public education. Levy's response was to write the custodian a memo, which he then posted next to the elevators in the lobby. The next morning, everyone working in the building saw the message as they reported for work. It directed the custodian to "clean up the pigsty in the bathroom" or "find yourself another job."

Levy also seemed eager to let New Yorkers know that 110 Livingston Street would be open to new ideas and intellectual ferment. He invited writers, some good, some not so good, to come and chat with him. I was troubled when I read that Levy not only met with Jonathan Kozol, but sent copies of one of Kozol's books to all of his principals (at Board of Education expense). I wondered if Levy was endorsing Kozol's destructive idea that inner-city schools were failing because they were segregated and then starved of resources by a heartless and racist society. Apart from being spectacularly wrong, this doctrine merely served to provide the system's many underachieving principals and teachers with an excuse for more failure.

On the other hand, I happily noted that Levy also invited education historian and critic Diane Ravitch in for a meeting. I hoped the chancellor listened well, since Ravitch had been saying for years that New York's "factory system" of education was a dinosaur, that the public education monopoly needed competition, and that providing vouchers for poor minority kids consigned to bad schools had become the right thing to do.

Levy responded quickly when I requested an interview. At the appointed time I walked into his suite of offices at 110 Livingston Street and found several other journalists with TV cameras milling around. An aide came out to tell me that Levy was running late. While waiting I jotted down some notes about our new chancellor from the business world:

Levy is the darling of the media right now and very popular. He's smart, articulate, dresses impeccably and comes across on TV as a breath of fresh air in a lifeless system. But the honeymoon will be over as soon as the latest disastrous test scores or dropout rates come out or there's the inevitable Board of Education screw-up. He needs to use his office as a bully pulpit constantly sending out messages like the custodian story, convincing the public that there will be no improvement until the system's perverse incentives are overhauled. Levy has 25 percent more money to spend in real dollars than Rudy Crew did at the beginning of his term. It's not the money, stupid, it's the system.

When the other interviews were over Levy came out of his office and apologized for the long wait. Unfortunately, he now had to get to a luncheon appointment with Terri Thomson, the Queens representative to the Board of Education who had provided him with the final vote he needed for a majority. He suggested that I ride out with him in his official car; we could talk during the thirty minutes it was likely to take to get to the restaurant in Queens. As we walked out of the building, I mentioned that I had been to the restroom while I was waiting for him and marveled at how clean it was. He laughed and I could see how pleased he was with his first victory over the system's fabled inertia.

In the car I asked Levy whether there was anything else about 110 Livingston Street that shocked him. I was surprised (not because of what he said but rather that he was willing to say it to me) when he launched into a litany of complaints about the quality of the work performed by middle managers and department heads at the board. He said many of these people were hardworking and dedicated, but their skills and knowledge were woeful. He had found no more than one or two people working at the board who could provide him with the basic information needed to make rational policy decisions. "No one seems to know the numbers around here," he said. As a result, his own desk was now piled high with pages and pages of raw data he was slogging through on his own in order to decide what his immediate priorities should be.

The second subject we discussed was the teachers' contract,

due to expire in November 2000. The UFT was already on the air with a $2 million ad campaign designed to convince the public that the city faced a critical teacher shortage because of the higher salaries paid in suburban schools. According to the UFT, city teachers were flocking to the suburbs and city schools would be doomed unless all eighty thousand teachers immediately received a huge across-the-board salary raise.

I told Levy that I was working on an article debunking the myth of the great teacher exodus to the suburbs. I didn't dispute that suburban schools were paying much higher salaries, but based on data published by the state education department, I estimated that the actual number of teachers transferring out per year was no more than 1 percent of the city's total teacher force. Being a numbers cruncher, Levy was interested in how I came up with my figures. He said I was probably right that the actual number leaving for the suburbs wasn't as high as the UFT was claiming, but also that I underestimated the effect of low salaries on the city's ability to entice talented teachers to work here in the first place.

The interview had given way to a dialogue, sometimes an argument. I said that new teachers were more demoralized by the way they were treated at 110 Livingston Street than by low salaries. I agreed with Levy on the need for more qualified teachers in the city's classrooms, but differed about the meaning of "qualified." He used it interchangeably with "certified," which I said wasn't the same thing. Since I hardly knew the man, I didn't yet have the nerve to bring up his own children's teachers at Dalton to prove he was wrong. I did tell him that my article would cite New Jersey's successful "alternate route" to certification for candidates who had an interest in teaching but were unwilling to invest the time and money to get a degree from an ed school. He wanted me to send him the material on the New Jersey program.

We agreed that the work rules in the teachers' contract were an obstacle to improved academic performance in the classroom. I was amazed at how knowledgeable he already was about the contract, chapter and verse. He knew of all the ways that seniority trumps excellence and how destructive this was. After I had railed against the contract for years, it was almost disorienting to hear the new schools chancellor tell *me* that it was virtually impossible to fire an incompetent teacher. "I am not going to sign off on any new contract unless the disciplinary process for teachers is completely revamped," he assured me.

Finally we reprised our argument of years earlier about the role of money in school improvement. Levy was still livid that Albany was shortchanging the city's schools; he wanted that money not only as a matter of fairness but as a means of improving teaching and learning. I agreed with him about the fairness issue, but I said he still had more money to spend in real terms than his predecessors did. If the system were well managed, and with the proper incentives in place, $11 billion (soon to be $12 billion) should be enough to provide a decent education for the city's kids. He wouldn't buy it.

After we arrived at the restaurant, our conversation continued for another ten or fifteen minutes. Finally, Levy said he couldn't keep Thomson waiting any longer. After shaking hands, he said: "Let's talk again. E-mail me if you think of other things I should be doing." He then stepped out of the car and asked his driver to take me to my home in Manhattan. All the way back to the city I had to keep convincing myself that the schools chancellor really did say the things I just heard him say.

It wasn't useful trying to figure out which cause was foremost on Levy's mind. Perhaps he was sincere about both: bringing effective reform to the system while continuing to complain about not having enough money to run it. I decided not to publish an account of what he said; rather, I would wait to see what he did. As requested, I sent him material on the New Jersey program of alternate certification.

In a speech at NYU a few weeks later, Levy announced that the recruitment and retention of qualified teachers would be a major priority of his new administration. He referred to a study by University of Tennessee researcher William Sanders showing that teacher effectiveness in the classroom is more important than all other variables—including class size, per-pupil expenditures, even the number of ed-school courses taken by the teacher—in explaining variation in student performance. Levy said this proved how important it was for the city to get all its teachers certified.

Well, I thought, he's got this one completely upside down. Sanders' study actually showed that there was little correlation between certification and teacher effectiveness in the class-room—something that many parents (including Levy) know instinctively about their own kids' schooling. In other words, it's better to have an effective teacher who is uncertified and never went to ed school than a weak teacher who is certified and has an ed-school degree. Levy also seemed unaware that Sanders' research supported education critics who were urging a radical overhaul of the nation's traditional teacher certification programs.

I continued to run into Levy at education events and we sometimes spoke on the phone. Soon he announced the creation of the city's first alternative teaching certificate program. I like to think it had something to do with the material I sent him. The program was aimed at "career changers," people in their thirties and forties who wanted to try teaching in the city schools but either didn't want to or couldn't afford to spend a year in a grad-uate ed school before they got into a classroom. In Levy's expensive program, they could now take a summer crash course run by the city and then be allowed to teach. The candidates would then take extra graduate credits while they were teaching, all at city expense.

Despite my view that Levy hadn't gone far enough, I praised him in an op-ed piece for taking the first step toward breaking the state's monopoly on deciding who teaches in the public schools. In another piece I said that Levy deserved "at least two cheers and maybe more" because he was also the first chan-cellor in recent memory to acknowledge that the system needed drastic reform. In that article I described Levy's response to a sit-uation that came up at a town hall meeting. Levy was told that alumni of Bronx Science High School were not allowed to pur-chase new seats for the school auditorium because of an obscure school board regulation. "That's just crazy," Levy announced to great applause. "If there is such a regulation I can assure you it is now rescinded."

True to his word, Levy refused to let go of the issue of incompetent and dysfunctional teachers who couldn't be fired, and he made this a priority in the board's contract negotiations with the UFT. Another reform initiative was his announcement of a visiting committee of five Nobel laureates to study the curriculum and the "staffing and organizational structure" at Levy's alma mater, Bronx Science. His intent was to have the committee then move on to assess Stuyvesant High School. Some in the media snickered about the "Nobel Prize" project. Knowing first-hand how many ineffective teachers there were at Stuyvesant, I thought the idea of a review committee was a wonderful idea. Levy confided to me that he intended to use the committee as a wedge to free the two schools from the destructive union work rules.

There were enough other promising moments during Levy's first year in office to keep me hoping; yet his incessant harping on the money issue was beginning to trouble me. By his second year in office the Board of Education budget was $12 billion, an increase of 24 percent in inflation-adjusted dollars in just three years. The total number of teachers working for the board had reached eighty thousand, which meant a ratio of one teacher for every thirteen children. Despite these substantial resources, the schools under Levy's command were still incapable of graduating more than 50 percent of each year's high school entering class in four years.

Instead of pressing for more radical reforms and following up on initiatives like the Bronx Science/Stuyvesant review committee, however, Levy complained more and more about being shortchanged by the state. He also cast his money crusade in starkly partisan terms. At one point he said that the only way the city would finally get its fair share of state education funding was for the people to work harder to oust the Republicans from control of the state senate.

Levy seemed to have accepted the UFT's propaganda campaign about the teacher shortage crisis. He frequently repeated the following argument: The city is getting screwed financially by upstate Republican legislators. As a result, we lose many of our best teachers to suburban schools and can't recruit other qualified teachers to take positions here in the first place. With fewer certified teachers in the system, the children's academic performance suffers. If the city is to fulfill its obligation to educate all the children, it must somehow find the money for huge across-the-board raises for teachers.

In the private sector whence Levy came, this analysis would be regarded as not only amateurish but ruinous management. By siding with the UFT's salary demands even before negotiations began, Levy made it harder to get the union to compromise on issues like merit pay or work rules. Levy's money complaints were also blinding him to the possibility of improving performance by changing the way the school system does business. Just because 1,200 city teachers (by the board's very questionable count) were leaving to take jobs in the suburbs didn't mean big across-the-board salary increases were warranted for all 80,000 teachers. Levy should have done some research first. If a significant number of those departing teachers were in shortage areas such as math, science and foreign languages, a more affordable remedy would be to offer higher salaries or bonuses for those in the shortage areas. On the other hand, if the teachers leaving city schools were in easy-to-fill areas, like English and social studies, their leaving was a less critical issue.

Levy always said that getting more money for the teachers was more than a matter of equity and fairness, that it was also good business. He invoked the law of labor markets, saying the city had no choice but to compete with neighboring school districts for teaching talent. Clearly he wasn't willing to consider offering higher salaries to teachers in shortage areas, because that would have brought him into conflict with the UFT, which was committed to the single salary schedule for all teachers.

Because Levy never spent a day in an education school, yet was given the biggest job in American public education, it wasn't unreasonable to hope that he would think somewhat more creatively about how to bring new talent into the schools. Yet aside from the small alternative certification program, Levy was as adamant in defending the closed monopoly system of teacher training and recruitment as any education bureaucrat. It all came to a head for me when I appeared with him on the city council's sponsored panel on education that I discussed in chapter four. Levy was visibly upset when I mentioned that he didn't seem troubled about the quality of the classroom instruction his own kids were getting at the Dalton School despite the fact that none of the teachers was certified.

Afterward I wrote a letter to Levy apologizing for seeming to personalize our disagreement and using his private life for a debating point. But I also elaborated on my argument that breaking down the barriers for entering the teaching profession might be one of the best tonics for the city schools. Given how bad the schools were doing, shouldn't this at least be tried? He never responded.

Instead of reforming the teacher recruitment and pay system, Levy now staged as many events and photo ops as possible with the likes of Hillary Clinton and assorted Democratic politicians in order to press the case for more dollars. For me, the low point occurred in March 2001 at Levy's national conference celebrating "Exemplary Education Practices in New York City." The three-day extravaganza cost the supposedly deprived school system over $400,000 (of which $80,000 went to pay for a "tasting event" at the Brooklyn Museum of Art). A few dozen educators from around the country accepted Levy's invitation to come and see how well some of the city schools were doing and to participate in a lot of panels. Hundreds of the city's teachers, principals and other personnel got two days off to attend the conference because there were not enough out-of-town educators to fill the seats.

Levy had started off promising an administration open to new ideas and respectful of intellectual discourse. Yet at his big event (UFT president Randi Weingarten jokingly called it "Harold's second bar mitzvah") there was no intellectual controversy, no new ideas. Not one of the hot issues roiling American education—vouchers, tax credits, charter schools, teacher certification reform, whole language instruction—came close to being discussed. It was a combination of a PR event for Levy's administration and a joint political rally with the UFT for the cause of getting more money for the system.

The two emotional high points of the gathering were the

welcoming address of Mayor Giuliani and the keynote speech by Joseph Weyland, the lawyer who had just argued a successful lawsuit against the State of New York to bring equity to the distribution of state education funds. (The state then appealed the decision.) Giuliani dared to suggest that, while it was always good to have more money, the school system already had enough to educate the kids if it reformed its practices. For this he was practically booed off the stage. Weyland on the other hand, after being introduced by Levy as one of the city's genuine heroes, received a standing ovation as he broke down and cried while describing the utter scandal of the city having only $12 billion to spend on its 1.1 million schoolchildren.

No one at Levy's event noticed the paradox of celebrating dozens of exemplary New York City schools (as good as any schools in the country, according to Levy) while simultaneously protesting that there's not enough money to produce good schools. No one bothered to figure out why those schools were performing at a high level while so many others were failing. It certainly wasn't because they had more money. (Poorly performing schools are always given more money and it rarely helps.)

Knowing some of the schools that were showcased at Levy's extravaganza, I would say that the biggest reason for their success was that their principals managed to find ways to escape the central bureaucratic regulations and oppressive union work rules that Levy was no longer crusading against. Many of these principals created their own republics of reform, places where teachers and administrators were guided by the needs of students instead of the rules of 110 Livingston Street or the union contract.

In 2001, about halfway through Levy's tenure, the *New York Times* published an article by education reporter Abby Goodnough describing how new teachers became demoralized because of senseless school board regulations and procedures. To me this old/new story was one of the saddest commentaries on Levy's tenure. In the article, teachers complained that they were forced to travel long distances to Board of Education headquarters in Brooklyn and wait in line to hand deliver their completed paperwork. Apparently Levy was so preoccupied with getting more money for the system that he hadn't managed to teach his employees at 110 Livingston Street how to process mail. Soon afterward Levy allowed the visiting committee for Bronx Science and Stuyvesant High Schools to lapse without bringing any change to the two schools.

Levy lasted for two years and seven months, a half-year longer than the average tenure of his six predecessors. I went to see him again at 110 Livingston Street a few days before his last day on the job. This time there were no TV cameras competing for his time and the phones not only weren't ringing off the hook, they weren't ringing at all. In fact, the executive suite was almost deserted. Levy was all alone in his office, taking pictures off the wall and packing his files. He made a persuasive case to me that he had achieved a lot during his two and a half years. He mentioned the alternative licensing program, making the system more transparent and giving parents more data about their children's schools, a successful summer school program and finally, and most importantly, negotiating a new contract with the teachers' union in which charges of incompetence against teachers would be more quickly resolved.

These were not insignificant. In fact, I would grant that Levy was a more effective chancellor than any of the six certified professional educators who preceded him at 110 Livingston Street. At the very least he proved that the elaborate state regulations governing the qualifications needed for running schools and school systems—a throwback to the "one best system"—were now out of date. Unfortunately, Levy wasn't able to see that almost everything else about the system's rules, including the process for finding quality teachers, was also out of date and irrelevant.

In the normal course of events, Levy's accomplishments would have been sufficient to have his contract as chancellor extended for another few years. But these were not normal times. Despair about the performance of the school system had reached the point that even the political establishment in Albany recognized that something desperate had to be done. Power over the city's schools was then stripped from the Board of Education and handed to the mayor. The theory was that the mayor—any mayor—knowing he would be held accountable by the electorate for the condition of the schools, would have the political incentive to cut through the bureaucratic morass and reform the system.

Mayor Michael Bloomberg didn't start out with any ideas for improving the schools. Like Levy, he apparently didn't think he could learn much of value from the private schools he sent his own children to. Bloomberg did, however, hire Joel Klein to replace Levy. Klein, too, was a lawyer and a businessman, not a professional educator. He had served as a deputy attorney general in the Clinton administration and made his name prosecuting Microsoft for antitrust violations—notably, for trying to eliminate competition. Like Levy, Klein also sent his children to private schools, but was sure that the choice he was taking advantage of wouldn't work in public education.

Then, out of the blue, Mayor Bloomberg delivered a Martin Luther King Day speech in January 2003 that I viewed as a vindication of what I had been saying about the school system. He called it an "Alice in Wonderland structure" suffering from "bureaucratic sclerosis" and "Byzantine administrative fiefdoms." He said he wanted to free principals from the "dead hand of bureaucracy" and defined the core mission of the schools as "classroom instruction for students, not jobs for bureaucrats." Standing in front of a portrait of Dr. King at Harlem's Schomburg Center, the mayor rightly termed the effort to reform the schools a civil rights battle.

Mayor Bloomberg's unsparing analysis represented a radical departure from the "lack of adequate resources" rationale for school failure used by Chancellor Levy. The mayor made a point of emphasizing that the city was spending the whopping sum of $12 billion a year ($10,000 per pupil) on K–12 education, yet 1,000 of the city's 1,200 schools were failing and most of the children still weren't learning to read and write. To Bloomberg this was a "disgrace" and the city's "shame." No one was to blame but the bureaucratic system that the city itself had created and tolerated for so long.

Unfortunately, Mayor Bloomberg didn't follow up on the

civil rights metaphor by recognizing the right of poor children trapped in failing city schools to attend parochial or private schools that might work for them. Instead, he proposed an inside-the-system revolution from the top. In place of the bureaucratic "blob," he said he would create a military-style, centralized chain of command from his own office right down to every school in the system.

We had now come full circle. Out of desperation New York seemed to be back to the "one best system" instituted by Nicholas Murray Butler at the beginning of the twentieth century. Despite my mistrust of top-down management in education, no one would cheer louder if Bloomberg manages to turn around a substantial number of the city's schools. But if he fails, if in a few years we are still in the Twilight Zone, there will no longer be any excuses. And then—even in New York City—the argument for school choice and competition will be irresistible.

6

Shake the Money Tree

I t is unfortunate but at least understandable that teachers' union leaders think it's in their members' interests to keep pushing the idea that lack of money and resources is at the root of urban school failure. But what excuse is there for those public figures sworn to protect the interests of the children in the public schools—politicians like Mario Cuomo, David Dinkins, Ted Kennedy and Bill Clinton, who took the union's money and political support and then helped keep millions of poor children locked in failing public schools while they sent their own kids to private schools?

Yet merely because they called for more money for the public schools, these politicians were portrayed in the media as the "education president" or the "education governor." This charade, in turn, was made possible by the fact that most of the elite media and many education writers reflexively accepted the notion that money was the key to educational success.

No single writer has done more harm in this regard than Jonathan Kozol. In *Death at an Early Age* and other best-selling books, he has worked hard to convince Americans that inner-city minority children are languishing academically only because their schools are segregated and starved for resources by a heartless society. In this, Kozol has been a shill for the teachers' unions and education officials who keep calling for bogus reforms, while the real causes of school failure—the monopoly public school system, the union work rules—continue to wreak damage and inner-city schools sink even lower.

Kozol's many fans see him as a heroic explorer of America's

slums whose painful discoveries about the institutional racism that stunts poor children go unheard and unappreciated. He presents himself as a rebel, a prophet without honor; but the truth is that the capitalist society Kozol so disdains has rewarded him extravagantly, turning him into a cultural icon, and a rich one at that. The Ford, Rockefeller and Guggenheim Foundations have showered him with grants; colleges and ed schools nationwide have made his books required reading. He has won the top awards given by both the American Federation of Teachers and the National Education Association, and both unions have paid handsomely for his speaking appearances. When Kozol's signature book on underfunded ghetto schools, *Savage Inequalities,* first appeared in 1991, *Publishers Weekly*—unprecedentedly—dropped five pages of paid advertising to run excerpts, printing on its cover a plea to the first President George Bush to pour billions more into the nation's inner-city schools.

The son of a prominent Boston-area doctor, Kozol attended prep school and graduated with honors from Harvard, his father's alma mater. After a Rhodes Scholarship to Oxford, he spent a few years in Paris working on a novel. Returning to Boston in 1964, he decided to try his hand as a substitute fourth-grade teacher at a run-down school in the largely minority Dorchester district—only to be fired after six months. The charge: that he had departed from the official curriculum by reading the poems of Robert Frost and Langston Hughes to his students. When the Boston papers picked up the story—HARVARD MAN FIRED FOR TEACHING LANGSTON HUGHES POEM TO BLACK CHILDREN—the public school authorities appeared terminally stupid.

The Langston Hughes episode gave the first-time author advance publicity and instant credibility, and his artful book engaged the reader with flesh-and-blood characters and tales of good and evil inside a school that Kozol paints as a racist hellhole. Reviewers praised Kozol's unsparing exposé of the "destruction of the hearts and minds of Negro children in the Boston Public Schools." *Death at an Early Age* won the National Book Award and went on to sell over two million copies.

The book's key idea is that institutional racism, embodied in segregated schools and twisted white teachers, is the sole cause of the failure of black children. For Kozol, no other explanation is worth considering—not family breakdown, not the underclass culture. Indeed, Kozol rationalizes the self-destructive behavior of black youngsters. After one of his students is accused of stealing, he writes: "I do not think that he had stolen anything, but I would consider it quite understandable and almost natural if he had. Any Negro child who stole anything movable out of any home or Boston schoolhouse would not have stolen back as much as has been stolen from him."

Kozol movingly profiles black children whose radiant souls and unrealized potential shine out from their impoverished circumstances. They suffer a continual assault on their spirits, as their teachers belittle their aspirations and abilities. In Kozol's telling, not one white adult—except him—exhibits a flicker of sympathy for the black children or teaches them anything useful. There's only one problem with this portrait: it is utterly false. For all my criticism of public school teachers in this book, I can't imagine such a school as Kozol depicts, where not a single teacher accomplishes anything of value. We will never get to hear from those accused teachers, however, because they don't exist. "With the exception of certain named public figures, characters in this book do not have counterparts in real life," Kozol acknowledges in a "Note to Readers." "Nevertheless, important attitudes, character traits, acts or stated viewpoints ascribed to faculty, administration and pupils in this book accurately reflect the author's experience in the Boston Public Schools." In other words: Don't pin me down with nitpicking questions about whether my school's teachers actually said everything I attribute to them. In short, *Death at an Early Age* is creative writing.

Undeterred by the author's admissions, Kozol's admirers insisted that *Death at an Early Age* revealed the grim truth about the segregation and racism that were damaging black students. At almost the same moment that it appeared, President Johnson's Kerner Commission was concluding that segregation in the North as well as the South was driving America "toward two societies, one black, one white—separate and unequal." As white liberals searched their souls, powerful voices in Boston, ranging from the *Boston Globe* to the local NAACP, pressed for judicial intervention. Kozol later wrote that *"Death at an Early Age* appears to have had some effect in heightening the pressure that would lead in time to the court-ordered integration of the Boston schools."

Indeed, a few years after the 1967 publication of Kozol's book, federal judge W. Arthur Garrity issued his draconian decree, causing thousands of black students to be bused halfway across the city every day, while thousands of white students unwillingly made the reverse trip. Most of the white liberals who cheered Judge Garrity's decision didn't enroll their own children in the public schools, of course; nor did the childless Kozol. But the white, predominantly Catholic, working-class families of the city who did send their children to public schools eventually voted with their feet against this experiment in social engineering. "In just four years, Boston's schools lost nearly 20,000 [out of 54,000] white students—to parochial schools, private academies, the streets, or because their families had left the city altogether," wrote Anthony Lukas in *Common Ground,* the most detailed account of Boston's busing wars.

Busing had achieved the very opposite of what it was meant to do, leaving the Boston schools more segregated than ever. The Dorchester school where Kozol taught was about 60 percent black when he excoriated it as a segregated hellhole, but Boston soon had not a single public school with as much as 40 percent white enrollment. Eventually, even Kozol had to acknowledge that forced busing "may prove at last to be a Pyrrhic victory. Today we see an integrated underclass in Boston in the process of gestation. Poor whites, poor blacks, and poor Hispanics now become illiterate together." All the energy and resources and passion that had gone into the busing effort were worse than wasted.

Death at an Early Age left another destructive legacy—a truly ironic one, given Kozol's dream of racial harmony. By its false portrayal of white educators as wantonly destroying the minds of black children, it helped legitimate curricular Afrocentrism. In this case the cure has been far worse than the alleged disease. School districts from Portland, Oregon, to Washington, D.C., have institutionalized a new form of racism, using curricular guides like the "Portland Baseline Studies" to stuff the minds of black children with racialist humbug about a mythical glorious African past in which black people flew gliders in the shadows of the pyramids, instead of teaching them the basic skills they need to succeed in an information-based economy.

In *Death at an Early Age,* Kozol presented himself as a non-political, idealistic young man shocked by a glaring injustice. But soon enough, he revealed himself as a hard-line leftist. In his next two books he argued that it was America's capitalist culture that gave rise to its racist public schools. Good schooling, therefore, shouldn't focus primarily on teaching literacy and numeracy but rather on encouraging children to free themselves from capitalism's competitive mindset and the false patriotism that traditional teachers and textbooks inculcate. Racism was merely the symptom. Mainstream America was the disease.

Kozol honed these views in (of all places) revolutionary Cuba, whose government invited him in the mid-seventies to study its education system. Dictatorships don't make such offers without knowing what kind of review they will get, and sure enough, Kozol's account of his visit, *Children of the Revolution,* is a nauseating apologia for the Castro regime's indoctrination of children and adults. Almost everyone else in the world knew about Castro's appalling human rights record by this time, with poets such as Armando Valladares languishing in jail and teachers finding themselves purged if they did not parrot the party line. But such issues don't make their way into Kozol's rhapsodic account. The dissident truth seeker had become a crude propagandist for a coercive Marxist state.

The first thing Kozol learned in Cuba was to get over some outworn ideals—that education is about the objective search for truth, for example, or that objective truth exists. When he asked Cuba's education minister why turgid political propaganda filled the texts for Cuba's adult literacy course, he got the standard Marxist line: "All education has forever had a class bias. No society will foster schools that do not serve its ends." Kozol accepts this doubletalk as gospel and urges the reader to discard the naïve view that education can be politically neutral. Even in the "so-called" free world, it is an instrument of state indoctrination, says Kozol. Why expect anything different from Cuba?

Kozol's visit to the Lenin High School, an indoctrination academy for future leaders of the revolution, stands out as the highlight of his trip. "[S]omething here is really different," he enthuses. "There is a sense of shared achievement, of hard work that remains...one good notch below the level of competitive obsession"—unlike capitalism's dog-eat-dog way of life. The school is "able to combine...a reverence for productive labor and an impressive level of true humanistic education of the whole man and the whole woman." No alienation here: socialist man is at peace with himself and his comrades. Like all Cuban schools, of course, this one is based "on a firm and vivid grasp upon the concrete truths of life itself. Almost all ideas and skills that are acquired in these schools are meant to lead to action, to real work, and to real dedication.... There is a sense, within the Cuban schools, that one is working for a purpose and that that purpose is a great deal more profound and more important than the selfish pleasure of an individual reward." Radically anti-intellectual as well as anti-individualist, this is a pretty good description of the totalitarian frame of mind.

Fortunately for Kozol's subsequent career, *Children of the Revolution* sold few copies and quickly went out of print. But Kozol obviously continued to brood over the ideas he had taken away from Cuba and slowly molded them into a new theory for reforming American education. Taking as his starting point the crude Marxist view that education in all societies is "a system of indoctrination" and "an instrument of the state," he worked out a method by which teachers could subvert capitalist America's bad indoctrination and—cleverly and subtly—substitute some good left-wing indoctrination in its place. His next book, *On Being a Teacher,* is a manual on how to do that.

A typical chapter, "Disobedience Instruction," tells teachers how to encourage skepticism of authority by calling attention to "those ordinary but pathetic figures who went into Watergate to steal, into My Lai to kill—among other reasons, because they lacked the power to say no." According to Kozol, teachers should also invoke mass murderer Adolf Eichmann, whose "own preparation for obedient behavior was received in German public schools"—which resemble our own in aiming to produce "good Germans, or good citizens, as we in the United States would say."

All the book's model lessons aim to teach little children to withstand America's state-sponsored brainwashing and to open them up to the self-evident truths of feminism, environmentalism and a Marxist interpretation of history. At the end of the book, Kozol thoughtfully provides a long list of left-wing publications and organizations—including the information agencies of the Chinese and Cuban governments—where teachers can get worthwhile classroom materials. But, he warns teachers, be stealthy about all this; you can't altogether neglect teaching the basic skills, because administrators or parents would then see how politically motivated you are.

Parents, particularly those of minority children, should dread the prospect of having one of Kozol's guerilla cadre in charge of their children's classrooms; such teachers are almost never much good at imparting basic skills, because they almost always embrace the ed schools' latest progressive pedagogical fads. The teacher who feels compelled to denounce every one of Columbus's depredations against the Arawaks—as my son Dani's fourth-grade teacher at P.S. 87 did—is also likely to believe that standardized tests are bunk, that math and reading should never be taught through drill, that children should not be taught "mere facts," and that the very idea of literacy is merely a Western conceit.

Unlike Kozol's Cuban book, *On Being a Teacher* is still in print and still widely read in ed schools, especially by activist teachers. To the degree that elementary and high school teachers take to heart Kozol's vision of the classroom as an arena for political indoctrination and the deconstruction of Western culture, they limit the life chances of inner-city children. As education critic E. D. Hirsch and noted black educator Lisa Delpit have warned, disadvantaged children desperately need drilling in basic literacy and numeracy skills—even more than do middle-class children from educated families. Those poor children will grow to adulthood not in the collectivist society of Jonathan Kozol's fantasy but in a competitive global economy. Education theories and practices inspired by another Marxist dystopia are the last thing they need.

Kozol's next bestseller, *Savage Inequalities,* picked up the teachers' unions' money argument. He claimed to have visited schools in thirty neighborhoods. But in the book, he chooses to highlight only the most glaring contrasts between the worst inner-city schools and nearby suburban schools. The disparities between urban and suburban schools should surprise no one, of course. White flight—partly caused by the forced busing that Kozol helped bring about—shrank urban tax bases while filling the suburbs with new, upwardly mobile parents who cared deeply about their children's schools and were happy to lavish tax money on them, particularly since they were now paying less in taxes for welfare and policing.

Each of *Savage Inequalities'* six chapters focuses on the blighted minority schools of a different city, along with some comparisons with nearby wealthy suburban school districts. By comparing the worst urban schools with the richest suburban schools—two of Chicago's sorriest high schools, for example, with preppy New Trier High School in one of the nation's poshest suburbs—Kozol can avoid dealing with the real reasons that urban schools don't work, the nonfinancial reasons that his comrades in the teachers' unions do not want discussed. If he had visited one of the many Catholic schools within walking distance of some of the woeful public schools he describes—schools that are thriving academically despite spending less than half of what the public schools spend—he might have to consider reasons other than money that might explain public school failure, including the absence of accountability for teachers, principals and other employees.

Kozol's 1995 book, *Amazing Grace,* restates the argument of *Savage Inequalities,* though with a preachy religiosity in place of Marxist rhetoric. This time it is the Mott Haven section of the South Bronx—New York's poorest neighborhood—that prompts Kozol's sermon about racial injustice and the unwillingness of the dominant society to spend money on black children's schools. He relishes describing how he boards the subway right next to Bloomingdale's department store on Manhattan's opulent Upper East Side and, six stops and twenty minutes later, emerges from Mott Haven's Brook Avenue station into a moonscape of garbage-strewn lots and burned-out buildings.

Kozol describes Morris High School, which he also wrote about in *Savage Inequalities,* as "one of the most beleaguered, segregated and decrepit secondary schools in the United States. Barrels were filling up with rain in several rooms the last time I was there. Green fungus molds were growing in the corner" of one room, and the girls' toilets smelled too bad to use. But this description merely recycles material from *Savage Inequalities;* Kozol wasn't anywhere near Morris while researching *Amazing Grace* years later. In *Savage Inequalities* he had written that it would take at least $50 million to restore Morris's decaying physical plant, implying that the same racist society that created segregated Mott Haven would never spend that much money on a ghetto school. But New York actually *did* spend about $50 million to restore Morris by the time Kozol wrote *Amazing Grace,* which he conveniently neglected to mention. But all that money and the newly gleaming building had hardly any impact on the academic performance of Morris's students.

As I have noted in an earlier chapter, one of the heroic figures in *Amazing Grace* is Mario, an angelic-looking black child trapped in an awful, segregated public school. Like every other black child Kozol has ever written about, he's engaging, bright, innocent and brimming with untapped talent. If Mario is going nowhere, it's only because the rich, white taxpayers of New York refuse to spend enough money on his education. Unquestionably Mario was a victim of cruel unfairness, like every poor child sentenced to a dysfunctional school. But the unfairness has nothing to do with the reasons Kozol and the teachers' unions put forth. Money has been pouring into urban school systems since the early 1990s. The cities have benefited from more than $50 billion in federal Title I money for poor children and substantially increased state aid packages to poorer districts to make up for their local property-tax shortfall. Three of the six cities portrayed in *Savage Inequalities*—New York, Washington and Camden—now spend $11,000 per pupil or more. True, that's less than rich suburbs like Scarsdale and Great Neck allocate to their schools. But it is much more money than the average expenditure for the United States, and it is higher than the average of the states those three cities are in. With the proper organization and incentives, it should be sufficient to provide any child with a decent education. But it will never be enough for Jonathan Kozol, because it will never match the purity of purpose and the leveling of all human differences he thought he once glimpsed in revolutionary Cuba.

★

The one place where you might think Kozol's money arguments would get little support is in the business community. After all, who more than a businessman or woman ought to understand that it's not necessarily how much money a school system spends that determines outcomes, but how intelligently and efficiently the money is spent? Who more than someone who has prospered in a market economy has the experience and authority to say that no enterprise can prosper that doesn't hold its employees accountable for their performance, rewarding merit and punishing failure?

In Milwaukee, as I will show later on, the business community did arrive at a consensus that school choice was good for children and that competition was better for the public schools than monopoly. It's not that the business organizations opposed more spending on the schools. In fact, they often lobbied the state legislature on behalf of the Milwaukee Public Schools as well as for the voucher program. But they also understood how destructive and paralyzing it was to use the money argument as an excuse for school failure. Thus they helped line up support for the total transformation of public education in their city.

I wish I could say the same for most of the business leaders in my own city, the world's financial capital. I often wondered why it was so rare to hear the voices of business people supporting even the most reasonable reforms in the public schools —such as making it possible for the city to fire incompetent teachers or paying teachers commensurately with their knowledge and performance rather than their seniority. Business leaders certainly had a deep interest in the success of the public schools, frequently speaking of the new economy's need for educated workers. Yet instead of providing a coherent analysis of what prevented the system from accomplishing this goal, they were more likely to echo Jonathan Kozol's complaint from *Savage Inequalities.*

Typical of the kinds of initiatives that New York City business executives supported is the "Principal for a Day" program, sponsored by an organization called PENCIL (Public Education Needs Civic Involvement in Learning). The founding genius behind PENCIL was Lisa Belzberg, daughter of one of Canada's richest families and wife of Matthew Bronfman, son of Canadian tycoon Edgar Bronfman. Attractive and articulate, with degrees from Barnard College and the London School of Economics, Belzberg moved easily among the city's movers and shakers; her name on an invitation could draw willing supporters by the droves. She once served as a Principal for a Day when it was an obscure program run by the city's Board of Education, and she found a cause. She created PENCIL and then expanded it into the largest and most successful operation of its kind in the country.

Although Belzberg sends her own children to an exclusive Jewish day school, she bubbles with enthusiasm about the public schools. "I truly believe in the notion of public education in this country," she once told me. "It is the one place where everyone can be accepted. There are beautiful things going on in the system.... I believe that by putting the private sector into the schools, we are bringing the city together."

In the past few years, companies such as NBC, Primedia and HBO have poured millions of dollars' worth of computers, books and furniture into their assigned schools through Principal for a Day—as well as offering students a host of internships and tutoring programs. While these gifts are undoubtedly useful to the individual schools that receive them, there is little evidence that Principal for a Day has brought about any systemic school improvement.

But the program *has* brought a bonanza of glowing publicity for the public school system and for some of the celebrity "principals." For years I found myself bemused by the gushing columns by journalists from all four major New York dailies about their Principal for a Day stints. Somehow, none of these normally skeptical writers ever seemed to visit a poorly performing school, or to serve with a less than stellar principal, or to observe a lazy teacher. Friendly media coverage of Belzberg depicted her as an angel of mercy, mobilizing private-sector relief for the city's worthy but "underfunded" schools. Her efforts on behalf of public schools were often contrasted favorably with the work of philanthropists such as Peter Flanigan, Ted Forstmann, Richard Gilder and Roger Hertog who donated millions of dollars for private school scholarships—privately funded vouchers, really—that allowed thousands of poor kids to escape dismal public schools. *She* cared; *they* were mean-spirited, despite their massive giving and their rescue of thousands of kids.

These supporters of the private voucher programs were often accused of abandoning the public schools. Even if you believe that dubious proposition, it leaves unanswered this key question: What should business leaders actually be doing if they really want to help save public education? Is donating books and computers the best answer?

To find out, I decided to volunteer as a Principal for a Day during the last year of the Clinton administration. I joined about one thousand of the city's business executives, a dozen or so local politicians, and such luminaries as bad-boy actor Billy Baldwin, Diane von Furstenberg and designer Norma Kamali. One of my fellow Principals for a Day that year was First Lady Hillary Clinton, just recently arrived in New York.

I found, alas, that the businessmen left their managerial smarts in the office when they signed up for a day in the public schools. They came to their schools with the best of intentions and bearing gifts, yet unwittingly they conspired in propping up an indefensible, failing system.

I was assigned to be "principal" of Intermediate School 59, in Springfield Gardens, Queens, a solidly middle- and working-class black neighborhood near the Nassau County border. Surrounding the vast rectangular school building are small one-family homes with neatly kept lawns. The building houses over 1,500 students, virtually all of them black, most from intact families, and comparatively few in poverty.

When I called the principal, Antonio K'tori, to arrange my visit, I could sense his disappointment in getting a writer rather than a businessman. "What can you do for us?" he asked in a somewhat forlorn voice. Thrown off guard, I replied, with a chuckle, "Maybe I could fire some of your teachers."

K'tori took it in good humor. He told me that he had only a handful of below-par teachers, because over the past several years he had forced several others—by methods unspecified—to transfer or retire. This led us to the constraints that the teachers' union contract places on the school principal's managerial autonomy. K'tori told me that, despite the contract's well-known restrictions, he felt he could run a successful school.

I found much that was positive about I.S. 59. K'tori, who grew up in England, the son of Sudanese parents, was basically an education traditionalist. He imposed a dress code, he said, "because it takes the children away from the feeling that school is unimportant and that they can get here any way they please." All of his math and science classes were tracked for ability. He was a believer in high standards. By chance I wandered into an advanced seventh-grade science class and watched John Como, twenty-nine, teach a magnificent lesson on human genetics and DNA. The thirty-five students—all black, all wearing neat school uniforms—were totally involved, answering Como's probing questions and asking intelligent questions of their own. Here was a scene, I thought, that certainly confirmed Lisa Belzberg's insistence that "beautiful things" are happening in the city's schools and that more New Yorkers should be made aware of that fact.

Just as certainly, however, Como's employment status was an indictment of the system's dysfunctional personnel policies—and New Yorkers should have known about that, too. In fact, it was a repeat of how Stuyvesant High School's brilliant math teacher, Iftimie Simion, was treated. After high school on Long Island, Como enlisted in the Navy and served on an attack submarine during the Gulf War. He then went to Tulane on an ROTC scholarship and graduated with a B.S. in molecular and cell biology. Returning to the New York area, he turned down the opportunity to work in industry and opted to try teaching for a while. The Board of Education granted him a temporary license, provided that he go back to school and take twelve education credits within the next three years. After that, he would have to earn a master's degree to become permanently certified.

Anyone who walked into Como's classroom could have testified that he was already a master teacher. With his military background, his knowledge of a difficult academic subject and his energy, Como should have been worth his weight in gold to any school. Yet despite his three stellar years in the classroom, the city and state education bureaucracies, obsessed with their absurd credentialism, were still hounding him to complete this or that petty education course before they would give him his permanent teaching license. Moreover, Como was mired at the bottom of the salary scale, earning about $32,000 a year. Out of that munificent sum, he had to fork over $800 per year (after taxes) in compulsory union dues and then spend thousands more on his education courses and on various fees to get the state eventually to process his license applications.

After leaving Como's classroom, I struck up a conversation in the hallway with a math teacher with graying hair who identified himself as "Mr. Denmark—like the country." He had been at the school for more than thirty years and seemed embittered with the system as well as with his own union leadership for accepting a contract with insufficient raises. Without a hint of embarrassment, he told me that because the city didn't show any appreciation for teachers, he had decided that he would work to the contractual minimum (six hours and twenty minutes a day) in return for his nearly $70,000 salary. His tenure protection meant that as long as he met with his assigned classes for forty-two minutes and did a reasonable job of keeping to the prescribed curriculum, there wasn't much that his principal or anyone else could do about it.

Near the end of the day, I spent a final few minutes with Principal K'tori. I asked him to name the one thing he would ask for if his Principal for a Day had the power to grant his wish. His answer: he'd request money for an after-school remedial program for the underperforming students in the school.

This was an excellent choice, reflecting K'tori's educational values. Despite I.S. 59's overall good numbers on standardized tests, too many students were way behind in crucial academic skills. More than new computers or other hardware, K'tori recognized, nothing would be as valuable to his at-risk children as extra time with a talented and productive teacher.

Still, if I could wave a magic wand, that isn't the gift that I would have offered. Instead, I would have granted K'tori the authority to control his own budget and staff. On the books, I.S. 59 was spending about $9 million per year; but it was the central Board of Education, not the principal, that allocated those dollars to the various school functions—making our school system one of the last examples of a command-and-control economy since the Berlin Wall fell. Bureaucrats at central headquarters decided that I.S. 59 would have so many teacher and assistant-principal positions, so many cafeteria workers, so many clerks and secretaries, so many security guards, so many custodial workers. If K'tori could have decided on the most efficient allocation of staff and resources, he could have found a way to pay for that extra remediation out of his own budget. To put it another way, were public education a rationally managed enterprise, K'tori would have had the authority to allocate the school's resources and staff to accomplish his educational mission, rather than have the central authority's bureaucratic rules subvert that mission from afar. Private school principals enjoy just such discretion—one reason that their schools are almost always more cost-effective and productive than public schools.

As I left I.S. 59 and drove back to Manhattan, I wondered why the business executives who served as Principals for a Day were either unable or reluctant to grasp this fundamental management issue—the bedrock principle of their own professional lives. I was soon to get an answer.

All one thousand Principals for a Day, plus many of the real principals, were invited for a town hall meeting in a large, ornate hall at the New York Public Library. Eight days earlier, in the same hall, Ted Forstmann's Children's Scholarship Fund had staged its own gala to celebrate the granting of forty thousand private school scholarships to poor public school kids. I had attended the Forstmann event, and the comments of Andrew

Young and Martin Luther King III at that ceremony still rever-
berated in my mind. The two civil rights leaders had pleaded for
a new civil rights agenda for the twenty-first century: the right of
poor minority children to choose a school that really would educate them. Another theme, sounded by Mayor Rudy Giuliani,
was that when public schools have to compete with private
schools for students, they tend to get better, so that vouchers
ultimately *improve* public education, rather than "abandon" it.
In his remarks, Mayor Giuliani stressed that 168,000 poor New
York City families with kids in the public schools—fully one-third
of all those eligible—had applied for the Forstmann scholarships,
an astonishing indictment of the existing system.

I hardly expected to find much support at the Principal for a
Day gala for using vouchers to spur competition in education.
Still, I did wonder if any of the business executives had taken
note of the Soviet-style workplace practices in the schools they
visited. Before the ceremony, I found myself in a seat next to a
Principal for a Day named Amy Larkin, president of a consulting
company that puts together private/public ventures. She told me
that she'd been assigned to an elementary school in Brooklyn
with a new young principal who was being sabotaged by the old-
guard clerical and secretarial staff. Larkin was surprised to learn
that the secretaries and clerks—just like the teachers—were covered by rigid civil service and union protections and couldn't be
fired or transferred.

Any hope that the Principals for a Day would get to air such
issues quickly evaporated. It became clear that the event was part
political rally and part revival meeting to drum up support for
the New York City education status quo and for the people who
run it. Seated in the first two rows of honor were Chancellor
Rudy Crew, Board of Education president William Thompson,
United Federation of Teachers president Randi Weingarten, and
principals' union president Donald Singer. Sprinkled among
them were lots of eager politicians, including Hillary Clinton,
who were hankering to run for higher office as candidates of the
no-change-in-education interests.

Casual and elegant, Lisa Belzberg opened the meeting by
asking everyone to pull together to "combat negative perceptions

of the system." She then turned the microphone over to TV talk show host Charlie Rose and sat down at the front of the stage, her legs draped over the edge. "All of you have had a remarkable experience," said Rose. "We now want to hear what happened to you today." Rose then worked the crowd, offering the mike to anyone who wanted to stand up and speak.

Larry Greengrass, a senior partner in the law firm of Mound, Cotton and Wollan, recounted his visit to P.S. 176 in Bay Ridge, Brooklyn, where, he said, he was thrilled to find a huge banner welcoming him, and where the "entire fifth grade" put on a performance for him. "The most amazing part of the day," he said, occurred when he sat in on a conference about a pupil who may have been the victim of abuse. "It was inspiring to me that there were all those professionals working so hard to help one kid," he said.

Jolie Schwab, a senior general attorney for ABC, spoke of the "dedicated and talented" teachers at the junior high school she had visited. Then, addressing Chancellor Crew directly, she voiced her concern that "our teachers were leaving for the suburbs."

Union boss Weingarten nodded approvingly as Crew stood up and took the mike. "What you saw," Crew told Schwab, "is what it is like every day. And it's true that our teachers are being cherry-picked by the suburbs. We have become a training ground for teachers for the suburbs." To prevent this, Crew said, the teachers had to get the salaries they deserved. The audience broke into applause. None of the business executives in attendance thought there was anything unusual about the CEO (Crew) of the public school system stating in public that his employees should get a huge raise without asking anything from the employees in return.

Not to be upstaged, principals' union chief Donald Singer stood up to say that the city's talented principals were also leaving for the suburbs. Turning directly to Crew, he urged: "Let's get a contract [for the principals] now." More applause. The same executives, of course, would have laughed instead of clapping if, back in their home offices, someone had proposed that because their companies had lost a couple of middle managers to a competitor, they should give a huge raise to each and every one of their existing managers, regardless of merit.

Strauss Zelnick, the CEO of B.M.G. Entertainment, then told of his visit to Midwood High School in Brooklyn and of the difficulties its principal was having keeping up the maintenance of his grand old building. Zelnick announced that he had committed $25,000 of his company's resources to help out. "We used to build beautiful schools in this city," Zelnick said. "It's time to say to the federal government and the state: Why don't you start putting up some money?" More applause. Everyone in the room seemed to have erased from their memory banks the fact that hundreds of millions of dollars in school construction money had disappeared into a dark hole because of the featherbedding work rules and rank incompetence at the Board of Education's School Construction Authority. Instead of trying to figure out how to eliminate the waste that virtually defines the system, the assembled business executives, despite their M.B.A.s and years of real-world experience, were applauding a proposal to keep shoveling money to the very people responsible for the failure. Only in the world of public education, I thought.

Inevitably, Charlie Rose turned the mike over to the First Lady. She told us of her visit to I.S. 226 in Queens. "It was interesting to hear the students talk about how they are always stereotyped," she said, and then remarked, somewhat vaguely, that we all "have a lot of stereotypes about public schools." Rehearsing a theme of her coming Senate campaign, she then went into high policy mode: we can't improve the public schools without new money for "reducing classroom size" and for "new facilities," she said. Touting her husband's plan to spend federal dollars to hire a hundred thousand more teachers, she compared it to the Dinkins administration's successful effort to put more cops on the street. "If you have more police, you have a better chance of reducing crime. If you have more teachers, you can do a better job of teaching the students," she remarked, ignoring the fact that New York City was living proof that more teachers didn't necessarily improve education outcomes.

It went on like this for forty minutes, as one after another of these highly successful men and women stood up and heaped praise on the "hardworking" and "dedicated" people who were doing such a "great" job of educating our children. Were they talking about the same school system that I had gotten to know so well as a parent? The system that virtually guarantees lifetime jobs for all its teachers, regardless of how little or how much they work? The system in which fewer than half the children who enter high school manage to graduate in four years? The system in which two-thirds—67 percent—of all fourth graders can't pass a very basic reading test administered by the state?

After the meeting, Donald Singer of the principals' union told me, "You can't apply the principles of competition to the schools, because education is not a business." I expected him to say that; his union exists to shield its members from the risks of the marketplace. But why did so many of the businessmen also accept it? I was dumbfounded that these shrewd, talented individuals, some of whom run the most entrepreneurial and competitive companies in the world and rightly boast that they can manage *anything* efficiently, would willingly draw down an iron curtain of denial when it came to the enterprise of public education.

In a more personal way, I was also angered. Few of the executives who were gushing about the schools they visited would actually consider sending their own children to those schools, just as Hillary Clinton hadn't sent her daughter to the Washington, D.C., public schools that she said shouldn't be "scapegoated" and "stereotyped." They all seemed to be saying the public schools were doing an excellent job for other people's children. As one of those other people, I resented being told that the quality of the education *my* children were receiving was good enough, when it so clearly wasn't.

I didn't begrudge those wealthy executives the extra money they spent on their children's private schooling; and what I had wanted for my children's schools had nothing to do with money. I wanted a system based on the fundamental idea that the interests of schoolchildren had to come first, ahead of the interests of the system's employees. These executives praising public education expected excellence from their own children's elite schools, yet in their rush to feel good about themselves they showed no interest in applying the same standard to the schools that my children attended.

After the town hall meeting, Lisa Belzberg told me she was "not in the business of trying to reform the system." On the contrary, she said she envisioned the (by now) thousands of business executives who have participated in Principal for a Day and "who have influence in this city" becoming a force to help persuade elected officials to pour ever more resources into the existing public education system. I didn't have the heart to tell her that despite all her enthusiasm and goodwill, her priorities were upside down. Business executives are better off allowing the education establishment and the unions to fight their own battles in Albany and Washington for more money and power—something these groups excel at anyway. The business community should have been prodding the public schools to change their dysfunctional workplace habits and to adopt the entrepreneurial talents that have made American enterprises the envy of the world. If they had done that, then when one of their own, Harold Levy, became schools chancellor, he would more likely have been able to bring fundamental reform to the system.

Although I could understand why the teachers' union would keep demanding more and more money for the system, it was exasperating to hear not only from a Marxist like Jonathan Kozol, but from a businessman that money was the key to school improvement. Everything I had learned in my sons' schools refuted this. It was a matter of observation and simple common sense that our public schools needed fresh ideas, innovation and competition more than they needed money.

THE IMPERATIVE
OF SCHOOL CHOICE

7

Catholic School Lessons

For almost seventy-five years after the American founding it was commonplace for private religious schools to receive some form of public funding. This essential historical fact about American education can't be repeated too often. Though not all children went to school in the first half of the nineteenth century, those who did could exercise some degree of choice in a mixed system of public and religious schools. It never occurred to any state or federal court that the straightforward words of the First Amendment—"Congress shall make no law respecting an establishment of religion, or prohibiting the free exercise thereof"—meant that the states or localities providing such funding were violating the U.S. Constitution.

Religious tensions and political interests, not the Constitution, were the prime factors in the push to create an exclusive system of taxpayer-supported, government-run public schools. By the 1840s a powerful social movement dominated by Protestant ministers and upper-class laypeople was pushing for the radical restructuring of the nation's inchoate school system, or nonsystem. These men regarded themselves as reformers and patriots, bringing uplift to millions of poor and uneducated immigrant children. To accomplish this holy mission they proposed the creation of a system of "common schools," as Horace Mann of Massachusetts, the leading light of the movement, called them. "Let the Common School be expanded to its capabilities," Mann prophesied, "let it be worked with the efficiency of which it is susceptible, and nine tenths of human ills would be abridged."

The reformers' near-utopian faith in the healing power of

government schooling masked a nasty streak of bigotry. Many of the education leaders were panicked by the specter of hordes of poor, ill-mannered Catholic immigrants pouring into the country. They regarded Catholic schooling as an abomination—not least because of their fear that the children would grow up with divided loyalties between America and the hated papacy. To prevent this, the reformers proposed steering all Catholic children into the new public school system where they would be cleaned up and "Americanized." At the very least they were determined that public funds never go to any remaining Catholic schools.

The reformers actually welcomed the teaching of religion in the schools, but only the Protestant brand. Thus, in the new "common schools" all children were required to read the King James (Protestant) Bible every morning, say prayers and sing hymns. The official school textbooks distributed to the children regularly derided the "superstitious" Catholic religion and warned about America becoming "the common sewer of Ireland."

The battle against Catholic participation in the emerging public school system was fought primarily in the legislatures, but also in the press and the streets. Riots broke out in New York City, Philadelphia and Boston over school funding controversies. Anti-Catholic mobs destroyed the residence of Bishop John Hughes, leader of New York City's Catholics.

In New York, the Protestant-led public school movement succeeded in its campaign to exclude Catholic schools, even though the popular governor, William Seward, stood with the Catholics in demanding equal treatment. To emphasize again, this was a *political*, not a judicial defeat for the principle of "school choice," or aid to religious schools. The courts actually had no constitutional problems with religious instruction in public schools per se. Thus, Massachusetts' highest court ruled that requiring children to read the Protestant Bible in public school every morning was no infringement of any child's religious liberty.

Despite their victories in the states, the public school reform movement felt that not enough had been done to guarantee that

Catholic education would remain marginalized. In 1875, President Ulysses S. Grant proposed a constitutional amendment prohibiting any public funding of religiously affiliated institutions, including schools. Congressman James G. Blaine of Maine, a prominent leader of the country's growing nativist movement and a Republican candidate to succeed Grant, sponsored the amendment in the House of Representatives. Blaine was the Pat Buchanan of his day—except that he hated Catholic immigrants more than others. What came to be known as the "Blaine amendment" fell short by four votes of achieving the necessary two-thirds margin in the U.S. Senate. Held together solely by their anti-Catholicism, the coalition (now also aided by the Know-Nothing Party and the Ku Klux Klan) took the campaign to the states. Eventually twenty-nine state legislatures, including New York's, added "Blaine amendments" to their state constitutions.

Clearly, there was widespread popular support during the latter half of the nineteenth century for keeping Catholicism out of the public square and for creating a wall separating religious schools from the government-operated school system. It was not until the middle of the next century, however, in the 1947 *Everson* case, that the U.S. Supreme Court weighed in on the issue.

The question before the Court was whether New Jersey's program of paying school transportation costs for all children, including those attending parochial schools, violated the U.S. Constitution. According to the Court, it did not. In the words of Justice Hugo Black, "New Jersey cannot hamper its citizens in the free exercise of their own religion. Consequently it cannot exclude Catholics, Lutherans, Mohammedans, Baptists, Jews, Methodists, Non-believers, Presbyterians, or other members of any other faith, or lack of it, from receiving benefits of public welfare legislation."

In other words, the "free exercise" clause of the First Amendment allowed New Jersey to pay school transportation costs for Catholic school kids, because this was a public benefit (the Court would later call it a "child benefit"). If government denied such funds to children attending Catholic schools, it would amount to religious discrimination and violate the Constitution.

The case could then have been disposed of without further commentary. However, the Court decided this was the historical moment to offer a definitive interpretation of the First Amendment's "establishment of religion" clause as well. Writing for the majority, Justice Black laid down this general rule:

> No tax in any amount, large or small, can be levied to support any religious activities or institutions, whatever they may be called, or whatever form they may adopt to teach or practice religion.... In the words of Jefferson, the clause against establishment of religion by law was intended to erect a wall of separation between church and state.

No matter that Thomas Jefferson was in Paris as American ambassador when the Bill of Rights was drafted and passed by the U.S. Congress. No matter that the "wall of separation" metaphor was in a heretofore-obscure letter written by Jefferson in 1803 to a group of Connecticut Baptists. Justice Black wrote the comment into Supreme Court precedent.

Historical ironies and unintended consequences surrounded the *Everson* decision. First, consider the judge who wrote the opinion. Black's appointment to the Court by President Roosevelt had almost been derailed by the revelation that as a young man in Alabama he had been a member of the Ku Klux Klan. Black atoned for his youthful indiscretion by becoming the most reflexively liberal member of the Supreme Court, a First Amendment "voluptuary" and defender of minority rights. Yet Black's opinion in *Everson* was a reminder of the nativist, anti-Catholic origins of the monopoly public school system. Furthermore, the "wall of separation" doctrine would in the future have less to do with religion than with the efforts of a new political coalition seeking to preserve the public school monopoly against all forms of outside competition. Teachers' unions, public education officials, civil liberties groups and Democratic politicians would soon cite Black's formulation to justify keeping poor minority children who might have been liberated by parochial schools locked up in failing public schools. These students were effectively denied a fundamental civil right—the right to equal educational opportunity.

This could not have been Justice Black's intention. At the time of the *Everson* decision he and the other justices reasonably assumed that the public schools would continue to fulfill their historic mission of educating poor and minority children and inculcating in them the nation's mainstream culture and shared civic ideals. In 1947 no one could have foreseen that a catastrophic decline of public education was about to hit the inner cities.

Even less could Black and the other justices have anticipated the extraordinary changes that were about to take place in Catholic education. After losing its battle to continue receiving a share of public education funds in the mid-nineteenth century, the Catholic school system retreated into a kind of cultural isolation. Its mission, first and foremost, became the defense of the faith against outside assault. The children enrolled in the schools were almost exclusively Catholic and the Catholic clergy performed virtually all the teaching.

Classes were hideously overcrowded and the curriculum and teaching methods were dogmatic. Not much changed in those schools for the next one hundred years. According to the best and most sympathetic account of contemporary Catholic education, *Catholic Schools and the Common Good* by Anthony Bryk, Valerie E. Lee and Peter B. Holland, "In the 1950s, Catholic schools might appropriately have been described as culturally isolated, doctrinaire, and racially segregated." Daily life in a typical Catholic school, the authors said, "perpetuated traditions and mores that had originated in medieval institutions."

The social turbulence that rippled through all of American society in the 1960s fundamentally changed the equation. The calamities visited upon the urban public schools by the decade's "liberationist" agenda have been well documented elsewhere. Less well know is the fact that in the 1960s and 1970s America's Catholic schools went through an entirely different, almost opposite kind of transformation. For Catholics the revolutionary 1960s also meant Vatican II and a renewed engagement with the modern world. As public schools were deteriorating in the cities, urban parish schools, inspired by Vatican II's universalism and its call for an end to racism and social injustice, opened their doors to the new poor. The traditional white, Irish and Italian parishioners might have left the inner city for the suburbs, but the Catholic schools stayed in the old neighborhoods and kept their doors open. Most of the new students were minority and many weren't even Catholic. For example, minority enrollment in New York State's Catholic schools shot up from 12 percent in 1970 to 36 percent in 1991. In New York City the figure is now almost 60 percent; in the boroughs of Manhattan and the Bronx, 85 percent. Catholic educators, now almost entirely laypeople, have renewed their commitment to an American ideal that even Horace Mann would have endorsed: that poor minority children can and should share in our civilization's intellectual and spiritual heritage.

Indeed, if Mann stepped out of a time machine into the twenty-first century, he would be astonished by what has happened to his beloved "common schools," as well as to the Catholic schools he once despised. He would find that in many urban public schools, classroom discipline, objective academic standards and a coherent curriculum have been discarded; in their place is a new edu-babble of "student-centered" learning, relativism, multiculturalism, diversity. Mann would be dismayed to see that, as the civil liberties lobby and other special interest groups pressed their narrow agendas, the public schools lost most of the authority they need to maintain order and deal with children from dysfunctional families.

Mann would be equally surprised by the Catholic schools, which no longer see their educational mission primarily as preserving the canons of the faith. Instead, they have been transforming the lives of millions of poor black and Hispanic children, whatever their religious convictions. Even more amazing to Mann would be the discovery that the Catholic schools, once suspected of "dual loyalties," are now among the last bastions in American education upholding the ideal of a common civic culture. In fact, the Catholic schools look far more like the "common schools" he dreamed about than today's public schools do.

Mann would also be astonished to learn that Catholic schools are doing a better job than the public schools at getting the children of the poor to meet minimum academic standards. The evidence for this remarkable turnabout began surfacing in the 1980s. A landmark 1982 study by education scholars James Coleman, Thomas Hoffer and Sally Kilgore, for instance, demonstrated that Catholic school students were one grade level ahead of their public school counterparts in mathematics, reading and vocabulary. A study by Andrew Greeley revealed that the differences between Catholic school and public school performance were greatest among students from the most disadvantaged backgrounds.

The early scholarship attributed Catholic schools' superior performance to their more rigorous academic curriculum and their greater degree of discipline. But researchers also credited the distinctive organization of Catholic schools. Free from the central bureaucratic controls then beginning to weigh heavily on public schools, the Catholic schools seemed more like autonomous communities—yet were accountable to their students' families. James Coleman observed that whereas the public school system had become an arena for the clash of political and economic interests, Catholic schools were infused with an atmosphere of trust and cooperation between teachers, administrators and parents, based on a shared moral vision.

During the next decade, a growing body of research confirmed these intimations of Catholic schools' benefits. In 1990 the RAND Corporation compared the performance of children from New York City's public and Catholic high schools with similar demographics. Only 25 percent of the public school students graduated at all, and only 16 percent took the Scholastic Aptitude Test. By contrast, over 95 percent of the Catholic school students graduated, and 75 percent took the SAT. Catholic school students scored an average of 815 on the SAT. By shameful contrast, the small "elite" of public school students who managed to graduate and took the SAT averaged only 642 for those in neighborhood schools and 715 for those in magnet schools.

A 1993 New York State Department of Education report compared New York City public and Catholic schools with the highest levels of minority enrollment. The conclusions were striking: "Catholic schools with 81 to 100 percent minority composition outscored New York City public schools with the same percentage of minority enrollment in Grade 3 reading (+17 percent), Grade 3 mathematics (+10 percent), Grade 5 writing (+6 percent), Grade 6 reading (+10 percent), and Grade 6 mathematics (+11 percent)." And the seminal study by Bryk, Lee and Holland, based on a national database of student performance, found that attending Catholic school reduced by almost half the adverse statistical impact of a student's minority background on academic achievement.

As these reputable research studies piled up one on top of another, it might have seemed that educators and elected officials would have stampeded to get to a microphone to spread the good news. Here were schools that were obviously doing something right, while public schools in the same neighborhoods were abject failures. Even more startling was the fact that the Catholic schools had half as much money to spend as the public schools. Surely something could be learned from the Catholic school experience that could benefit the kids relegated to the failed system.

But public education interest groups—more interested in perpetuating a monopoly position with millions of jobs than in acknowledging that there might be better, more effective ways of educating children—first tried to ignore the emerging story of Catholic school success, then tried to explain it away, and finally attacked it.

The most common argument used to undermine the record of Catholic school success was that a "self-selection" bias distorted the data. The charge was that while public schools were required by law to take every single child, Catholic schools had the advantage of being able to "cream" motivated children and reject those from the most troubled families who also happened to be the most difficult to educate.

Albert Shanker, who understood the data about Catholic school success as well as anyone in American public education, was a master of the "self-selection" argument. In November 1991 he was discussing the relevance of the data on Catholic school performance at a City University of New York education conference. With a dramatic flourish, he announced to the audience: "I challenge the Catholic schools to accept the lowest-scoring 5 percent of our public school students. Let's see how they do then." After a moment of silence, a soft-spoken, middle-aged lady stood up to respond. She introduced herself as Catherine Hickey, superintendent of schools of the Archdiocese of New York. "Mr Shanker," she said, "in the name of the Catholic schools, we accept your challenge."

Dr. Hickey represented the new face of Catholic education in this country. She was a homemaker who raised three children (she now has five grandchildren) and then went into teaching. She worked her way up the ranks in the Catholic schools from classroom teacher to administrator and took her doctorate in a university education program—much the same path followed by most public school administrators. In 1989 she became the first woman ever appointed to head the New York Archdiocese schools, the largest Catholic school system in the country, with 235 elementary schools, 54 high schools and 113,100 enrolled students. She still serves as superintendent. During her tenure, the city public school system, rife with political patronage and clashing special interests, has seen nine chancellors come and go.

Having been challenged in public to put up or shut up, Shanker's union and the New York City Board of Education had little choice but to engage in exploratory discussions with the archdiocese about the possibility of transferring some students to the Catholic schools and then monitoring their progress. The discussions continued for about eighteen months. Then the perennially revolving doors to the schools chancellor's office revolved again: the incumbent chancellor was out and the new chancellor let the project die.

Of course, public school officials always knew that Shanker's challenge to the Catholic schools was nothing but an empty rhetorical gesture. A publicly funded transfer of students from public schools to Catholic schools was impossible because of two legal obstacles. First there was New York's Blaine amendment, prohibiting public funding of religiously affiliated institutions. Second, Justice Black's "wall of separation" was now constitutional writ, a fortified barricade behind which the monopoly public school system remained sheltered throughout the 1990s.

The Catholic school system continued trying to engage the larger educational community. In his weekly column in the archdiocese newspaper, Cardinal John O'Connor repeated his willingness to take in the lowest-performing 5 percent of students from the public schools. The cardinal even sweetened the offer, inviting city officials to come and study the Catholic school system, "to make available to public schools whatever of worth in our Catholic schools is constitutionally usable. The doors are open. Our books are open. Our hearts are open. No charge."

There was virtually no media coverage of Shanker's challenge or O'Connor's response. The only official who even noted the cardinal's offer was Mayor Rudy Giuliani. In 1995 the mayor publicly extolled the Catholic schools for their success in educating minority children and suggested that they could teach something to the public schools. The *New York Times* responded to the mayor's comments by carrying extensive quotations from public school teachers and principals angry at the comparison between public and Catholic schools. The *Times* also editorialized that "the two systems are simply not comparable," repeating the old canard about "self-selection." But the paper didn't publish a word about the large body of scholarly literature supporting Catholic schools' success.

In a more rational world, one without metaphorical walls of separation, education officials would have jumped at the cardinal's offer. First of all, it might have been a huge financial plus for the city's school system. The annual per-pupil cost of Catholic elementary schools at the time was $2,500 per year, about one-third of what taxpayers were spending for the city's public schools. Assuming that the Catholic schools really could absorb 50,000 public school students (roughly 5 percent of the one million enrolled) and educate them for that amount, the city might pocket the difference—between $2,500 and $6,000 per student, adding up to over a quarter-billion dollars a year. The money could then have been put to good use in improving education for the vast number of students remaining in the public schools.

But the city would have enjoyed an even greater benefit in that thousands more of its disadvantaged children would have finished school and become productive citizens. The experience of a wealthy New Yorker named Charles Benenson illustrated the point. As part of financier Eugene Lang's "I Have a Dream" program, which paid college tuition for minority children who finished high school, Benenson adopted several classes at P.S. 44 in the South Bronx. Disappointed by how few students even made it through high school, Benenson decided to offer to pay the tuition of any of the eighth graders who wished to attend a Catholic high school. The results for his first adoptive graduating class: of the 38 students who stayed in public high schools, only 2 made it to college; of the 22 who attended Catholic high schools, only 2 failed to go to college.

"They were the same kids from the same kinds of families and the same housing projects," said Benenson, a non-Catholic. "In fact, sometimes one child went to public school and a sibling went to Catholic school. We even gave money to the public school kids for tutoring and after-school programs. It's just a fact that the Catholic schools worked, and the public schools didn't."

John Chubb, co-author along with Terry Moe of *Politics, Markets and America's Schools,* wrote an op-ed piece for the *New York Times* that partially explained why "the public schools didn't work." He described how he had attempted to get some accurate data on the number of people working in the central bureaucracies of the New York City public school system versus the archdiocese school system. When he contacted the press office of the Board of Education and asked how many people worked at central headquarters at 110 Livingston Street, he was told that it would take days to get the information. Chubb never did get an accurate headcount, although it was widely suspected at the time that the number was somewhere between 6,000 and 7,000. (Years later Mayor Giuliani decided to force out schools chancellor Ramon Cortines after Cortines still couldn't tell him how many people worked at 110 Livingston Street.)

Chubb then made his call to the offices of the archdiocese

schools. He immediately reached an aide to Dr. Hickey. When Chubb asked how many people worked in central administration, the aide said that if he stayed on the line he would have an answer shortly. As he waited, Chubb could hear someone counting heads—"one, two, three, four." The aide then got back on the phone and told him that a total of twelve people worked at central headquarters.

Chubb's article appeared after my older son, Jonathan, had spent his first few years at P.S. 87. I took it as confirmation that the absurd bureaucratic practices I had observed at the school were not merely the product of ordinary human shortcomings to be found at any institution. Instead, it was becoming clear to me that they were the results of a system that had compromised its primary educational mission and all too often served as a jobs agency for adults.

I also became more curious about the school system that was doing so well with twelve people working in central administration despite spending less than half the sum allocated to the public schools. I decided to start by exploring Catholic schools in Community School District 3, where my own children studied.

The Upper West Side was, of course, one of the most liberal communities in the country. Many white, middle-class parents not only sent their children to public schools like P.S. 87, but through their activism assured that the elected school board remained in the hands of like-minded "progressives." Nothing the activists did, however, could change the grim reality of the low performance of almost every minority school in the district. Yet no one was thinking about the network of Catholic schools in the district that somehow managed to do a better job with the same minority children. Complacent behind the Berlin Wall of separation, the progressive parents just *knew* that Catholic schools were still run by a rigid, regressive church hierarchy and had no relevance to our situation.

The first Catholic school I visited was Saint Gregory the Great, an elementary school on West 90th Street. For years I had passed by the drab-looking parish building while walking my kids to P.S. 87. I would notice the well-behaved black and Hispanic children in their neat uniforms entering one side of the building. Yet my curiosity never led me past the imposing crucifix looking down from the roof, which evoked childhood images of Catholic anti-Semitism and clerical obscurantism. Finally I made an appointment with the principal.

I learned that not one of Saint Gregory's 280 students was white, almost all were poor, and some came to school from Harlem and Washington Heights. If Saint Gregory's didn't exist, these children would likely have been attending one of the public schools in the district which are annually cited by state evaluators for performing below the minimum academic standard. In some of those schools less than one-third of the third and fourth graders scored above the state's minimum standard in reading. By contrast, over 60 percent of Saint Gregory's third graders were reading above the minimum standard, and 92 percent were above the standard in math. In fact, I learned from the state records that Saint Gregory's students held their own even in comparison with some of District 3's predominantly white, middle-class schools.

After a few days at Saint Gregory's, I realized that it was constituted much like a charter school, one of the most touted of the public school reforms. Public charter schools, now legal in over thirty states, receive varying degrees of relief from constricting regulations and teacher contract rules. The group holding the charter—it may be a consortium of parents or a university or a nonprofit organization—is accountable for the school's performance: if a school fails, it can be closed. In theory, such freedom will lead to better performance.

That's almost exactly what was already happening in many urban Catholic schools. At one point Saint Gregory's had been in dire financial straits, with enrollment down to 209 from a high of over 300 a decade earlier. The archdiocese was getting ready to close it down. In a last-ditch effort to save the school, the parish hired a determined African American woman named Deborah Hurd as the new principal.

Hurd was one of the new generation of lay educators that was rapidly replacing the priests and nuns who used to staff Catholic schools. Herself a Catholic school graduate, Hurd originally had no intention of pursuing a teaching career. She took her first job as a substitute teacher in a Catholic school to help put herself through business college. But one day she got a desperate call from a nun at Saint Joseph's School in Harlem. "I didn't want to teach," Hurd told me, "but she kept asking me to 'just take this class.'" Hurd took the job because she believed in the moral discipline and academic structure that Catholic schools provide.

Hurd's own seven-year-old daughter served as a yardstick. "I had her in a progressive kindergarten run by the Quakers, but she was floundering. So I moved her to Saint Gregory's. Now she's learning how to study and concentrate. What we do in first grade is set the tone. The children learn to sit in a chair, to put their coats away, to raise their hand when they want to be called on, to understand when an assignment begins and ends. These things, and the uniforms they wear: they are all signs—and our kids are decoding them. So right from the start they are learning structure and skills."

When Hurd became principal of Saint Gregory's, the parish gave her five years to turn the school around. She did it in less then three. Taking charge right away, she did some fundraising and found a few patrons who helped her add new programs, including preschool and kindergarten classes. To build enrollment, she advertised in local newspapers.

During her first summer, Hurd had the school painted and the restrooms renovated. She cut the auditorium in half to make space for more classrooms. Unlike a public school principal, she didn't have to wait years for a central building maintenance office to approve her renovation requests. "I just went out and found a contractor and a plumber who gave me a good price," she told me. "There's no magic to it. It can all be done if you have half a brain and you don't have a bureaucracy breathing down your neck."

The school still had to pass the test of the market: it could survive only by meeting the needs of its students, whose parents paid up to $1,700 in tuition. (The rest of the school's $2,500-per-pupil budget came from the archdiocese, private donors and government grants for books, transportation and school lunches.) Catholic schools are "called into being by the community," according to Hurd's colleague Pat Kelley, principal of Saint Angela Morrici School in the South Bronx. "The community comes. The community pays. And the school goes. If the people didn't want to come, it would be closed." In return for the $100-per-pupil subsidy that Saint Gregory's received from the archdiocese scholarship fund, the only requirements were that all students study religion for one period a day (non-Catholics aren't required to accept the sacraments) and that the school follow a standard curriculum, which parallels the state's.

In public schools, teachers almost automatically get tenure—a lifetime job guarantee—after three years. Most Catholic schools around the country have no tenure system whatsoever, though in New York City, where the teachers are represented by a union, many do get tenure after three years of successful teaching. But it is the principal who grants tenure, not some distant bureaucrat being prodded by a union shop steward. And unlike the public schools, tenured teachers have no claim on job openings in other schools. The labor contract imposes few work rules that tie a principal's hands in the area of teacher hiring and assignments. Even tenured teachers can be fired for incompetence or nonperformance far more easily than in the public schools. And there is no rigid credentialing system: principals can select teachers for their talent and commitment.

Consider how Deborah Hurd hired Susan Viti, Saint Gregory's fourth-grade teacher when I visited. Viti had been a public school teacher near Chicago when her fiancé was transferred to New York. The young couple found an apartment a few blocks from Saint Gregory's. While trying to decide what she wanted to do in New York, Viti befriended some of Saint Gregory's students, who played in a small playground next to the school. One day, on a whim, she walked in off the street in her tennis clothes to meet the principal. Hurd was impressed, and when a position opened up just before the first day of school, she offered it to Viti.

Only nominally Catholic, Viti took the job because she believed she could make a difference in the lives of some of the children she had met. She could not have been hired in a public school at the time because she lacked a New York State teaching credential. But at Saint Gregory's, Viti was in front of the classroom a few days after being offered the job.

When I visited Viti's fourth-grade classroom it was nicely decorated with students' artwork and writing samples. On one of the walls there was a poster:

CLASSROOM RULES
1. Follow directions.
2. Be prepared for class.
3. Respect others and their property.
4. Be a good citizen.

CONSEQUENCES
1. Name written down.
2. No recess.
3. Discuss with parent.
4. A meeting with principal.

Viti's students, all black and Hispanic, reflected an admirable tone of civility and seriousness. The boys were dressed in gray slacks, light blue shirts and ties; the girls all wore the same plaid jumpers and blue shirts. They sat in matched pairs of desks, their books and notebooks stacked neatly under their chairs. It was a far cry from the worst public schools—exhibitions of pandemonium with principals unable to expel disruptive students. In many ways it reminded me of P.S. 6 on Vyse Avenue of my own youth. Catholic schools, after all, never went through the rights revolution of the 1960s, which eroded the order-keeping authority of schools and discouraged teachers and principals from disciplining violence-prone students.

Whenever Ms. Viti asked a question, hands shot up enthusiastically. When she returned graded assignments, each child would say, "Thank you, Miss Viti." "You're welcome, darling," she answered cheerfully. I sat in as Viti conducted a review lesson on the geography of the western United States. All the children were completely engaged and had obviously done their homework. They were able to answer each of her questions about the principal cities and capitals of the western states—some of which I couldn't name—and the topography and natural resources of the region.

"Why do the Rocky Mountains have lower temperatures?" Ms. Viti asked. One of the children explained the relationship between altitude and temperatures.

"Which minerals would be found in the Rocky Mountains?" Hands shot up. Viti called on several children, each of whom contributed an answer. She used the lesson to expand the students' vocabulary and understanding of concepts such as the differences between crops and minerals. When the children wrote things down, she insisted on proper grammar and spelling.

Without pausing for a break, Viti moved on to the day's math lesson. She had the children go to the blackboard in teams to do multiplication problems with fractions and decimals. She praised those who solved the problems and gently corrected mistakes.

I was amazed at the children's ability to endure more than two hours of learning without losing their concentration. The students at Saint Gregory's, as at most Catholic schools, had very few breaks. Saint Gregory's was not able to afford art and music classes and scheduled only one gym period per week. Thus, from first grade on, children were expected to sit quietly and learn for most of the day.

Viti, too, enjoyed few breaks. On some days, other than a lunch period, she was on her feet in front of her class for almost six hours. Because she assigned considerable homework, she also did a lot of grading at home. She was constantly on the phone or writing notes to parents. Four days a week she stayed after school to do remedial work with some of her struggling students; twice a week she gave up her lunch hour to do extra work with her more advanced math students. On weekends she sometimes dropped in on students' Little League games.

She was earning a few thousand dollars less than a first-year teacher in a public school. "I've taught in an all-white, affluent suburban school, where I made over $40,000," she told me. "This time I wanted to do something good for society, and I am lucky enough to be able to afford to do it. I am trying to instill in my students the idea that whatever their life situation is now, they can succeed if they work hard and study. I involve the parents, and they know that I am serious about holding their children to a high standard."

Saint Angela Morrici's principal, Pat Kelley, echoed this sentiment: "Those of us who are doing the work do it not only for a paycheck. We're doing it because we get to practice a profession that we love."

Of course, not all Catholic school teachers were as impressive as Susan Viti. I visited some classes where the teachers overemphasized rote learning and focused too narrowly on the textbook. But in every classroom I visited, the teachers were deeply, personally engaged with their students. They were on top of them constantly, refusing to let them fall behind. It was inconceivable that I would see what I witnessed in the several junior high schools in our district, where children were literally asleep in the classroom. I was reminded of an epigram of Bryk, Lee and Holland: Catholic schools take the position that "no one who works hard will fail," whereas the prevailing approach in too many public schools is that "no one who shows up will fail."

★

My next stop was Holy Name of Jesus Elementary School on Amsterdam Avenue, six blocks north of Saint Gregory's. It began serving the neighborhood's Irish and Italian immigrants a century ago. When I visited the school, I learned that 99.5 percent of its six hundred students were black or Hispanic, 40 percent were from single-parent families, and 98 percent were poor enough to qualify for the federally funded free school lunch program.

Holy Name's principal was Brother Richard Griecko of the De La Salle Christian Brothers, one of the Catholic Church's teaching orders. Griecko created a technological wonderland that would have been the envy of the city's best high schools—on a budget of less than $1.5 million per year, or just $2,500 per student. The school had two computer labs, each with thirty state-of-the-art computers. Every classroom was also equipped with two computers, one for the students and one on the teacher's desk. A satellite dish on the roof received interactive programming; the seventh-grade English class was able to turn on the television and receive a live lesson from a poet in Boston.

Some public schools have modern computer labs where the students play games while their teacher gets a period off. At Holy

Name, by contrast, the computers were an integral part of the curriculum. Students used them to write journals and reports, work with special educational programs, and learn computer languages. When I visited the school, I saw first graders in the lab working intently on an IBM phonetics program called "Writing to Read."

While some students came from homes where no English was spoken, there was no bilingual program. "We believe it's important as quickly as possible to have the children reading and speaking English," Brother Griecko told me. "Sometimes we take children from public school. The parents put them here because they want them to finally learn English."

Sitting in an office cluttered with videotapes and papers, jazz playing softly in the background, Griecko explained how he managed to acquire the elaborate technology on a shoestring budget. "Its pretty simple: I have the freedom to control the budget and how our money is spent. I can see areas where we underspend, and I can transfer funds to another project—such as the computers." He also applied for private grants. Griecko estimated that the technology cost about $250,000 over eight years; he was able to squirrel away $30,000 out of his budget each year for his dream project.

Like Deborah Hurd, Griecko was grateful for his freedom from bureaucratic regulation in the selection of staff. "Some of my best teachers don't have an education degree, but they happen to be born teachers," he said. "Then you have teachers with all the credentials, but they can't manage a group of kids. Our curriculum is not that difficult to pick up. What can't be learned is self-assurance and classroom management."

One of those noncredentialed teachers that Brother Griecko hired was Frances O'Shea, a striking young blonde woman born and raised in Limerick, Ireland, who arrived in America with a science degree from Dublin's University College. In O'Shea's seventh-grade life science class, I observed the same combination of academic rigor and personal engagement I had seen in Susan Viti's classes at Saint Gregory's. Addressing the students in her rich brogue, O'Shea held forth on topics ranging from white and red blood cells to bacteria and infectious diseases. Her sense of humor livened up the proceedings: when a student got an answer completely wrong, she gently said, "Well, Steven, you are way out in the Wild West."

A slightly built black boy named Jonathan read a report he had researched on cystic fibrosis. O'Shea frequently asked him to pause while she made sure the students understood such concepts as the difference between malignant and benign tumors. At one point the coed class had a mature and unembarrassed discussion of the female reproductive system.

O'Shea told me that even if she had the required credentials, she would not have considered teaching in a public school. "I just can't accept the lack of discipline. I am a believer in structure and self-control. The idea of a fourteen-year-old wielding weapons—I just can't adapt to something like that. We have the same children. They are very poor and their parents are scrimping. But we think they will overcome their bad surroundings. In the public schools little is expected of the children, and they sense that."

It became clear to me that the success of schools like Holy Name and Saint Gregory's, despite their penury, was no miracle; it was more a matter of simple common sense. The strong discipline in Catholic schools does not rest on an authoritarian ideology, but rather reflects an age-old, well-tested understanding of human nature. "The discipline in our school comes down to one word: respect," Brother Griecko reminded me. "It is respect by students for teachers and teachers for students. We expect the students to listen and be respectful in class, and if they can't do it we will call in the parents. And it really works."

The other salient aspect of Catholic schools is that teaching there is quite literally a religious calling. "We are here to educate and empower these kids, to do two things with them," said Pat Kelley, the principal of Saint Angela Morrici. "One is to make sure that they learn how to read, write, and do math—every day. The other is to form their character. We believe in the divinity of being; we believe in the holiness of our existence. That infuses the culture we're in."

In the Catholic schools I visited, there was a greater sense of community, of collaboration between teachers and parents, than in any public school I knew of. Yet Saint Gregory's and Holy Name had no official school council or even a parents' association. What they did have was a foundational credo that no interests mattered but the children's. To put it another way, the idea that the interests of other school "stakeholders" such as teachers or administrators can supersede those of children— plainly immoral when stated so bluntly—had no force in these schools.

The Catholic schools also worked because they focused on the basic human encounter that is at the heart of all good education. Pat Kelley put it best: "Parents walk into my office once a week, twice a week, and I know they pay my salary. They say, 'I want to know why Junior failed this test. I want to know why Junior has detention.' So I spend a lot of time dealing with families, who are the backbone of the school. The school exists for their kids. There's no other reason this school exists. None."

★

The article I wrote on my observation of the Catholic schools was first published in *City Journal* and then excerpted in the *Wall Street Journal*. It produced a greater response than any other piece of journalism I had done since the late 1960s, when I exposed the CIA's penetration of American and international student organizations during the Cold War in *Ramparts* magazine. The article on Catholic schools didn't expose anything or break any new ground—or so I thought. Yet ordinary people calling in to the numerous talk shows to which I was invited thanked me for telling an important story that wasn't getting the attention it deserved.

Among the many letters I received was one from the late Cardinal John O'Connor. He too thanked me for telling a story "that I have been trying to get across since I arrived in New York as Archbishop." The cardinal invited me to have breakfast with him and I gladly accepted. When we met a few weeks later at his official residence, he told me a few things I wished I had known when writing the article. He said that raising money for the always financially strapped schools was one of the most difficult challenges for the archdiocese and it consumed an inordinate amount of his own time and energy. It would have been an easy way out to drop some of the more marginal schools, which had the fewest Catholic children. But O'Connor said he considered it a personal mission to preserve as many of the city's Catholic schools as possible, particularly those in the most distressed neighborhoods. He pointed out an astonishing fact that I wasn't even aware of when I wrote the article: There was not a single public high school left in Central Harlem. However, the archdiocese continued to maintain Harlem's famous Rice High School with its predominantly non-Catholic student body.

Mayor Giuliani cited my article several times in trying to get a pilot voucher program that would liberate several thousand kids from failing public schools and allow them to attend Catholic schools. This was essentially the same idea that had been discussed with Al Shanker and the archdiocese seven years earlier. But Giuliani could not convince schools chancellor Rudy Crew or a majority of the members of the Board of Education or the *New York Times* editorial board that things were bad enough in the city schools that this was something worth trying. Even Giuliani's own corporation counsel warned that the voucher program would not pass legal muster because of the Supreme Court's *Everson* decision and New York State's Blaine amendment.

But Giuliani wouldn't give up; he was convinced by the evidence that Catholic schools could help the underprivileged children of the city. Stymied on the government side, he threw his support behind a private voucher program initiated in 1997 by a group of New York philanthropists, some of them affiliated with the Manhattan Institute, which publishes *City Journal*. Called School Choice Scholarships, the program offered 1,200 poor public school children vouchers worth $1,400 to be used for tuition at any private or religious school that would accept them. The children were picked by lottery from a very long list of applicants who met the family income criteria.

The private voucher program was designed to produce a randomized sample of children who transferred to Catholic and other religious schools and whose academic progress could then be evaluated against a statistically identical sample of children who remained behind in the public schools. But the scholarship program produced one immediate and incontrovertible piece of evidence that many of the city's poor and minority parents already believed that Catholic schools could give their children a better chance of success. In the two months from when the scholarship program was announced to the deadline for applications, over twenty thousand public school families responded. Since the scholarships were available only to children in grades one to three and there were stringent family income limits, it was clear that a significant percentage of the target population were ready to transfer their children out of the $7,500-per-pupil public schools and into a Catholic school that had only one-third of that to spend. Moreover, these parents were so desperate for change that they were even willing to scrape together an extra few hundred dollars to pay the difference between the voucher amount and the tuition actually charged at the Catholic school.

To anyone who was paying attention, this should have been a clear warning that the public school system's poor and minority parents were ready to vote with their feet. All they needed was a chance to go to the ballot box.

But once again the response was denial. The School Choice Scholarships program was derided by public school officials and the teachers' unions as a "diversion" from the main task at hand—which, as usual, was to find more tax money for the public schools. The UFT newspaper noted that the money for the scholarships came from "right wing" philanthropists. Schools chancellor Rudy Crew waved off questions about the plan. "I came here to defend the public school system," he said at a public forum. Likewise, the *New York Times,* ever hostile to school choice, editorialized that the supporters of the private scholarship program could do more good by helping to improve the public schools.

To me this indicated how twisted the education debate had become. Liberals and leftists—otherwise self-styled champions of disadvantaged children—should have been singing the praises of educators like Deborah Hurd, Richard Griecko, Susan Viti, Frances O'Shea and Pat Kelley. People who believed that America was not doing right by its most vulnerable children should have been looking for ways to help the financially struggling schools where these people worked to fulfill their mission. Instead, these *bien pensant* advocates of the disadvantaged and oppressed were doing their best to make sure that Catholic schools remained just as marginalized as they had been throughout the nineteenth century.

Liberal child advocates have touted an endless array of "prevention programs" that are supposed to inoculate inner-city children against delinquency, dropping out of school and teen pregnancy—yet they have deliberately ignored Catholic schools, which have a superior record of preventing these pathologies. Why were Catholic schools taboo among those who claimed to speak for the downtrodden? Certainly, liberal groups found the Catholic religious tradition anathema on issues like abortion, feminism and gay rights. And many liberal commentators in the 1980s and 1990s sincerely believed that the Constitution required maintaining a wall of separation between religious schools and government. Yet these explanations seem inadequate to explain the total silence, the refusal to admit that something worthwhile was going on behind the parochial school gates that would help all poor children escape the pathologies of inner-city neighborhoods.

Whatever the reason for this liberal denial, it lost one of its major props on June 26, 2002, the day the Supreme Court announced that it had voted 5-4 to uphold the constitutionality of a Cleveland choice program giving a few thousand parents vouchers that could be used at religious schools or other private schools. Liberals and public school interest groups will continue to fight tooth and nail to ensure that minority kids are relegated to schools that do not educate them. But they can no longer say the Constitution made them do it.

8	

The Schools That Vouchers Built

The modern school choice movement was born in the late 1980s in the streets and churches of Milwaukee's black neighborhoods. It was nurtured through community protest that called attention to the glaring lack of equal educational opportunities for poor black and Latino children in the city's public schools. Despite decades of court-enforced busing schemes and more and more money spent on the public school system, the Milwaukee schools were performing terribly. The dreary statistics would have been familiar to observers of inner-city school systems anywhere in the country: Overall dropout rates were above 50 percent and much higher for black children; 70 percent of black children couldn't read at grade level.

Polly Williams, a single mother of four and a former welfare recipient, became the Rosa Parks of the school reform movement. Like Parks, she resorted to civil disobedience when school authorities told her that her daughter would have to be bused to a school all the way across town. To Williams this meant exchanging a failing neighborhood school for one many miles away that was failing just as badly. When her request for her daughter to be transferred to a school near her home was refused, Polly Willams walked into the superintendent's office and placed a note on his desk. It said: "My daughter will stay home before I let her be bused. You may send the police to arrest me." Very soon the transfer request was approved.

Soon afterward, Williams entered politics and became a Democratic state legislator and the Wisconsin chairperson of Jesse Jackson's 1988 presidential campaign. A fierce cultural nationalist, she first proposed that the black community be allowed to create its own separate school district. Her argument was that nothing could possibly be worse for black children than the education status quo. When the separatist option failed to gain traction, Williams introduced a bill in the Wisconsin legislature to allow a few thousand poor children escape the dismal public schools with tax-funded tuition vouchers that could be used at private secular schools. The legislation was passed with the support of Republican governor Tommy Thompson and many Republican legislators. Hard opposition came from the teachers' union, state education officials and some Democratic politicians. The first thousand recipients of the tax-funded vouchers left the Milwaukee Public Schools and enrolled in private secular schools in 1991. In 1998 the program was expanded to include religious schools.

This was the first major breach in the century-old wall of separation between public and religious schools in America. The irony was that it occurred not in a reactionary, antilabor town, but in the epicenter of modern progressivism. (Wisconsin had been the home of Senator La Follette, and Milwaukee was the last major American city to have an avowed socialist as mayor.) This city was a proud bastion of the public school ideal, where few people would even have questioned whether a government monopoly of education was a good thing for children.

Today, after the revolution sparked by Polly Williams, Milwaukee has a mixed system of public education. One suspects it is how American public education as a whole might have looked had there not been a widespread anti-Catholic panic during the second half of the nineteenth century. About 12,000 Milwaukee children receive government-funded vouchers which they use at over a hundred different Catholic schools, Protestant denominational schools or independent secular schools. Another 7,000 to 8,000 students attend autonomous charter schools that are accountable to the government agency that funds them, but are free of most bureaucratic regulations and union work rules. The voucher students get about $5,600 for tuition, the charter schools receive allocations of about $7,000 per pupil, and the Milwaukee Public Schools spends close to $10,000 per pupil.

When the first voucher program for Milwaukee was passed in 1990 by the state legislature, it seemed as if it might tear the city apart. The Milwaukee Teachers Association did everything possible to sabotage the program, beginning with a massive ad campaign in which the union charged that if the voucher program was allowed to continue, it would not only undermine public education but also erode the very foundation of democracy. The teachers' union ran its own slate of anti-voucher candidates for the school board. The city's major newspaper, the liberal *Milwaukee Journal Sentinel,* weighed in with very strong anti-voucher editorials. The national liberal lobbying groups, People for the American Way and the American Civil Liberties Union, camped out in Milwaukee, determined that the voucher menace be stopped here before it spread to the rest of the country.

There was even a nasty public battle between the academic experts studying whether the voucher program benefited the students who transferred from public to private schools. Officials at the state department of education, where there were few friends of the voucher program, appointed a University of Wisconsin political scientist named John Witte to analyze the limited data available to determine whether the academic performance of the students receiving vouchers surpassed that of the students who remained behind in public schools. Although Professor Witte concluded that the parents in the voucher program were very satisfied with the education their children were getting in their new schools, he claimed there was no hard evidence that the students were making significant academic gains as a result of receiving the vouchers.

Witte's conclusions were challenged by Paul Peterson, a Harvard University political scientist. Using the same data base, Peterson concluded that substantial academic improvement was shown by the voucher students after three years in their new schools. During the mid-1990s Witte and Peterson battled it out at academic conferences and in professional journals, charging each other with misinterpreting the data. Eventually another academic researcher, Celia Rouse of Princeton University, did yet a third study and concluded that the students receiving vouchers made some gains.

The battle over vouchers was political and it would not be settled, one way or another, by student performance studies. It took a decade-long protracted struggle for key municipal leaders and constituency groups to be convinced that giving dissatisfied public school parents a chance to send their children to a private school that worked was a good thing for the city of Milwaukee. Meanwhile, as they have done everywhere else in the country, the teachers' union and its allies worked hard to convince the public that every tax dollar spent for vouchers was a dollar snatched away from needy public schools. Those supporting even the most minimal school choice program were accused of abandoning the public school ideal and of being duped by a right-wing cabal intent on dismantling public education in America. A major target of this assault was the Bradley Foundation, headquartered in Milwaukee, which played an important role in keeping the voucher coalition together with money and strategic advice.

But the neoconservative Bradley Foundation was embedded in Milwaukee's social service community and widely respected for the generous grants it made to community development and education projects in the city's minority neighborhoods. Michael Joyce, Bradley's president throughout the 1990s, preached "compassionate conservatism" long before George W. Bush adopted the term. In the mid-1990s, after the courts issued a temporary injunction against the use of vouchers for religious schools in Milwaukee, the Bradley Foundation put up the money that allowed several thousand children to continue attending those Catholic and Protestant schools.

Michael Joyce once told me that one of the things that spurred him to become a backer of the voucher plan was his experience of driving through some of the city's desolate neighborhoods every morning on his way to work. "I would see these black kids, standing at bus stops in the middle of winter at 6:30 or 7:00 A.M. waiting for a bus to take them clear across town to a school in another neighborhood that the system had consigned them to. Their families had no choice in the matter. They looked demoralized and hopeless. In the meantime there were private schools with empty seats right there in the neighborhood where these kids might have succeeded, but their families couldn't afford the tuition. It made no sense."

Despite the importance of the Bradley Foundation's contributions, the school choice insurgency in Milwaukee was led by liberal African Americans. After Polly Williams moved on to other causes, Howard Fuller became the most persuasive and visible leader of the movement. Tall and athletic, Fuller had been a star basketball player in college before earning a Ph.D. and then turning to community organizing in the most crime-ridden and depressed black neighborhood in Milwaukee. His position on most social and economic issues would have located him politically within the Democratic Party's left wing. Yet when it came to understanding why public schools in Milwaukee were failing black children, Fuller had no patience with the traditional explanation favored by the teachers' unions and most liberal Democrats—lack of money and resources. Instead, he put much of the blame squarely on the teachers' union, the entrenched city and state bureaucracies and the Democratic Party politicians who took the union's campaign contributions.

Fuller had learned his public school lessons from inside the system. For three years in the mid-1990s he was superintendent of the Milwaukee Public Schools. When he resigned in 1995 he said there was no chance of reform without the challenge of competition from the outside. Today Fuller is chairman of the Black Alliance for Educational Options, a new national organization working in black communities throughout the country to build grassroots support for voucher programs and to radically reform public schools.

Another major Milwaukee voucher leader was John Gardner, a self-styled "radical democrat" and former labor union organizer from New York. Gardner's lessons in the public schools (his three sons attended city schools) paralleled mine. They led him to run for the school board as an at-large representative. In 1995 he won that election with 52 percent of the citywide vote, and then, after declaring his support for the voucher program as a necessary spur to public school improvement, he was reelected in 1999 with 60 percent of the vote. Gardner recently wrote a monograph titled *How School Choice Helps the Milwaukee Public*

Schools. He insists that his favorable view of vouchers doesn't change the fact that he remains "a passionate partisan of American public education which, with all its faults and limits, richly deserves the place it has assumed in national civil religion as prerequisite fundament of democratic promise"—an arcane way of saying he is still in the school choice battle primarily to improve his beloved public schools.

Yet another key player in the Milwaukee voucher movement was the city's Democratic mayor throughout the 1990s, John Norquist. Looking back at his own involvement in the struggle, Norquist says, "Originally, I opposed school choice. While I was in the state senate, Polly Williams finally converted me, because I found myself mouthing arguments that I really couldn't believe, that I thought were ridiculous. Many of the arguments against school choice were based on fear. What has happened now is revolutionary. It's made a difference. The public schools are getting better. There are more Montessori schools, more language-specialty schools, more schools that people want. Schools with wacky ideas that parents wouldn't choose aren't being created, but rather public, private and parochial schools that parents want to choose."

The teachers' union might attack the Bradley Foundation, but it could hardly demonize good liberals like Howard Fuller, John Gardner and John Norquist as instruments of a right-wing assault on public education. Their crossover politics made it possible to have a rational public discussion of school choice in Milwaukee. One by one, major constituencies came around to the view that choice was good for the whole city. Among the early converts were the city's business groups. Tim Sheehy, president of the chamber of commerce, now sits in on strategy meetings on the choice program alongside Fuller, Gardner and Norquist. Eventually, the *Milwaukee Journal Sentinel* did a 180-degree turn and endorsed the voucher program. Even Professor John Witte acknowledged that the program was good for the city and should be continued. The public consensus for school choice is now as deep and wide in Milwaukee as it ever was for an exclusive public education system. Only the Milwaukee Teachers Association, People for the American Way and the American

Civil Liberties Union continue to pine for a return to the *ancien régime.*

★

The voucher schools I visited in Milwaukee had all taken children previously consigned to violent and dysfunctional schools and integrated them into an atmosphere of innovation and achievement. I can't imagine that any fair-minded person spending time in those schools could fail to be impressed by their orderly, energetic atmosphere and solid academic foundation. Yet the schools I saw couldn't have been more different from one another: they ran the gamut from an evangelical Christian academy to an independent Catholic high school to a secular elementary school with a Hispanic cultural theme.

The one thing these schools had in common was that, at their creation, their founders and many of their staff did not qualify as professional educators. They did not have degrees from the education monopoly's favored ed schools or credentials issued by government education boards, and they certainly did not belong to the teachers' unions of the monopoly system. Yet every one of these outsiders had all they needed to educate and inspire children: a sense of mission, a willingness to work long hours for little pay, and common sense about the discipline and the core knowledge that inner-city children need in order to succeed. Unconstrained by the official school system's suffocating bureaucratic regulations, they were able to develop an entrepreneurial, problem-solving approach that helped overcome hurdles likely to sink any rule-driven public school.

Believers in Christ Christian Academy, for instance, lights up a desolate, crime-ridden Milwaukee neighborhood. At this school, everyone arrives early and stays late. By 8 A.M., the children, staff and many parents have filled the basement auditorium with its plain folding chairs for an assembly that is part gospel-singing prayer meeting and part academic pep rally. Up on the stage, three parents form a makeshift orchestra of two pianos and a tambourine to accompany the singing. At the lectern, swaying to the hymns and exhorting the children to work hard in their classrooms, is the school's founder, a tall, attractive African American woman named Cheryl Brown. Invoking the scriptures, she reminds the children, all of them black and from the city's worst neighborhoods, that they were made in God's image. "No matter what anyone tells you and no matter what messages you hear from society, you can each achieve great things," she exhorts them. "But you have to work for it. Are you going to work hard in your classes today?" she demands. "Yes!" the children shout back in unison. "No excuses," she intones again and again.

Cheryl Brown's school is the hardest possible sell for the pro-voucher forces. Dire warnings about "witchcraft" schools, "Farrakhan" schools and "creationist" schools greedily waiting to get their hands on voucher money have been the bogeymen of teachers' union propaganda. Well, Believers in Christ is definitely a "creationist" school. The people running it believe in a literal interpretation of the Scriptures. Nor do they separate their faith from their role as educators. Bedecking the hallways and every classroom are posters that proclaim such inspirational messages as "I can do all things through Christ" and "God gave me a brain." Many teachers expound the biblical story of creation in the classroom. Cheryl Brown herself teaches biology, offering her students a perfectly mainstream scientific account of DNA and RNA, while also telling them: "God created everything; it all began with Him. Science can't contradict that. Science can explain how everything works physically in relation to everything else."

I watched Reginald Johnson, a young African American with a degree in physics from Xavier University, teach seventh graders a fairly sophisticated lesson on black holes. I asked Johnson, who is an evangelical Christian, whether he also teaches the children the biblical version of creation. "Sure," he said. "I don't see it as a conflict. It's going to make them stronger adults. When they get to college and all through life, they will have to reconcile their faith with science."

"We absolutely believe in our faith," Cheryl Brown explains, "but we also believe that there is a body of knowledge that our children must know in order to survive in the real world." Brown is adamant that if the condition of receiving voucher students were that she had to separate Believers in Christ's religious teachings from the rest of the school's educational mission, she would instantly forgo the vouchers: "This is who we are," she said.

The teachers' unions believe that giving poor kids tax money to go to Cheryl Brown's school is a stain on the Republic and a subsidy for superstition. Never mind that her kids are learning something and might actually complete school. Never mind, too, that nothing in the school's curriculum has been forced on the parents against their will—unlike the graphic and inappropriate sex education lessons or texts such as *Heather Has Two Mommies* that public schools inflict on children. As Mayor John Norquist put it, "If a family in Milwaukee believes that their child should go to a Lutheran school that teaches creationism, that's okay with me because at least they'll learn how to spell 'creationism.'"

Cheryl Brown never recruited any unsuspecting families into her school under false colors. Rather, the school itself was called into existence by the community—by minority parents who felt that the public schools were trashing their most cherished values as well as mortgaging their children's futures. In 1990, Brown was a director of nursing at Milwaukee County Hospital and also a lay pastor for Believers in Christ, an independent evangelical congregation that began as a Bible study group a few years earlier. For two years she ran a six-week summer school for the children of the congregation and other poor families in the neighborhood. So successful was the summer program—and so dysfunctional were the regular public schools the children would have to return to in the fall—that many parents begged Brown to start a year-round school. So in 1992 she agreed to give it a try. Within a year she had resigned her job at the hospital and was embarked on her new career as an educator.

It was a rocky start. Space wasn't a problem, because the ministry had already leased an abandoned Catholic school from a nearby parish for a modest rent. But there was almost no money for books or teachers' salaries. Brown recruited parents as volunteer teachers, and she herself took no salary the first few years, subsisting on savings and offerings from the church. Most of the parents were too poor to pay more than $50 a month in tuition.

"We felt it was our mission, our personal responsibility," Brown says. "We just trusted that somehow our needs would be met." One of the parents explains further: "We stuck it out because we felt our children would escape the violence and lack of religious values" of the city's public schools. When this parent mentioned "religious values" she also meant, as I understood her, that the public schools had abandoned the most rudimentary values of all: the very idea of a shared civility and reverence for individual achievements that all parents, secular ones included, should be able to endorse.

Brown's faith was vindicated; the school's needs were met, although it was through political, not divine, intervention. In 1990, the Wisconsin state legislature passed the Milwaukee Parental Choice Program, the first publicly funded voucher program in the country. The lawmakers initially restricted the program to one thousand low-income Milwaukee public school students, who could use the vouchers only at nonreligious private schools—which didn't include Believers in Christ. This legislation, however, prompted an organization of philanthropists called Partners Advancing Values in Education (PAVE) to launch a parallel private voucher program that poor children could use in religious schools. This enabled Believers in Christ, for the first time, to get a number of customers paying something close to full tuition. Finally in 1996 the legislature expanded the program to include up to fifteen thousand students and allowed them to take their tuition vouchers to religious schools. At this point, hundreds of students at Believers in Christ began carrying public vouchers that are now worth $5,600. That allowed Cheryl Brown to begin to pay her teachers and herself real salaries and meet some of the school's other basic financial needs.

Even so, Brown still hires her staff not on the basis of state credentials or education courses taken, but on other vital qualifications. "We want people who are committed to children and to values," she explains. "We want staff here who view this school as a mission in life. I believe that if you are committed to children and love them, they will respond and learn anything."

All the classes I visited kept a sharp focus on a traditional, skills-based curriculum. The lack of state-certified teachers didn't seem to create any problems. The fifth-grade class was typical: the children were working over a map of the United States with no place names. They eagerly showed off their knowledge of the states and their principal cities. Each of the twenty-odd children was engaged, polite, enthusiastic and informed. Anyone who has been in an inner-city school in the past generation knows how exceptional, and precious, such a scene really is.

These children might be learning creationism along with basic science, but they are much more likely to become productive citizens than if they had remained in the public schools. Social science research has shown that children involved in faith-based institutions are less likely to drop out of school, to end up as teenage parents, or to get caught up in the criminal justice system. Most of the graduates of Believers in Christ go on to college. Considering the staggering 80 percent dropout rate among black males in the Milwaukee Public Schools, who can say that these parents made anything but an excellent choice for their children?

Just as Cheryl Brown was called into urban education by poor minority parents desperate to save their children, so too was Brother Bob Smith. When Smith, an African American, took his vows as a Capuchin friar nearly twenty years ago, the last thing he ever thought he'd be doing was running an inner-city high school. After graduating from Wayne State University in Detroit with a degree in criminal justice, he did his first service for his religious order as a youth worker and then taught social studies and economics in a Catholic high school. He arrived in Milwaukee in 1984, just when an inner-city Catholic archdiocesan high school named Messmer was going through a crisis. Its run-down neighborhood had been abandoned by the white ethnic former parishioners. That left Messmer with a predominantly black, largely non-Catholic student population, whose parents had difficulty paying the tuition.

With almost no warning to parents and staff, the Archdiocese of Milwaukee abruptly decided to stop making up Messmer's growing deficits. In the middle of the spring 1984 semester, the school closed. Determined not to send their children to public schools, many parents refused to take no for an answer. They organized a Save Messmer committee. After surveying the available talent, the parents' committee turned to Smith to lead the efforts to save the school and become its new principal. Then all of twenty-seven years old, he had offered Messmer his services as a teacher, but he had zero experience as a school administrator.

When I met him, Smith, an athletic forty-two-year-old who refereed men's Division 1 college basketball games in his down time, reminisced about his fourteen years of struggle to rebuild Messmer into one of the Milwaukee area's premier high schools. "For years, we just lived hand-to-mouth," he recalled. "The parents worked as volunteers in the business office, in the cafeteria, all around the school. Some of them even took out second mortgages to help cover the payroll. At one point we were half a million dollars in debt." With a trace of bitterness in his voice, he remarked that the Archdiocese of Milwaukee had not only refused to offer any help in getting Messmer on its feet again, but denied it the right to advertise itself as a Catholic school.

All around Smith's office were testimonials to Messmer's miraculous resurrection: plaques honoring students for outstanding academic performance, photographs of visiting notables such as William Bennett and George Will, and copies of laudatory newspaper articles about the school. But the acknowledgment that Smith cherishes most is the April 1998 decree by the Archdiocese of Milwaukee recognizing Messmer once again as a Catholic school. The signer of the decree was the same Archbishop Rembert G. Weakland who had ordered Messmer closed in 1984.

Smith rebuilt Messmer on a foundation of merit and accountability. His code applied to students as well as staff. He took no student solely because he or she could pay or came with a scholarship, and he turned away no student solely for lack of funds. Every student he accepted had to make a firm commitment to strive for academic excellence and to complete the school's very demanding curriculum, which requires many more courses in math, science and foreign languages than do most of Wisconsin's affluent suburban high schools. As for the teachers,

Smith recounted, "We looked for people we considered the best, the most knowledgeable, the most committed, whether they had state teaching credentials or not."

One of those teachers was Jeff Monday, a first-class educator hired without any graduate education-school training. "Jeff is the only person I ever hired on the spot," Smith said. "There were people with teaching credentials and more experience, but I have never met anyone with a greater sense of mission." Smith decided to groom the young math teacher to become Messmer's next principal, so that he could kick himself upstairs and focus on fundraising. In 1997, Monday took over as principal at the age of twenty-nine, and Smith became Messmer's president. Since then, Monday has been recognized as one of the most talented high school principals in the state and has turned down high-paying offers from other private schools.

Monday's starting salary as a math teacher was $13,000. As principal he still makes far less than the top salary paid to teachers in the Milwaukee Public Schools. He routinely puts in seventy-to-eighty-hour weeks. Monday's own Catholic education is part of the reason he is making the financial sacrifice. "What also inspired me about Messmer," he says, "is the sense of mission here, of working with poor students yet holding them accountable and helping them strive for excellence. We are not in the business of making excuses or allowing the kids to make excuses for themselves."

Visitors to Messmer can see evidence of the school's culture of decorum and seriousness throughout the ornate building. It shows up even in the cafeteria. Look at a typical inner-city public school cafeteria and you will see everything that's wrong with the system. The room is generally the noisiest place in the school building, filled with tension and chaos. To keep the students from erupting into violence, burly security guards and a platoon of teachers and aides are usually on patrol. Central school district employees serve the unappetizing meals mess-hall style. At Messmer, by contrast, a variety of outside vendors, including Pizza Hut, have set up several food stations. The students—from very tough, very violent neighborhoods—line up quietly and pick their favorite foods. Some Messmer students, working part-time for the vendors, are behind the counters serving food or manning the cash register. When I had lunch in the cafeteria there wasn't a single security guard or faculty member on duty, yet everything was quiet and orderly.

One of Messmer's secrets of success is its inculcation of a culture of civility, through sensible rules enforced fairly and consistently. For instance, no hats in school, no lying, immediate expulsion for violence. I sat at a cafeteria table with two seniors, Jennifer Vega and Shalonda Greer. They told me that the existence of those rules was the major difference they perceived between Messmer and the public schools that some of their friends attended. "They are very tough here," Jennifer said. "You can't break any rule without being punished. And you have to work hard to stay in the school. In the public schools, there's a lot of violence, and you don't have to work hard."

If there were no voucher program, some of Messmer's students would have had to attend a hellhole called North Division High School, about two miles away in the same school zone as Messmer. North Division was built twenty-two years ago with a capacity of 1,900 students. The 600 students currently enrolled are there only because they have no other option. It is sometimes referred to as the "Siberia" of the Milwaukee Public Schools, because no sane parents would willingly consign their children to this school, where gangs roam the halls and teachers don't teach. This disgrace to public education is known far outside Milwaukee because it was the subject of an exposé on NBC's *Exposed* news program a few years ago. A student at the school was able to get a hidden camera in and the resulting video showed kids running wild in the halls and teachers reading comic books in their classrooms. The MPS board of directors were so embarrassed that they voted to close the school down, move the teachers and students elsewhere and start again from scratch. However, the teachers' union sued in court to stop the closing, charging that it was a violation of the teachers' contract. The union won and they now have this totally segregated, demoralized and violent school, costing the taxpayers just under $10,000 per pupil, as a monument to the glories of the monopoly public education system.

Messmer's per-pupil cost is around $5,000. Yet no Messmer

student pays more than $3,000 and no student who keeps up his grades is ever turned away for inability to pay. The difference is made up by the state-supported vouchers valued at $5,600, plus dozens of scholarships donated by several Milwaukee foundations and businesses.

Clearly the taxpayers are getting their money's worth. With a student body that is 85 percent black and 10 percent Hispanic, with 60 percent of the children from single-parent families and a similar number below the poverty line, Messmer manages to get academic results more typical of middle-class, suburban high schools. Its graduation rate is over 95 percent, and almost all the graduates go on to college—the favorite destinations being Notre Dame, Marquette, the University of Wisconsin at Madison and a number of black colleges, including Howard and Spelman. Those who don't attend college go either into the military or straight into the workforce. "I have been here twelve years, and I have never had a kid on graduation day say, 'I don't know what I am going to do,'" says Smith.

Such is the popularity of Messmer that parents in the neighborhood came to Brother Bob and told him that they didn't want to wait until high school for their younger children to experience the "Messmer miracle." Two years ago a new K–8 school, also named Messmer, opened up about a mile from the high school. It wouldn't have been possible without vouchers.

Needless to say, Smith is an enthusiast for school choice, not only for helping his school achieve its goals, but also for what it is accomplishing for the pupils in the public schools. "The Milwaukee Public Schools started out hating vouchers," he says, "but it was a real wake-up call for them. They have created a lot of new schools in the last few years, and every one of them has a big banner over the front of the building that says, 'High standards begin here.' Even the district superintendent now says, 'We ought not to be fighting with the choice schools; we should be working with them.' I want to see the public schools learn the lesson that when they stop making excuses about having to work with poor, minority kids, they will improve."

★

While some Milwaukee parents have chosen to take their vouchers to religious schools such as Messmer or Believers in Christ Christian Academy, others have chosen to use them in secular private schools. On the city's near south side, a school called Bruce-Guadalupe benefited from the voucher program for many years before switching to charter school status, because it brought more money to the school. (Charter schools not only receive about $1,500 more per pupil than voucher schools, but all students are eligible, no matter what their financial status.) Once part of the Catholic archdiocese, Bruce-Guadalupe is now a secular school owned by the United Community Center.

The school was the brainchild of the center's executive director, Argentine-born Walter Sava, who had been a student activist at the University of Wisconsin at Madison in the sixties. After taking a Ph.D. in romance languages at Wisconsin and teaching at Carroll College, Sava took over the reins of the United Community Center fourteen years ago. In those days, the center had little more than a gymnasium, an after-school program for children and a drug prevention program for adults. Since then, Sava has been able to raise several million dollars (from the Bradley Foundation and a long list of major corporations) to build two new buildings and expand the range of the center's activities. By far his biggest innovation was bringing the Bruce-Guadalupe elementary school under the aegis of the United Community Center.

The school is housed in a building attached to the main community center. Strikingly beautiful, it has a Spanish architectural flavor, with a pyramidal front entrance that evokes Mayan culture, and traditional Mexican murals and mosaics decorating the corridors. The school and community center share many facilities, including the gym, a health clinic, dance studios and a large auditorium. The center houses a popular, handsomely decorated Hispanic restaurant, which also prepares the meals for the school's cafeteria. This joint usage of facilities not only makes for efficiency and enhances productivity, but also provides a sense of shared community values and civility. Parents and grandparents mingle with the students, since they often come to the center to attend English classes, visit the health clinic or eat at the restaurant.

What is immediately conspicuous about the school is that it is multicultural in the old-fashioned sense of the word. The second- and third-grade classes I visited were full of Hispanic children, many of them recent immigrants, with varying degrees of limited English-language proficiency. In public schools in Milwaukee (and indeed, in most parts of the country), many of these children would have been shunted into bilingual-ed classes. Here, though, teachers were drilling students in the English alphabet and sounding out words in English.

This approach largely reflects the educational philosophy of Walter Sava, who, of course, is not a "professional educator." "People think that because this is a school in the *barrio,* we are only interested in preserving our culture and our language," he told me. "Of course we are, but we are also eager to see to it that our kids become proficient in the English language. They are learning to read through phonics. The curriculum is knowledge-based, with clear benchmarks that the teachers can't deviate from very much. At the end of each grade, there are certain things the kids have to know and are tested on." In addition to the full traditional curriculum, the children get plenty of extra work in Hispanic history and literature.

Despite a per-pupil expenditure that is still less than that of the city's public schools, Bruce-Guadalupe is able to cap its classes at about twenty-five students and offer sports programs, a full arts program, and a health clinic with a full-time nurse. This cornucopia of resources results partly from the sharing of facilities with the community center and partly from the administrative and budgetary flexibility that Sava enjoys by not being burdened with either a centralized school bureaucracy or a teachers' union contract.

With a requirement that students wear uniforms and a strict disciplinary code, the school has the feel of an orderly Catholic school stressing character and values. The results in academic performance have been impressive. Around 80 percent of Bruce-Guadalupe's third graders usually score at or above grade level on the state's standardized tests—not only a better outcome than most public schools in Milwaukee, but close to what some of the wealthier suburban Wisconsin schools achieve. These results are all the more remarkable when you consider that 100 percent of Bruce-Guadalupe's students had to take the test, whereas public schools often exempt students with English-language deficiencies from taking it.

Although Sava pays his beginning teachers the same rates as the public school system, he regards the union culture as the kiss of death. Without the constraints of the Milwaukee teachers' union contract, for example, he can have his teachers come into the school for two weeks or more before the opening of the school year for staff training sessions. He is also able to offer a longer school day and to assure parents that if their children somehow wind up with an incompetent teacher, that teacher can be fired.

Sava has nothing against the public schools. Indeed, he persuaded a retired Milwaukee public school principal, Allan Nuhlicek, to be Bruce-Guadalupe's principal for its first two years. "Being a public school person," Nuhlicek told me, "I wasn't for vouchers for private schools when I came here. I didn't like to see money drained off from the public schools— until I saw what you can accomplish with half of the per-pupil costs of the public schools." Nuhlicek also told me that in twelve years as a public school principal, he had been able to hire only two teachers that he personally selected; all the rest were forced on him because of the union contract. "Now I'm for schools like this," he concluded, "to give the union some competition."

Everything in Walter Sava's political background—his student radicalism at the University of Wisconsin, his belief in socialism—should have inclined him to support the teachers' union agenda and the governmental monopoly over the public schools. But like Howard Fuller and John Gardner, Sava too had his public school lesson.

"When we started out fifteen years ago trying to improve the public schools in this community, we became more and more frustrated," he said to me. "We realized that trying to change the system from within simply did not work. It was like moving the deck chairs around on the *Titanic.* The bureaucracy and the system were too powerful to be affected by small community groups getting an occasional quote in the newspaper, or one protesting angry Latino or black school board member. I realized that choice is the only radical way to change the system. It meant the parents were choosing and they were listened to. Before, we spent endless hours trying to remove the nonperforming principal of the local public school. Now we created our own school and it's working for the community. That's the kind of power choice gave us."

Sava's venture into the school construction business also answers one of the most frequently raised objections to choice programs—namely, that there aren't enough seats in the small private school sector for the students who might want to leave the public schools if they could. In the early 1990s Sava and his colleagues built an extraordinary new elementary school with choice funds. Then, knowing that charter school funding and vouchers had been institutionalized in Milwaukee and that Bruce-Guadalupe could count on a steady funding stream, Sava was able to add a middle school building to the complex and expand by several hundred the number of children who could be served.

★

If school choice spreads outward from Milwaukee to more cities and states, the space issue will be critical. David Brennan—a colorful, cowboy-hat-wearing resident of Akron, Ohio—can advise on how to get new schools up and running in a hurry. A wealthy industrialist, Brennan discovered that many of the young workers in his manufacturing firms were functionally illiterate and innumerate. To help them, and to improve his workforce's productivity, Brennan created "learning centers" at his facilities. These company schools quickly and inexpensively boosted the employees' math and reading skills. Then he focused on the Akron public schools as the root cause of the problem. He soon concluded that without the pressure of competition from outside, the existing system would never be able to produce the educated workforce that employers like himself will need in the twenty-first-century economy.

As a prominent Republican fundraiser, Brennan began to work on persuading Ohio governor George Voinovich to support the legislation that resulted in Cleveland's voucher program for two thousand low-income students. The experimental program was challenged in the courts by the teachers' unions and other opponents of choice, and ultimately it became the case that resulted in the historic Supreme Court decision of 2002 in favor of the vouchers.

When the state officially announced the voucher program in April 1996, Brennan was on the spot to make sure that all the children who opted for the program actually had a school to attend. After all the spaces in the existing private schools were filled, three hundred or so students were left over. So Brennan enrolled them in two new secular schools that he promised to open virtually overnight. He called them the Hope Academies.

I visited one of those schools after its first year of operation. I saw that over three hundred poor, mostly minority children, whose parents fled in desperation from the public schools, had found in Hope an orderly, quiet place to learn without the need for security guards or metal detectors. Under incredibly tight time pressures Brennan had found reasonably competent teachers for each classroom. A few were defectors from public schools; some were substitute teachers who didn't have regular, full-time licenses; some were completely unlicensed recent college graduates who just wanted a chance to teach young children.

Nothing came easy for the rest of that first year. Unaccustomed to a demanding workload, none of the former regular public school teachers lasted until summer vacation. Even the most dedicated teachers found themselves challenged by the job of taking public-school children with poor work habits and inculcating them with a disciplined approach to academic work. "I was shocked to find that many of my third graders couldn't spell their names, couldn't add four plus three, couldn't even sit still," recalled teacher Wynne Udovich, a veteran of the school's first year.

Under these tough conditions, David Brennan was able to offer a real-life demonstration of his theory that open markets and freedom from bureaucratic constraints can work wonders in education. At the beginning and at the end of the first year, all the Hope Academy students in the third grade took standardized achievement tests in reading and math. According to an analysis by respected scholars from Harvard, Stanford and the University of Texas, the students scored, on average, 5.4 percentile points higher at the end of the year on the reading test and 15 percentile points higher on the math test. Noting, correctly, that "many of the poorest and most educationally disadvantaged [of the voucher] students went to the Hope schools," the three scholars concluded that these students nevertheless appeared to be "learning at a faster rate" than their counterparts in other public schools.

Another analysis by Indiana University professors found that the next group of third graders didn't show as much improvement. But while standardized test scores are one appropriate yardstick of the voucher schools' success, another, equally pertinent, is what parents value. For them, even more important than whether their children score a few points higher on a standardized test is the certainty that their kids are in a safe environment where they are being taught good study habits and appropriate moral lessons. The Hope Academies clearly met that test.

As in Milwaukee, the Cleveland program offers more money for charter schools than for vouchers, and eventually Brennan decided to close the Hope Academies and take advantage of the more generous funding stream in charter schools. Nevertheless, he remains one of the more optimistic and visionary voucher advocates in the country. Conducting a survey in his hometown of Akron, he discovered that the city has enough room in existing churches and community centers to create new schools for all the city's public school students if a voucher program should impel them to abandon the public schools en masse.

Brennan is certain that more school choice will bring more and more creative Americans into education. "I know that when choice becomes universal, there are a million people out there who are smarter than we are, who are going to solve all these problems of inner-city education," he says, with infectious enthusiasm. "There is nothing more impressive than American innovation. Let's give it a chance."

The voucher experience in Milwaukee and Cleveland seems to vindicate that optimism. Cheryl Brown, a black evangelical Christian; Brother Bob Smith, a black Capuchin friar; Walter Sava, a Hispanic community activist—here is a taste of what American diversity at its best can achieve. What these three exemplary Americans have accomplished is to rekindle some of those "thousand points of light" that one of our former presidents liked to talk about. In their schools, they have given thousands of disadvantaged children the best possible chance to grow up to be productive adults. They did this not by portraying the children as victims needing special privileges, but by holding them to a common standard of excellence and hard work.

But these three individuals are also accomplishing something even more significant. In their separate ways, they are disproving the widely accepted dogma that only government-certified education professionals know what and how to teach children. This notion has spawned a vast, interlocking industry of education schools, certification boards, teachers' unions and school board officials, and it has certainly boosted the material interests of those same certified professionals. But the dogma has done little for America's schoolchildren. These three educators, and hundreds of others like them, are showing us a different—and better—way. The public schools have much to learn from them.

9

The Imperative of School Choice

S tarting in the early 1990s, a new education reform movement rose up to tackle the unfulfilled agenda of the 1960s civil rights revolution. By proposing that poor inner-city parents be given the right to get their children out of dismal public schools, the movement stepped into the vacuum created by the mainstream civil rights organizations' abandonment of this territory. First by giving generously to private choice programs, then by creating publicly funded voucher programs in Milwaukee and Cleveland, the school choice movement has already rescued tens of thousands of minority children otherwise probably doomed to failure.

As the year 2002 opened, much more than philanthropy and activism was needed. To protect its gains, the school choice movement had to have the votes of five justices of the United States Supreme Court. On January 22 the Court heard oral arguments in the case of *Zelman v. Simmons-Harris*. The issue was whether the Ohio legislature violated the First Amendment's Establishment Clause when it created an experimental school choice program for the city of Cleveland. Up to two thousand poor children were receiving publicly funded vouchers worth $2,250 that paid tuition costs at religious schools or private secular schools. If the Court approved the five-year-old program, it would constitute the first breach in the legal "wall of separation" that for more than a century had shielded the nation's public education system from outside competition.

On the other hand, if the Court decided that the Cleveland program was unconstitutional, it would be a devastating setback for the school choice movement. The Cleveland children would be forced back into what Ohio attorney general Betty Montgomery called "one of the most dramatically failing school systems in the country"—where only one out of ten children passed the state's eighth-grade proficiency test and two out of three failed to graduate high school. Twelve thousand poor children in Milwaukee would have faced the same fate.

Two rather large men in their seventies sitting in the Supreme Court's front row VIP seats seemed to personify the clash of ideas and interests in the Cleveland voucher case. One was Senator Ted Kennedy. With the Democrats' loss of the White House, Kennedy became the public education industry's most important political asset. During the Clinton years he worked to block poor children from getting tax-funded vouchers that would have allowed them to leave the dismal public schools of Washington, D.C. Nina Rees, a high-ranking Bush administration education official, was once asked why the president had accomplished so little of his own school choice agenda. "The answer consists of two words," Rees replied. "Ted Kennedy."

Kennedy had never found a public school good enough for his own children. Why, then, was this erstwhile champion of civil rights supporting the teachers' union lawyers who were pleading with the Court to squash Cleveland's voucher program?

The conventional explanation is that Kennedy is a principled Jeffersonian on the issue of church and state, that he sincerely believes in the "wall of separation" doctrine that rules out any public money ending up in the coffers of religious schools. Perhaps. But it's also good politics. Most of the five million government employees who work in public education are organized into highly effective unions, which support candidates like Kennedy and policies he favors, such as national health insurance and affirmative action. With support from Kennedy and others, the unions have built a Berlin Wall that protects the public education system from competition and prevents poor children from leaving bad schools. It also prevents educators who were not trained, ideologically molded and licensed by the system from entering the teaching ranks. Which partly explains the hegemony of curricular progressivism and political liberalism in most public school classrooms. It also explains how the public education industry, with over $400 billion in annual expenditures, became one of the key political constituencies of the Democratic Party.

Sitting a few seats away from Senator Kennedy that day was David Brennan, the spirited businessman from Akron, Ohio, who almost single-handedly nurtured the Cleveland voucher program until it could get to the Supreme Court. Like others in the movement, Brennan became convinced that no matter how much money was budgeted, public education wasn't going to improve without the pressure of outside competition. If Kennedy represented the old civil rights movement that was now in league with the public school establishment, Brennan represented the new civil rights movement fighting to liberate black children from deadly schools like Milwaukee's North Division High School.

The opposing camps represented by Kennedy and Brennan each knew that the *Zelman* case involved more than a disinterested search by the justices for the true "meaning" of the Establishment Clause. At its heart, it was really about whether the government school system could be made to relinquish any control over the education of poor children to their parents. The school choice movement's lawyers went in counting on the conservative bloc of justices—William Rehnquist, Clarence Thomas, Antonin Scalia and Anthony Kennedy—who tended to believe that the words of the Establishment Clause, "Congress shall make no law respecting the establishment of religion," should be read literally, to mean simply that government was prohibited from "establishing" or favoring any religion as the nation's official creed but not required to banish religion utterly from the public square.

Senator Kennedy's anti-voucher side was just as confident that they were starting with the votes of Ruth Bader Ginsburg, David Souter and John Paul Stevens. In earlier church/state cases the three liberal justices were guided by Justice Hugo Black's creative appropriation, in the 1947 *Everson* case, of Jefferson's "wall of separation" interpretation of the Establishment Clause. Thus, it was nearly certain that the three liberal justices would oppose transferring tax funds to the coffers of religious schools under almost any circumstances.

This meant that the lawyers for the Cleveland voucher program had to persuade at least one of the two remaining justices, Sandra Day O'Connor or Stephen Breyer. "We knew we had to have O'Connor's vote," said former Whitewater prosecutor Kenneth Starr, who choreographed much of the school choice movement's legal strategy in the case. In pursuit of O'Connor, Starr asked Stephen Gilles, a constitutional law professor at the Quinnipiac University School of Law and, not coincidentally, a former law clerk for Judge O'Connor, to write an *amicus* brief. Gilles emphasized a point he hoped would sway O'Connor, namely, that the Cleveland voucher program was totally neutral on whether the eligible children selected a religious school, a private secular school or a public school in another district. "We tried to show that this was true private choice and that all schools were eligible for the vouchers," said Gilles. "But we also thought O'Connor would need something more. We had to prove there was no pressure on parents to choose religious schools."

In her concurring opinion eventually upholding the constitutionality of the Cleveland program, O'Connor highlighted the neutrality issue and the fact that the parents were making free choices. For the school choice movement, the 5-4 decision was a political, legal and moral victory all wrapped up in one.

On the morning after the *Zelman* decision, an amazing editorial supporting school choice appeared in the *Washington Post.* It highlighted the equity issue that leaders of the old civil rights movement still refuse to acknowledge. Said the *Post:*

> The failure of many public school systems around the country to offer any semblance of an education to millions of children is not a matter of serious dispute. Wealthy and middle-class people have an out: private schools or a move to a jurisdiction with better public schools. The poor often have no option.

But the *Washington Post* also understood that vouchers were not merely a matter of justice for poor minority children. Equally important, school choice had the potential to force public schools to do a better job for all children. The *Post* continued:

> In fact our quarrel with the Cleveland program would be that the vouchers are too small. Imagine how much competition might be generated, and with what respect poor parents might be treated, if they were given an $8,000 voucher for each child, and public schools really had to prove they were worth what society now spends on them.

The editorial could not have been improved on if Dave Brennan or the team of lawyers arguing the school choice issue before the Court had written it themselves. Appearing in one of the bastions of the liberal media establishment, it was a clear sign that after *Zelman* the foundations of the public education monopoly would be questioned as never before.

The teachers' unions and their allies immediately began their political counteroffensive. Robert Chanin, the principal litigator for the National Education Association (NEA) and the lead lawyer arguing against the Cleveland voucher program, had already made it clear that no matter how the case turned out in the Supreme Court, the union would fight on. He candidly (some would say arrogantly) acknowledged that for his clients this wasn't a question of constitutional right or wrong, or even of educational philosophy. His job was to protect the union's interests and he promised to continue to use every available legal stratagem to derail any measure that helped children transfer out of the public schools.

The teachers' unions have accumulated a huge political war chest that allows them to keep fighting against school choice on many fronts. The money rolls in from the $2 billion in dues the unions take from their three million members. My wife, a New York City public school teacher, now has $882 (after taxes) deducted from her paychecks by the union every year (the exact same amount that all other teachers in the city pay, no matter what their salary is).

The dues coerced from millions of teachers allow the unions to keep a full-time staff of thousands, deployed strategically around the country. Hundreds of those employees spend all their time on political lobbying and electoral politics. Teacher dues also pay for hours and hours of political advertising. For example, in the two months after the *Zelman* decision, the

Florida Education Association (the state affiliate of the NEA) spent $3 million in media buys for the union's preferred candidate in the Democratic primary for governor. In the process, the FEA anointed a relatively unknown Democrat named Bob McBride over Janet Reno only after he assured the union that he would work to repeal all of Florida's recently enacted laws that created vouchers or private school scholarships for thousands of children.

One of these Florida laws allows corporations to take a tax credit for contributions to scholarship funds that then pay the costs of tuition for poor children switching from public schools to private schools. The other, called the "McKay Scholarships" legislation, pays private school tuition for children designated as having "special needs" (the equivalent of special education). These two publicly funded programs have allowed twenty-three thousand poor children throughout the state to leave the public schools.

With another forty thousand children on scholarship program waiting lists, the popularity of this legislation with poor families threatens the hegemony of the public education system and thus the jobs of union members. That's why the FEA wants all those children returned forthwith to the public school system before the contagion spreads. The union got closer to that goal when McBride pulled off an upset victory over Reno in the Democratic primary. Many more millions of teachers' union dollars then became available for McBride's losing campaign against the incumbent governor, Jeb Bush.

As if the unions' war chest weren't already overflowing, the American Federation of Teachers (AFT) pushed through a resolution at its summer convention in Las Vegas authorizing an additional levy of $1 a month per member. The extra $12 million went into a special "Solidarity Fund" designed to thwart vouchers and privatization initiatives in school districts. In proposing the new fund, AFT vice president Herb Magidson warned the 3,700 convention delegates that "there is a well-funded, extreme group of ultraconservatives led by millionaire ideologues who seek to do away with unions and, failing that, to bleed us dry." Translation: $2 billion a year isn't enough because in the battle against vouchers, the villain is—you guessed it—the "vast right-wing conspiracy."

★

I know something about the people the AFT is so scared of. In fact, around the same time the AFT was holding its 2002 convention, I attended a conference in Jackson Hole, Wyoming, that the union must have regarded as the evil empire of the voucher conspiracy. Children First America, a national organization based in San Antonio, Texas, sponsored the meeting. CFA serves as a coordinating group for a choice movement that still remains largely decentralized. About seventy or eighty school choice activists from all over the country met to exchange information and gird themselves for the unions' counterattack in the wake of the Supreme Court's decision.

The AFT was right about one thing: There really were a lot of millionaires at the meeting and at least one billionaire, John Walton. Instead of being slandered by the AFT as extremists, however, these men and women ought to be celebrated for their contributions to civil rights and education reform.

Walton, for example, may be the heir of the Wal-Mart Stores fortune, but he's no silver-spoon rich man's son. He attended the public high schools in Bentonville, Arkansas, served in the armed services in Vietnam, worked as a crop duster and a boat builder. He now lives in Jackson Hole with his wife, Christie (also a public high school graduate), and their son, who has attended public schools in Wyoming. The Waltons are hardly ideologues. In fact, they seem like free spirits in their lifestyle and their approach to education. They spend three months a year on a boat off the coast of Baja California, are interested in the environment, and have founded charter schools in California. John looks as if he would be uncomfortable in a suit. Christie, with her long blond hair and peasant dresses, appears almost to have stepped out of a poster from the 1960s counterculture.

Nor is there anything secretive or conspiratorial about Walton's philanthropy. He has been totally up front about the $100 million or so he has given to the school choice cause. Almost all of this has been in the form of scholarships to poor families to enable them to get their children out of public schools that don't educate and into private schools that do.

Walton told me he gave this money not because he is in favor of abandoning public education, but rather in an effort to save it. "Choice is a vehicle for improving all education, not just those who get to choose," Walton said. "The reason choice is capable of doing that is that we now have a top-down, bureaucratically driven system. However, by funding students instead of the system, choice turns the power structure on its head. In the process our entire public education system has to become more responsive."

Like Walton, the other philanthropists who attended the Jackson Hole meeting are trying to make the public schools fulfill the promise of providing educational opportunity for all children. Many of them are businessmen who had public school experiences similar to that of David Brennan (who was also at the meeting). This made them concerned that the schools were not doing their job of preparing young people for an economy requiring more and better skills.

Of course, they are not the only Americans who are worried. Politicians, elite opinion makers and many of their fellow businessmen have been expressing alarm at the poor performance of the public schools for almost half a century. National commissions were set up and issued numerous and voluminous reports with ominous-sounding titles like "A Nation at Risk." For the better part of three decades the commissions and "education summits" kept coming back with the same proposals for fortifying the existing public education system with more money and resources. It's the same approach to school improvement of the business groups I described earlier, such as New York's Principal for a Day.

What most characterizes the wealthy activists I met at Jackson Hole is their conviction that they have hit on a better idea. They realized that public school failure has less to do with lack of resources than with the fact that the system operates like a monopoly and offers few real incentives to maintain high standards. To them this is just basic Economics 101: Enterprises that never have to worry about losing their customers, and therefore face no consequences for failure, will usually have a high failure rate.

One by one, they had come up with a different and—as recent history has proven—a more useful approach to education philanthropy. Rather than throw more money at an unaccountable system, they decided to give money in the form of scholarships to families living in the inner cities who were most victimized by the public school system's failures. This allowed the parents some measure of choice over their children's education and generally produced better outcomes.

Many of these philanthropists also believed in the principle of publicly funded vouchers. But as recently as a decade ago, there seemed to be insurmountable political and legal obstacles to enacting voucher legislation. (The Milwaukee voucher program was in its infancy and appeared about to be strangled by onerous state regulations. Cleveland didn't yet have vouchers.) Moreover, there was the fear that even if state legislatures passed publicly funded voucher programs, the federal or state courts would kill them by declaring them unconstitutional. In creating what were essentially "private voucher" programs, the philanthropists were able to help a lot of poor kids immediately, while simultaneously building the constituencies and political coalitions that could eventually bring about tax-funded school choice.

Children First America began in the early 1990s as a clearinghouse of sorts for these proliferating and spontaneously created private voucher programs. "The word spread through our efforts and also because people would hear about scholarship programs through their own contacts or through the media," said Fritz Steiger, the group's executive director since its founding. "We would get calls from business leaders and philanthropists who would say 'I read about this. How can I do a scholarship program?' " By 2002, CFA counted over 115 private voucher programs operating in almost 100 different cities and communities. The programs were serving more than 60,000 poor students nationwide at a cost to their sponsors of close to $100 million per year, all of it privately donated.

Peter Flanigan, CFA's chairman from 1999 to 2002, founded the first program, New York's Student Sponsor Partnership, in

1986. Flanigan is a former World War II combat carrier pilot who went on to a career as an investment banker with Dillon, Read and Company. His first experience in education philanthropy was with the public schools. In the mid-1980s he participated in the "I Have a Dream" program, adopting a class of eighth-grade public school students and promising to pay their college tuition if they worked hard for four years and graduated from high school. Flanigan then had his own public school lesson: The high schools were so chaotic and poorly run that many of the students he adopted were dropping out and squandering the extraordinary opportunity he was offering them.

Flanigan figured out something better to do with his time and money. Starting in 1986, he created a charitable foundation called Student Sponsor Partnership. This program placed at-risk students from public schools—exactly the sorts of kids Flanigan had previously adopted—in Catholic high schools. Their tuition was paid by individual donors or "sponsors" who also agreed to serve as mentors to the scholarship students. The results have been spectacular. According to a RAND Corporation study of the program, the scholarship students far outperformed similar students who went to public high schools in every category—graduation rates, SAT scores, college admissions.

Another private voucher innovator who was at the CFA meeting was a tall, middle-aged Texan named James Leininger. He too was mobilized into the school choice movement by what he learned about the performance of inner-city public schools. Leininger was a practicing physician in San Antonio, Texas, who started up a very successful medical supply company called Kinetic Concepts, of which he then became CEO. One day his vice president for human resources came to him and sheepishly admitted that a number of employees on the payroll were functionally illiterate, despite having valid high school diplomas. Leininger realized that the San Antonio public schools were not preparing students for the workplace. By coincidence he had just read an article in the *Wall Street Journal* describing a private voucher program in Indianapolis, and he decided to launch something similar in San Antonio.

Leininger was stunned by the overwhelming response to

the ad he and his friends placed in the *San Antonio Express-News* offering a few hundred scholarships that would pay up to half the cost of tuition at private schools. In three days there were three thousand applications from poor Hispanic parents. The local teachers' union immediately attacked the scholarship program and demonized Leininger as an extremist trying to undermine public education. He smiled and shrugged as he described this experience to me. "Until then it never occurred to me that there was anything wrong with helping poor families educate their children."

The San Antonio scholarship program eventually became one of the biggest of its kind in the country. It's also an example of how the private scholarship approach was able to lay the groundwork for an eventual political campaign to get publicly funded vouchers. Leininger and one of his colleagues in the program, a businessman named Robert Aguirre, used the program to launch a statewide citizens' effort to convince the Texas legislature to enact a full voucher program. Aguirre also founded a new national organization called CREO (Spanish for "I believe") to mobilize support for school choice within the Hispanic community. To advance the cause, Leininger ended up contributing lots of money to Republican candidates, but he would gladly have supported Democrats if they had shown any sympathy for the school choice approach.

During the late 1990s several voucher bills came very close to being enacted by the Texas legislature. The *Zelman* decision may help change some votes. Whether it's this year, or next, or the year after, Texas gives the school choice movement its best opportunity for a victory in a big state. (School choice programs funded by tax credit arrangements already exist in Florida, Pennsylvania and Arizona.)

Each successful school choice initiative will have to be defended against new attacks by the teachers' unions. Much of that task falls to Clint Bolick of the Institute for Justice, the lawyer for the school choice movement who has crossed swords with the NEA's Robert Chanin in many courtrooms around the country. Bolick promises that he and his colleagues aren't going to sit back and wait for Chanin's expected legal offensive.

The *Zelman* decision gives the school choice movement an opportunity to strike at the "Blaine amendments" in dozens of state constitutions that strictly prohibit public funds going to religious schools. The teachers' unions have counted on these relics of the late-nineteenth-century anti-immigration and anti-Catholic panic as their second line of defense against voucher programs. But school choice lawyers will launch preemptive attacks on the amendments by arguing that they are inconsistent with the Court's new reading of the Establishment Clause and violate the First Amendment's guarantee of religious freedom. "We will show the courts that the Blaine amendments were the product of anti-Catholic bigotry," said Bolick.

After four years of service, Peter Flanigan turned over the chairmanship of CFA to Richard Sharpe, the CEO of Circuit City and a major player in the choice movement in Virginia. CFA's new executive director is thirty-nine-year-old John Kirtly, a school choice activist from Florida who played a big role in lobbying for the state's tuition tax credit bills. Sharpe and Kirtly now share the task of taking what has been a largely decentralized and often spontaneous grassroots movement and turning it into a more effective national political force for transforming American public education.

In contrast to the unions' massive organizational and political resources and their ability to pour millions of dollars into pivotal elections at the drop of a hat, the school choice movement still has virtually no professional staff, no clear national organizational structure, no significant advertising budget, no paid political cadres. It doesn't even have a national headquarters. It has established a significant base in about a dozen states, but in many others it hardly exists. The $3 million that the teachers' union spent in two months on one primary race in Florida on trying to kill tuition tax credits is probably more than all the school choice groups combined have ever spent on organization and infrastructure.

Despite this immense gap in resources, John Kirtly is convinced that the movement will prevail. He's counting on an idea—the powerful civil rights idea of education equality. "We may be underfunded and underorganized," says Kirtly. "We can always get more funds and become better organized. What we do have that our opponents will never have is moral justification."

★

To see the moral impact of the choice movement on the whole system, it is necessary to return to Milwaukee. There it was grassroots organizers from the black community, not white philanthropists, who agitated for alternatives to the monopoly public school system. Milwaukee is where the school choice movement that began in the 1990s most closely resembles the civil rights movement of the 1960s.

It took a protracted struggle to convince key municipal leaders and constituency groups that giving dissatisfied public school parents a chance to send their children to a private school that worked was not a threat to public education. Now, a decade later, teachers' union propaganda about vouchers being the devious work of rich, right-wing extremists is regarded as ridiculous. A virtual across-the-board consensus exists in the city that school choice works, not just for poor children who get to go to better schools, but for all children.

I have always thought that if I were trying to convince someone that school choice is good for kids, I would try to bring that person to see some of the schools that vouchers built in Milwaukee. And I would try to have them meet some of the talented people who would never have been able to make such enormous contributions to education if not for the opportunities created by the voucher program.

Of course, however much they might be taken by the charisma of Brother Bob Smith or Walter Sava, my visitors might still question whether the benefits of voucher schools came at the expense of the 85 percent of the kids who have remained in the Milwaukee Public Schools. This is the zero-sum notion that has been effectively used by the opponents of choice to scare off public school parents. But in Milwaukee, zero-sum has been turned into win-win for everyone: great new voucher schools, plus improvement of the existing public schools.

Enrollment in the Milwaukee Public Schools has risen by 4 percent since the voucher program began. Inflation-adjusted spending per pupil has increased from $7,600 to $9,500. Not only has there been no fragmentation because of the voucher schools, but there is now unprecedented collaboration between the city's public and private schools.

John Gardner, the displaced New Yorker, former labor organizer and self-described "radical democrat," is probably the most pro-voucher member of the Milwaukee school board. Yet during the two times he ran for and won an at-large seat on the board, he staked his reputation on his claim that vouchers would help make the public schools better. Now Gardner is proudly waving around documents proving that the academic perform-ance of Milwaukee public school students has improved since the voucher program went into full gear in 1997. Measured against a national sample, student test scores rose in 12 out of 15 cate-gories. The four-year high school graduation rate went from 60 percent to 67 percent during the last three years. The highly respected Harvard University economist Caroline Hoxby has published a peer-reviewed paper finding that students in some of the poorest schools in the Milwaukee system, and thus most under the threat of losing students to voucher schools, made the greatest gains in test scores.

Gardner also points to a long list of structural reforms within Milwaukee Public Schools that are directly attributable to the competition created by voucher schools. The most impor-tant of these changes was the adoption of "school-based hiring." Prior to the voucher program, MPS had one of the country's most onerous "seniority" clauses in its contract with the teachers' union. When voucher schools set an example of hiring on the basis of merit rather than seniority, the teachers' union was forced into making concessions to stay competitive. Now almost every principal in the Milwaukee Public Schools system is allowed to fill vacancies with candidates deemed the most qualified, without regard to seniority.

The MPS administration also gives principals more control over how money allocated to their schools can be spent. Here's an example: One public school took advantage of this new manager-ial flexibility to shift the money available for a librarian into expanding the school's highly regarded music program. The princi-pal figured out a way to keep the library staffed, but now almost every student could participate in the orchestra. This was highly popular with the parents, and it gave the school a selling point for attracting new students and preventing defections to voucher schools.

Another instance of how competition has forced improvement is the fact that many Milwaukee public elementary schools now offer "Direct Instruction." This is a carefully scripted, phonics-based reading program for the early grades that has produced very good results in schools around the country, particularly with low-income minority children. Previously, many public school principals in Milwaukee, influenced by progressive education orthodoxy, turned their noses up at phonics, instead using the "whole language" approach favored by the ed schools. But when these principals saw that most voucher schools were not only using Direct Instruction but advertising it to parents, they quickly changed their approach in order to avoid losing students.

For years, Milwaukee parents complained that there wasn't enough kindergarten space in the public schools. The district said it couldn't afford to expand. Then many voucher schools, despite having less money than the public schools, figured out a way to offer more kindergarten classes. MPS responded to the competition by conducting a survey among public school parents and eventually expanding the number of kindergarten seats. It is highly unusual for an entrenched bureaucratic system actually to listen to its customers (parents) and become more responsive. You could sum it up in a paraphrase of a well-known political slogan: It was the competition, stupid.

Yet it's important to note that the new school competition in Milwaukee has not developed into cutthroat rivalry. Instead it is fostering a process of cooperation and improvement through the power of example. Public schools and private schools are now sharing space; public school principals are visiting the private school down the street to see how the practice of requiring student uniforms might work for their own school; public and private schools in the same neighborhood are collaborating on joint after-school programs.

★

The person responsible for telling the Milwaukee voucher story to as many parents, school officials and politicians from around the country as possible is Susan Mitchell, the president of an organization called the American Education Reform Council (AERC). Mitchell, a fifty-eight-year-old mother of two, is regarded as one of the national school choice movement's key strategists and one of its most knowledgeable. Like almost every other school choice activist in Milwaukee, she got into this fight as a way to improve public education, not abandon it.

Like so many other movement leaders, Mitchell had her own dispiriting public school lessons. She tells the story of how she and her husband, George, and their two adopted daughters moved back to Milwaukee from Madison, the state capital, in the early 1990s. Being a public school person at heart, she tried to register her daughters for a school in the neighborhood. Because one of her daughters is Asian and the other of mixed Hispanic and African American lineage, the school authorities classified them as being of two different races for the purpose of school assignment. Mitchell was told that the girls would have to be bused to two separate schools, both far from the family's home.

Instead of giving up and abandoning the public schools, as many other white, middle-class families had done in Milwaukee for the better part of two decades, the Mitchells decided to fight for a more rational and more responsive public school system. Their vehicle was school choice. Susan in particular threw herself full-time into the struggle for the voucher program, becoming one of the Milwaukee movement's key leaders. Through AERC, Mitchell now makes sure the good news gets out about Milwaukee's new mixed education system. She arranges visits to the city for educators, community leaders and politicians from all over the country. She also offers strategic guidance on building political coalitions and drafting legislation to school choice activists in other states.

As Susan Mitchell and her colleagues convey the lessons of Milwaukee's voucher program to those visitors from all over the country, other cities may then begin to realize how much wasted energy goes into maintaining the Berlin Wall dividing their public and private school zones and how many opportunities to improve their schools have already been squandered. And then, hopefully, spreading across the land there will be one, two, three, many Milwaukees.

If the reader recognizes this locution from the 1960s (when Che Guevara called for "two, three, many Vietnams"), it wasn't included here by accident. Increasingly I have been struck by the similarities between the contemporary school choice movement and the protest movements I was part of many years ago. I joked about this with some of the wealthy businessmen I met in Jackson Hole, telling them that I once would have said their meeting was a gathering of the "ruling class." But now, I added, it's the teachers' unions that have become the ruling class in education. At the same time, the school choice movement is countercultural in the best sense of the word.

After all, today's school choice activists are challenging the coercive and bureaucratic culture of public education, just as we in the student protest movements of the sixties took on what we regarded as the authoritarian, top-down, factory-model universities (or "multiversities," as Berkeley chancellor Clark Kerr called them). Against this monopoly system of education, we demanded the right to choose our own modes of learning and even the right to create our own "free schools."

The ultimate irony is that many of my erstwhile comrades are themselves now entrenched in universities that are even more monocultural and authoritarian than the ones we rebelled against in the 1960s. These "tenured radicals" use their power to deny a fair hearing to all manner of politically incorrect and nonconforming ideas, including the idea of choice and freedom in elementary and secondary education.

This will never be the fate of the current school choice movement. That's because its leading activists are not in it for power or ideology, but rather for the same idea that enabled the civil rights movement: empowering the most powerless in our society. In one of my conversations with Susan Mitchell, she captured the essence of this idea:

"People can always make good decisions for themselves when they have the power to exit. In a job or in a school you need to be able to say: 'this isn't fair' or 'this isn't rational and I am leaving.' In Milwaukee, parents who had little else could at least now say, 'We are going.' It forced those in charge of the schools to respond. They said, 'What can we do to make you keep your child in our school?' "

Thinking about Susan Mitchell's comment, I realized that we all need that "power to exit." It applied to everything I had learned, primarily through my children's experiences, about the public schools. My first lesson was that the schools they attended, though supposedly among the best in the system, were burdened with too many unproductive or dysfunctional teachers, harmed by irrational personnel and recruitment practices, and affected by a deadening, systemwide bureaucratic culture. I was annoyed and angry about all this and did my best to expose these failings to public scrutiny. Nevertheless, I always distinguished between my sons' situation and the conditions faced by the hundreds of thousands of city kids, almost all of them poor and minority, forced to attend the schools that made it to the federal or state failure lists.

The distinction was this: If my children were stuck with a dysfunctional teacher, my wife and I could always step in and make up some of the slack. Even when one of my sons ended up with a lemon teacher at Stuyvesant High School in an advanced math class, we could still get him some extra tutoring. But the children of poor families stuck in bad schools had no remedies at all. First, they had more of those dysfunctional teachers, and second, they couldn't get the help at home to compensate.

From this I concluded that the remedy of school choice that I had begun to support and write about would make a huge difference for poor kids in bad schools, but was probably irrelevant to my own children's education in the public schools. Since I knew that neither my kids nor their classmates could ever qualify for a voucher, I assumed that this was a school reform meant for other people's children.

I now know this was wrong. School choice was relevant to my children's education and to their classmates even at schools like Stuyvesant. I am convinced that if I could have waved a magic wand and created a voucher program in New York City similar to the one in Milwaukee, my sons would have benefited greatly. They would have had fewer seniority transfer teachers who couldn't teach. Their schools—all of them, from P.S. 87 to Stuyvesant—would have had fewer bureaucratic regulations imposed on them from central headquarters and thus could have been more creative in structuring classes and designing curricula. Each of their principals would have had more freedom to move items around in their budgets in order to meet the real academic needs of the students. In other words, school choice would have kept the system honest and forced it to compete.

Suppose that about a hundred thousand students from low-performing schools in New York (about the same percentage as in Milwaukee) had moved to private schools with tuition vouchers. The now-forgotten Chancellor Harold Levy could have used the threat of losing students to push for radical innovations that would otherwise have been unthinkable. For example, he might have said that since our competitors, the private schools, are paying teachers for their performance and knowledge, not seniority, we must do likewise to stay even. Levy could have noted that kids are leaving for Catholic schools because they are safer and more orderly, and then he could have pushed to change the tangle of state laws and regulations that currently impede public schools from imposing reasonable discipline on students.

Unlike his immediate predecessor, Levy never revealed whether he was for vouchers or against. I always assumed he was just being politic, not wanting to completely alienate Mayor Giuliani, a vocal supporter of vouchers. In a way, it didn't matter. For all practical purposes, Levy operated as if the public schools were a world apart from the private and parochial school sectors. If not a Berlin Wall, he at least seemed to favor keeping an Iron Curtain between the two systems. And among the reasons he failed to move the public school system forward is that his mind remained closed to the possibilities of learning from the private schools.

After Harold Levy left, there was a very telling incident that revealed the cul-de-sac the city school system has gotten itself into because of its hostility toward school choice and competition. In September 2002, just after the school year opened, 280,000 parents received letters informing them that their children were in failing schools and thus were entitled to transfer out to other schools in their district. The letters were sent by the state education department as required under the new federal education law known as the "No Child Left Behind Act."

Under the Bush administration's original version of this legislation, the designation of a school as "failing" would have triggered a process that could lead to offering parents vouchers for private schools, thus giving them that vital "exit" power that Susan Mitchell talked about. However, once Ted Kennedy got finished cutting up the bill, all that survived as a remedy for kids in failing schools was "public school choice"—that is, transferring to another public school in the same district. Kennedy certainly must have known that in the horrific conditions of inner-city schools, public school choice is no choice at all.

It was a cruel hoax for the New York City parents who received those letters from the state. A total of 331 schools—one out of every three city schools—appeared on the failure list. In many districts, every single school was on the list, so there was nowhere to transfer to. In other districts, the schools that managed to stay off the list were already filled to capacity. For children and their parents, this was worse than moving around the deck chairs on the *Titanic;* it was more like being tied down to one of the deck chairs and not permitted a space on the life rafts.

As usual, the traditional civil rights organizations were completely silent about this scandalous case rife with injustice and discrimination. For a moment we almost had a new Rosa Parks (or Polly Williams). A mother in one of the Bronx school districts where every school was on the failure list went to the district office and insisted on a seat for her child in another district. When school officials said they couldn't accommodate her, she announced that she would keep her child home and dared the authorities to come and arrest her. An anonymous benefactor read about the mother's defiant stand and offered the child a scholarship to a private school. Thus a promising legal confrontation was averted.

Nevertheless, many other parents stuck with inferior schools were restive—so much so that Mayor Michael Bloomberg, with U.S. education secretary Rod Paige in tow, made an appearance at one school to try to calm things down. Both officials asked the parents to be patient, promising that help was on the way. "We are trying and you will see results and we have to do this together," Bloomberg assured them. Then Secretary Paige said he needed more time to work out the kinks in the No Child Left Behind Act.

But even with his new unfettered power over the city schools, Mayor Bloomberg may not have enough time or an effective methodology to bring these schools up from failure. Thus the contradiction between what the government is telling these parents about the sorry condition of the schools and the same government's inability to provide remedies within the existing public school system will only deepen. It is hard to believe that parents would willingly accept these contradictions year after year while watching their children's chances at a decent education go down the tubes—especially when they see that poor children in Milwaukee and Cleveland have been granted their manumission.

After *Zelman,* and with the church/state issue laid to rest, it will be more and more difficult to keep the lid on this discontent. Sometime in the future I can imagine an angry group of parents marching on City Hall, waving their latest official government letters about their children's dreadful schools and shouting, "We want out!" When this finally happens—an event that will be as momentous as the marches against segregation in places like Selma and Birmingham—the old monopoly system of public education will be finished. We will then have—even in New York, the bastion of teacher unionism—a mixed system of public schools and publicly supported private schools, much like Milwaukee's, and much like the rest of the industrialized world.

And when it happens I believe that the schools will begin to recapture for families in every neighborhood of the city the same dream that my parents had when they first sent me off to P.S. 6 all those years ago. It was a dream about competence and citizenship—a dream about America.

Acknowledgments

Portions of this book derive from articles I originally published in *City Journal*. I am grateful to *City Journal*'s editor, Myron Magnet, for encouraging me to write about what I saw in my sons' schools and then assigning me to cover other education issues. Larry Mone, president of the Manhattan Institute, first urged me to consider writing a book on urban education. I am grateful to Manhattan Institute and the John M. Olin Foundation for much-needed support for the project. Peter Collier, publisher of Encounter Books, not only is an old friend and a superb editor, but he exhibited uncommon patience with his wayward writer. My wife, Ruthie Stern, reassured me through many moments of doubt and also provided insights into how the public school system works (or rather doesn't work). My friend Fred Siegel listened patiently to my public school stories and encouraged me to believe that I had something useful to say about school reform.

This is a work of journalism, based partly on personal experience. Nevertheless, I benefited from the efforts of many scholars and writers who have previously explored the issues of urban school failure and school choice. I am indebted in particular to the body of literature on these issues created by Clint Bolick, Anthony S. Bryk, Jay Greene, Valerie E. Lee, Peter B. Holland, Caroline Hoxby, John Chubb, Terry Moe, Andrew J. Coulson, Chester Finn, Paul T. Hill, E. D. Hirsch, Myron Lieberman, Paul Peterson, Diane Ravitch, David Seeley and Joseph Viteritti.

Index